"Professor Brennan compellingly ⟨... his⟩ tory, the powerful have used language to dehumanize, and then victimize, the most vulnerable and powerless among us—blacks, Native Americans, women, and Jews in Nazi Germany. The unborn are the latest targets of this corruption of words. To every liberal, pro-choice American who believes that in our laws and in our hearts we should welcome all people as our brothers and sisters, I say—read this book. But be prepared for a sea change in your thinking. Professor Brennan will show you how the twisted lexicon of 'abortion rights' has prepared the present massacre of the youngest and most voiceless of our brethren—the unborn."

—Patricia Wesley, M.D.,
   Assistant Clinical Professor of Psychiatry,
   School of Medicine, Yale University

"William Brennan's new book, *Dehumanizing the Vulnerable: When Word Games Take Lives*, is an important contribution to our current debate on the issue of abortion. He reviews the damaging rhetoric that makes the abuse of classes of human beings possible. He shows convincingly that dehumanizing language has been used against a wide range of social groups, including women, American Indians, Black slaves, Jews, the unborn, and those with disabilities. . . . An excellent case for today's 'crimes against humanity.' Fortunately, in addition, he provides us with a guide to action. We begin by changing our language."

—Wanda Franz, Ph.D.,
   President, National Right to Life Committee

Dehumanizing
the
Vulnerable

Dehumanizing the Vulnerable

When Word Games Take Lives

by William Brennan

A Campion Book

Loyola University Press
Chicago

Loyola University Press
3441 North Ashland Avenue
Chicago, Illinois 60657

Library of Congress Cataloging-in-Publication data

Cover design by Frederick Falkenberg.
Interior design by Beth Herman Adler.

Brennan, William.
Dehumanizing the vulnerable : when word games take lives / by William
Brennan.
p.   cm. — (Values and ethics series ; v. 11)
Includes bibliographical references and index.
ISBN 0-8294-0822-3 (cloth : alk. paper). — ISBN 0-8294-0821-5 (pbk. : alk.
paper)
1. Language and ethics. 2. Semantics. 3. Stereotype (Psychology)
4. Pejoration (Linguistics) 5. Political persecution. I. Title. II. Series: Values &
ethics series; v.11.
P106.B6946 1995
306.4'4—dc20   94-41824
97 98 99 00 01 5 4 3   CIP

Contents

List of Tables   vii

Preface   ix

Acknowledgments   xi

Introduction: The Dynamics of Linguistic Warfare   1

Part One: Profiles in Oppression: The Plight of the Victims   25

  1. Global War on the Unwanted Unborn   27

  2. Assaults on Dependent and/or Disabled Discards   33

  3. Female Objects of Sexploitation and Violence   37

  4. Destruction of the European Jews and Others   43

  5. Genocide of the Soviet People   47

  6. Black Slavery and Kindred Atrocities   51

  7. Annihilation of Native Americans   57

Part Two: Dehumanizing Stereotypes   63

  8. Deficient Humans:
    On the Margins of the Human Race   65

  9. Subhuman/Nonhuman Entities:
    Below the Level of Humanity   77

 10. A Species of Lower Animals and Wild Beasts   89

 11. Repulsive Parasitic Creatures   99

 12. Diseases of Epidemic Proportions   113

 13. Inanimate Objects for Exploitation   127

 14. Waste Products:
    At the Bottom of the Subhuman Scrap Pile   139

 15. Legal Nonpersons: Nonexistence before the Law   147

Part Three: Challenges to Dehumanizing Rhetoric   173

16. The Reality Test:
    Refuting the Validity of Disparaging
    Designations   175

17. Statements of Semantic Impact:
    Assessing the Devastating Effects
    of Words on Deeds   185

18. Toward a Vocabulary of Life-Affirming Images:
    Replacing Dehumanizing Language with a
    Language of Humanization and Divinization   205

Postscript: Thinking the Unthinkable:
The Prospects for Expanding the Boundaries of Humanity   223

Notes   229

References   239

Index   267

Tables

The Semantics of Oppression   6

A Lexicon of Esteem   21

Preface

The capacity of human beings to justify their behavior, no matter how unconscionable, appears to be limitless. When the behavior consists of harming other human beings, degrading words serve as an extraordinarily effective weapon.

A group of teenagers climaxed a night of "wilding" with the gang rape and brutal beating of a female jogger in New York's Central Park. They joked to the police about what they had done. One of the perpetrators called the victim "nothing." Erik and Lyle Menendez rationalized gunning down their parents by portraying them as perverted "monsters." After cutting off the heads of fifty-two babies aborted alive, a medical researcher declared, "An aborted baby is just garbage and that's where it ends up. Why not make use of it for society?" An intensive care nurse observed that hospital staff who mistreat debilitated patients refer to them as "parasites" on the health care system.

Those resorting to such demeaning terminology are involved in a reckless game of verbal gymnastics. The intent is to bolster a wide range of violent actions. This game of playing fast and loose with words bears a striking resemblance to the distortion-ridden vocabulary of Newspeak responsible for tyranny and thought control in George Orwell's nightmarish world of *1984*.

The major focus of my book, accordingly, is on the significance of name-calling as a strategy for justifying massive oppression. Many of the dehumanizing phrases examined in this study are so extreme, outlandish, and shocking that it is easy to dismiss them as the ravings of crazed individuals and fringe groups. In most instances, however, this is not the case. Such language more often reflects and shapes the attitudes of people and organizations in the mainstream of societal life today and in times past.

Because these epithets seem so unbelievable, it is necessary to furnish extensive documentation to show that they have actually been said, who uttered them, the circumstances under which they were expressed, their ideological underpinnings, their function, and their impact on victims and perpetrators alike. The disparaging designations I have chosen for analysis represent typical examples culled from a vast assortment of historical and contemporary sources, including Supreme Court and lower court decisions; laws, ordinances, and decrees; press and media accounts; magazine articles; war crimes trials testimony; scientific, medical, legal, historical, philosophical, and anthropological journals and books; ancient and modern poetry and fiction; cultural practices; policy statements enacted by leading professional organizations; propaganda tracts; and papers presented before prestigious conferences.

In addition, I have examined the same sources in determining the extent to which positive, life-affirming expressions have played a decisive role in countering the dehumanizing expressions from antiquity to modern times.

My main purpose in writing this book is consciousness raising. By becoming aware of how the words used against today's most vulnerable individuals constitute a resurrection of the words deployed against some of history's most reviled groups, we are provided with an indispensable perspective for challenging this lexicon and replacing it with an expansive vocabulary of humanization encompassing all human lives despite their status, condition, or stage of development. Although exposing the pernicious nature of the degrading language and substituting life-affirming terminology will not alone put an end to massive oppression, these steps are necessary in achieving such a worthwhile goal.

Acknowledgments

I am grateful to the Office of Research Services of the St. Louis University Graduate School for a summer grant. This support was crucial in enabling me to complete the final phases of the book.

I wish to thank Mike Byers for introducing me to the word processing potentials of the computer. His patience and expertise aided me in gaining the skills needed to cope with the necessary drafts and revisions. I am likewise indebted to Professors David Murphy, Daniel Schlafly, and Philip Weeks; as well as Helen Valois and Dave Andrusko, who read earlier versions of the book and furnished a number of helpful comments.

Many thanks also to the staff at St. Louis University's Pius XII Memorial Library. David Shocklee of the interlibrary loan department did an outstanding job of obtaining hard-to-find documents and books from libraries throughout the United States. Archivist John Wade was extremely successful in tracking down historical sources and answering several important technical questions.

Special appreciation is due to Loyola University Press editors Jeremy Langford and Gary Von Euer for the thorough manner in which they went over the manuscript and the excellent observations they offered for its improvement. One could not ask for two more capable and perceptive editors.

Most of all, my deepest gratitude goes to my wife, Nancy, for her unqualified support. Not only did she provide me with the enormous amount of uninterrupted time required to carry out a project of this magnitude, but she also read and made many valuable contributions to various segments of the book.

Introduction

The Dynamics of Linguistic Warfare

T he power of language to color one's view of reality is profound. In many instances, the most significant factor determining how an object will be perceived is not the nature of the object itself, but the words employed to characterize it. Operating through the lenses of contrasting linguistic symbols, two persons looking at the same phenomenon are likely to come up with sharply divergent observations. Words can also act as a force for justice or a weapon of repression, an instrument of enlightenment or a source of darkness.

The Miraculous Word

The capacity of language to elevate understanding to the highest level of enrichment is compellingly portrayed in *The Miracle Worker,* the story of Helen Keller and her teacher, Annie Sullivan. When Annie entered Helen's world, Helen was a deaf and blind child who did not even possess the most basic rudiment of communication: she had no idea there was a connection between a word and the object it symbolized. With much patience, love, and dedication, Annie set about the task of opening up Helen's horizons. Just "one word," she reflected, "and I can—put the world in your hand." The image of reality conveyed to Helen was a place where "you can see five thousand years back in a light of words, everything we feel, think, know—and share in words, so not a soul is in darkness" (Gibson 1962, 104).

In her autobiography, *The Story of My Life* (1902), Helen recalled that momentous day when Annie's efforts resulted in establishing Helen's kinship with the world through language.

The decisive incident took place down at the water pump as Annie was spelling out the word "water" in Helen's hand:

> I stood still, my whole attention fixed upon the motions of her fingers. Suddenly I felt a misty consciousness as of something forgotten—a thrill of returning thought; and somehow the mystery of language was revealed to me. I knew then that "w-a-t-e-r" meant the wonderful cool something that was flowing over my hand. That living word awakened my soul, gave it light, hope, joy, set it free. . . .
>
> I left the well-house eager to learn. Everything had a name, and each name gave birth to a new thought. As we returned to the house every object which I touched seemed to quiver with life. . . .
>
> I recall many incidents of the summer of 1887 that followed my soul's sudden awakening. I did nothing but explore with my hands and learn the name of every object that I touched; and the more I handled things and learned their names and uses, the more joyous and confident grew my sense of kinship with the rest of the world. (1961, 34–35)

Annie had a special feel for language as a vehicle of love and understanding. She passed this legacy on to Helen, and Helen, through her writings and inspiring life, passed it on to the world.

A Classification of Semantic Warfare

Instead of unlocking the mysteries and wonders of the universe, language can serve an entirely different purpose: the spreading of deception, illusion, misinformation, and falsehoods.

An insidious form of linguistic abuse—name-calling—is considerably muted in the familiar children's adage "sticks and stones will break my bones but names will never hurt me." This maxim contains two flaws: it negates the impact of name-calling and minimizes the relationship between words and deeds. Disparaging designations may inflict greater damage than physical blows and foster a climate of antagonism leading to the actual breaking of bones and other forms of violence.

Although name-calling does not always result in violence, it is invariably an essential component of any large-scale oppression: discrimination, segregation, enslavement, or annihilation.

The annals of inhumanity are replete with an endless litany of disparaging expressions as well as scores of oppressive actions. The demeaning labels manufactured may become so pervasive that they constitute a full-scale *war of words.* Linguistic reduction of victims to an insignificant, despicable, or dangerous level helps stimulate the kind of destructive thinking that leads ultimately to destructive actions. The victims are cast in such a negative or inconsequential light that whatever is done to them, no matter how horrendous, is considered perfectly justifiable.

Sometimes the terms concocted are aimed at certain groups. "Hun," for example, was invoked to malign Germans during World War I, while the terms "gook," "slope," and "dink" were employed to revile the Vietnamese in the Vietnam War. The epithets "kike," "nigger," and "wop"—directed extensively in the past against Jews, blacks, and Italians respectively—still persist, although to a lesser extent than they did in prior times.

More often, a universal set of dehumanizing designations keeps recurring whoever the victims and whatever the period of their victimization. Much of this name-calling can be placed under eight categories: *deficient human* ("stupid," "defective," "inferior," "potential life," "lives not worth living"), *less than human* ("subhuman" and "nonhuman"), *animal* ("beast" and "lower animal"), *parasitic creature* ("parasite," "vermin," "lice"), *infectious disease* ("pestilence," "plague," "epidemic," "infection," "contagion"), *inanimate object* ("thing," "property," "material," "merchandise"), *waste product* ("trash," "rubbish," "debris," "garbage," "refuse"), and *nonperson* (social, psychological, or legal nonexistence).

This classification of linguistic devaluation furnishes a comprehensive framework for exploring the pervasiveness of defamatory rhetoric and its devastating effects on a diverse spectrum of victims. One of the most remarkable features of antilife rhetoric is the sheer consistency and stability underlying the denigrating concepts that engulf a wide variety of people rendered expendable. While the range of victims has fluctuated down through the years, the semantic assaults against them have remained stubbornly constant.

The Victims of Linguistic Oppression

Any war, whether semantic or otherwise, requires an identifiable enemy upon whom to impose the derogatory labels. At one time or another almost every imaginable racial, ethnic, religious, age, and social group has suffered the consequences of linguistic abuse, ranging from discrimination to outright annihilation.

The victimized groups selected for analysis in this study are among the most extensively oppressed on record: *the unborn* (unwanted human lives before birth in contemporary society), *the dependent and/or disabled* (mainly young children, people with disabilities, the elderly, and debilitated patients), *women* (unmarried and married females past and present), *those exterminated in the Nazi Holocaust* (primarily Jews, but also Gypsies, Germans with disabilities, Poles, and "asocials"), *the targets of Soviet tyranny* (peasants, religious groups, "deviationists" and others), *African Americans* (especially enslaved blacks in the antebellum American South), and *Native Americans* (North American Indians).

Although these groups have not all undergone the same kinds of oppression, the nature of their victimization has usually been of a longstanding duration and frequently lethal in outcome. North American Indians were robbed of their lands, massacred, forcibly removed to uninhabitable western territories, and herded onto reservations. Black people were sold into slavery, treated with the utmost cruelty, lynched, segregated, and subjected to numerous violations of human rights. The victims of Soviet tyranny were forced to undergo a multitude of atrocities: unjust imprisonment, massive starvation, torture, and extinction in the slave labor camps of the Gulag. Some of the barbarities perpetrated against the expendables of the Third Reich included gassing, shooting, deadly injections, starvation, and experimental exploitation. The lot of all too many women in contemporary society and in the past has been precarious at best: abduction, severe beatings, enforced prostitution, sexual assaults, and the denial of fundamental rights. The unwanted unborn in contemporary society are dismembered, obliterated, injected with toxic solutions, and increasingly appropriated for research. Individuals with handicaps are still being abandoned, neglected, abused, denied life-sustaining treatment, and starved to death.

This study is not intended to be an exhaustive coverage of all the possible victims of linguistic and physical violence. The need for an in-depth analysis requires confining it to a limited number of vulnerable populations. Although many severely oppressed groups are not included, this does not mean that their experiences are less significant than those that are included. The comprehensive framework of degrading categories provides a basis for future research regarding the impact of demeaning stereotypes on these and other past and present groups as well: Hispanics, immigrants, the poor, the Vietnamese, and people living in China, Russia, Africa, Bosnia, and various areas throughout the world.

Thus a major focus of this book is comparative; that is, an exploration of the similarities between the words manufactured to devalue today's most defenseless groups before and after birth and the words constructed to revile some of history's most oppressed peoples. The inclusion of vulnerable populations from times past during their respective periods of greatest victimization affords an opportunity to examine the hypothesis that these were also the very periods when the most extreme and extensive linguistic assaults were likely to occur. The same criterion underlies the decision to focus on the verbal attacks against two of contemporary society's most maligned groups— the unwanted unborn and dependent and/or disabled individuals after birth. Table 1, "The Semantics of Oppression," provides a sampling of the degrading linguistic classifications that cuts across the range of victims included in this study.

The Semantics

Dehumanizing Terminology

Vulnerable Victims		DEFICIENT HUMAN	NONHUMAN	ANIMAL	PARASITE
	Native Americans	"Indians [are] . . . inferior to the Anglo-Saxon." *(Henry Clay, Sec. of State, 1825)*	"The life of these [aborigines] is . . . not human." *(Author Hugh Brackenridge, 1779)*	"The Indian . . . is an untamable, carnivorous animal." *(Dr. Josiah Nott, 1847)*	"Clear the country of that vermin [Indians]." *(Colonel Henry Bouquet, 1763)*
	African Americans	"A subordinate and inferior class of beings." *(U.S. Supreme Court on the status of Black people, 1857)*	"The negro is not a human being." *(Buckner Payne, Publisher, 1867)*	"The negro is . . . one of the lower animals." *(Professor Charles Carroll, 1900)*	"They [Negroes] are parasites." *(Dr. E. T. Brady, 1909)*
	Soviet Enemies	"The uncivilized, stupid, turgid people in the Russian villages." *(Author Maxim Gorky, 1922)*	"Kulaks are not human beings." *(Lenin and Stalin, 1918-34)*	"[Peasants are] beasts of burden." *(George Plekhanov, founder of Russian Marxism, 1823)*	"The kulak, the parasite." *(Lenin, 1918)*
	European Jews	"The inferior Jewish race." *(Dr. Rudolph Ramm, Nazi medical educator, 1943)*	"Jews are undoubtedly a race, but not human." *(Adolf Hitler, 1923)*	"The prisoners here are animals." *(Nazi anatomy prof. Dr. August Hirt, 1942)*	"The Jew is a parasite." *(Nazi propaganda booklet, 1944)*
	Women	"They [women] form . . . the second sex, inferior in every respect to the first." *(Philosopher Arthur Schopenhauer, 1851)*	"Women are not seen as human." *(Report by women's group on pornographic images, 1980)*	"Women are domestic animals." *(19th-century poet Charles Baudelaire)*	"Women's sexual parasitism is innate." *(Philosopher Rene Guyon, 1950)*
	Unwanted Unborn	"The fetus, at most, represents only the potentiality of life." *(U.S. Supreme Court decision, 1973)*	"A fetus is not a human being." *(Rabbi Wolfe Kelman, 1984)*	"Like . . . a primitive animal that's poked with a stick." *(Dr. Hart Peterson on fetal movement, 1985)*	"The fetus is a parasite." *(Professor Rosalind Pollack Petchesky, 1984)*
	Dependent Discards	"A life . . . devoid of those qualities which give it human dignity." *(Assessment of child with disability, Dr. Harry Hartzell, 1978)*	"No newborn infant should be declared human until it has passed certain tests." *(Dr. Francis Crick, 1978)*	"Until a living being can take conscious management of life . . . it remains an animal." *(Prof. George Ball, 1981)*	"That's a real parasite." *(Medical staff characterization of a debilitated patient, 1989)*

of Oppression

Dehumanizing Terminology

DISEASE	INANIMATE OBJECT	WASTE PRODUCT	NONPERSON
"The Iroquois had proved more deadly . . . than the pestilence." *(Historian Francis Parkman, 1902)*	"[Indians are] anthropological specimens." *(American press coverage, 1904)*	"[Indians are] the very dregs, garbage . . . of Earth." *(Poet Christopher Brooke, 1622)*	"An Indian is not a person within the meaning of the Constitution." *(George Canfield, Am. Law Rev., 1881)*
"Free blacks in our country are . . . a contagion." *(American Colonization Soc., 1815–30)*	"A negro of the African race was regarded . . . as an article of property." *(U.S. Supreme Court decision, 1857)*	"The negro race is . . . a heritage of organic and psychic debris." *(Dr. William English, 1903)*	"In the eyes of the law . . . the slave is not a person." *(Virginia Supreme Court decision, 1858)*
"Every religious idea [is] . . . 'contagion' of the most abominable kind." *(Lenin, 1913)*	"[Gulag slave laborers are] raw material." *(Author Maxim Gorky, 1934)*	"A foul-smelling heap of human garbage [Purge Trial Defendants]." *(Prosecutor Andrei Vyshinsky, 1938)*	"Unpersons who had never existed." *(Designation for people purged by the Soviet government)*
"Some day Europe will perish of the Jewish disease." *(Joseph Goebbels, Nazi Propaganda Minister, 1939)*	"Transit material." *(Portrayal of Jews dispatched to Nazi death camps, 1942–44)*	"What shall we do with this garbage [Jews]?" *(Christian Wirth, extermination expert, 1942)*	"The Reichsgericht itself refused to recognize Jews . . . as 'persons' in the legal sense." *(1936 German Supreme Court decision)*
"The worst plague Zeus has made— women." *(Ancient Greek poet Semonides)*	"I considered my wife . . . my property." *(Former wife abuser, 1989)*	"Emptying refuse into a sewer [the woman's body]." *(Author Henry Miller, 1965)*	"The statutory word 'person' did not in these circumstances include women." *(British voting rights case, 1909)*
"Pregnancy when not wanted is a disease . . . in fact, a venereal disease." *(Professor Joseph Fletcher, 1979)*	"People's body parts [embryos] are their personal property." *(Attorney Lori Andrews, 1986)*	"An aborted baby is just garbage . . . just refuse." *(Dr. Martti Kekomaki, 1980)*	"The word 'person,' as used in the 14th Amendment, does not include the unborn." *(U.S. Supreme Court decision, 1973)*
"Those 'sicklers.'" *(Doctors' portrayal of patients with sickle cell anemia, 1986)*	"I came to see the patients as work objects." *(Nursing home staff member, 1977)*	"There's a lot of rubbish [patients] this morning." *(ER doctor, 1979)*	"New-born humans are neither persons nor even quasi-persons." *(Philosopher Michael Tooley, 1983)*

Playing with Words: The Psychology of the Big Lie

Phillip Knightley, a keen observer of wartime propaganda, emphasized that when war comes the first casualty is the truth (1975). Consequently, a feature common to any war of words against whatever victims is the patent falsehood of the designations concocted. They often constitute grotesque distortions of reality itself; reality in these instances being the innate humanity of those who are reviled. They are also part and parcel of an elaborate game of verbal corruption.

Their absurdity notwithstanding, derogatory stereotypes are readily transformed into the accepted "truth" when they are heard over and over again. The successful waging of semantic warfare does not rely solely on the sheer number of epithets conjured up, but frequently on the extent of their usage. A few key designations of denigration, continually intoned, like any persistent slogan, are apt to have a significant impact. This is in line with the psychology of "the big lie" so tenaciously advanced by Adolf Hitler in *Mein Kampf:* if the lies are repeated often enough they will be embraced.[1] Those who control language control thought, and eventually semantic corruption leads to the adulteration of thought itself.

An editorial appearing in the September 1970 issue of *California Medicine* contains a revealing statement on lying in the service of killing. The editorial proposes a linguistic strategy of *semantic gymnastics*—"avoidance of the scientific fact, which everyone really knows, that human life begins at conception" and separation of "the idea of abortion from the idea of killing"—as essential for obtaining widespread acceptance of not only abortion, but also euthanasia. Further, the article dubs semantic gymnastics "a schizophrenic sort of subterfuge."[2]

Semantic gymnastics is an exceedingly apt term because it connotes the severe twisting and distorting of language necessary to deny fundamental *scientific facts,* which include the facts that human life exists before birth and that abortion kills human lives in the womb. Likening these denials to a "schizophrenic sort of subterfuge" is considered so extreme that they are placed in the same league as a major mental disorder. However, what is admittedly a strategy comparable to pathological lying is actually endorsed as an appropriate way to promote abortion.

Ever since 1970, the policy of semantic gymnastics has been propagated so often and with such fervor that it has become deeply embedded in the public consciousness. What once had been "the scientific fact, which everyone really knows, that human life begins at conception" has been—through countless repetitions—obscured and reduced to the suspect level of an outmoded, sectarian bias. Thanks to the power of "the big lie," no longer does everyone know that human life begins at conception.

The *California Medicine* editorial did not confine its vocabulary of duplicity to aborted humans, but envisioned other victims as well:

> Medicine's role with respect to changing attitudes toward abortion may well be a prototype of what is to occur. . . . One may anticipate further development of these roles as the problems of birth control and birth selection are extended inevitably to death selection and death control. (p. 68)

Therefore, if semantic gymnastics can be used to deny the humanity of the unborn, they can also be employed to deny the humanity of the born. If semantic gymnastics can be invoked to call abortion something other than killing, they can be relied upon to cover up the destructive nature of euthanasia. Helped along by the enormous inroads made by "the big lie" in the promotion of abortion, euthanasia proponents are resorting to the same kind of linguistic distortions to justify getting rid of undesired humans after birth.

Prestigious Players

The extreme lies and deceptions emanating from this deadly serious game of verbal engineering and manipulation take on enhanced credibility when its most influential players are highly regarded individuals. In the early 1970s a distinguished-looking, authoritative-sounding actor was coached to give a lecture on "The Application of Mathematical Game Theory to Physical Education" to groups of professionals and educators. He was billed as Dr. Myron L. Fox of the Albert Einstein University and dressed up with a fictitious but impressive curriculum vitae. Dr. Fox was instructed "to present his topic and conduct his question-and-answer period with an excessive use of double talk, neologisms, non sequiturs, and contradictory statements. All this was to be interspersed with parenthetical humor and meaningless references to unrelated topics." Afterward, questionnaires were administered to evaluate his talk. Some typical responses were as follows:

> Excellent presentation, enjoyed listening. Has warm manner. Good flow . . . Lively examples . . . Extremely articulate . . . Good analysis of subject . . . Knowledgeable. (Naftulin, Ware, and Donnelly 1973, 630–35)

Moreover, not a single person in the well-educated audiences detected that the authoritative lecturer was a phony!

Prominent personages with impeccable credentials also play an important role in the successful imposition of language intended to denigrate human beings considered discardable. Contrary to popular belief, although despicable language is often primarily associated with crazed individuals or mobs in the streets, it is far more likely to emanate from highly educated, respectable circles. Eminent people throughout history rank among the most steadfast purveyors of demeaning expressions. In *The Republic,* Plato's advocacy of infanticide (book 5) proceeded from a perception of handicapped children as "inferior creatures" (1974, 241–43). Louis Agassiz, founder of the Museum of Natural History at Harvard University and a leading nineteenth-century scientist, called black people a "degraded and degenerate race" (Lurie 1960, 257). One of America's greatest historians, Francis Parkman (1823–93), associated Indians with "leeches" and "contagions" (1925b, 173; 1897–98, 1:243, 2:123; 1902b, 2:127; 1902 a, 1:244; 1925a, 1:444).

Such revelations are not intended to detract from the monumental achievements of these individuals, but to show that even *they* became agents of the prevailing rhetoric. In the hands of revered individuals, the degrading concepts were endowed with enormous credibility. This in turn greatly enhanced their acceptance and facilitated the appalling actions taken against those at the receiving end of the disparaging terminology.

The successful waging of semantic warfare on the contemporary unwanted unborn can likewise be largely attributed to the heavy participation of influential and respectable individuals and organizations. The 1970 *California Medicine* editorial advocating a policy of semantic gymnastics to justify the dehumanization and destruction of unborn humans put it this way: "The very considerable semantic gymnastics which are required to rationalize abortion as anything but taking a human life would be ludicrous if they were not often put forth under *socially impeccable auspices* [italics mine]." Nevertheless, the statement continues, "this schizophrenic sort of subterfuge is necessary" to obtain widespread approval of abortion (p. 68).

In other words, under the ordinary standards of honest discourse it would be ridiculous ("ludicrous") to maintain that the life taken in abortion is something other than human. However, according to one of the sacrosanct tenets of semantic gymnastics, such an outlandish canard ("this schizophrenic sort of subterfuge") is elevated to the status of an incontestable truth when disseminated by prestigious individuals and institutions ("under socially impeccable auspices").

Similarly, the extensive involvement of prominent people and groups is playing a major role in the proliferation of linguistic assaults against vulnerable human lives after birth.

Ideological Foundations of Name-Calling

The reason particular groups are earmarked for large-scale semantic devaluation and massive physical oppression is closely linked to ideology. Behind almost every escalation of linguistic derision is some kind of ideology; that is, a philosophy, a social theory, a set of interrelated ideas, concepts, beliefs, and values that generate and sustain the dissemination of dehumanizing terminology.

Few have probed the significance of ideology with keener insight than Aleksandr Solzhenitsyn. He writes:

> Ideology—that is what gives evildoing its long-sought justification and gives the evildoer the necessary steadfastness and determination. That is the social theory which helps to make his acts seem good instead of bad in his own and others' eyes, so that he won't hear reproaches and curses but will receive praise and honors. . . .
>
> Thanks to *ideology,* the twentieth century was fated to experience evildoing on a scale calculated in the millions. (1973–74, 1:173–74)

Semantic warfare, therefore, does not ordinarily burst upon the scene helter-skelter. It is not an accidental, spontaneous, or chaotic episode, but a deliberate and unremitting phenomenon usually undergirded by fully elaborated systems of concepts, beliefs, and myths.

Theoretical support for many past defamatory labels pinned on blacks, Indians, and Jews can be traced back to the work of eighteenth-century anthropologists and naturalists involved in the task of classifying human beings and other creatures in nature. What began as a legitimate attempt to comprehend the great diversity of human and animal life, however, degenerated into the construction of a great "chain of being," an imposing ideological Goliath for ranking the world's races according to a hierarchy of worth. The Anglo-Saxon, Teutonic white Americans and Europeans were placed at the top while the "colored peoples" of Africa and other "primitive areas" were relegated to the lowermost point on this scale of value.[3]

In 1982 the "chain of being" was resurrected to deny the humanity of the unborn and rationalize abortion. Drawing upon "one of the oldest of mankind's perspectives . . . that of the scale or chain of being" for support, Columbia University emeritus professor Robert Nisbet refers to "the fetus of four weeks" as "patently inhuman." Although Nisbet claims that "the chain of being" comprises "the very spinal column of Christian theology," he neglects to reveal the seamy side of an essentially elitist theory. While ideologues in prior times chose race as the major criterion for assigning the worth of an individual, Nisbet has selected the degree of one's development. The book in which his views are expressed bears the noteworthy title *Prejudices* (1982, 5–6).

The dogma of male supremacy—a set of beliefs that maintains men are stronger, smarter, better, and more important than women—has often functioned as a precondition for the torrent of degrading images and despicable actions imposed upon female members of the human race. Although all violence against women cannot be attributed to a patriarchal mindset, the ideology of male superiority is so deeply ingrained in numerous societies and cultures that it has had a profound influence on how men view and treat women. Historically and currently, an overwhelming preponderance of violence against women has been male-induced. And many perpetrators believe that their status as males entitles them to exploit the minds and bodies of women in any way they wish.

Today the quality-of-life ideology underpins many of the linguistic assaults directed against vulnerable individuals throughout all stages of the human life cycle. According to the quality-of-life ethic propounded in the *California Medicine* editorial of 1970, "it will become necessary and acceptable to place relative rather than absolute values on such things as human lives." The article goes on to emphasize that such an ideology "will of necessity violate and ultimately destroy" both "the traditional Western ethic" and "the Judeo-Christian ethic" of "intrinsic and equal value for every human life regardless of its stage, condition or status." Furthermore, it asserts, "the very considerable semantic gymnastics required to rationalize abortion as anything but the taking of a human life" are "necessary because while a new ethic [the quality of life] is being accepted the old one [the sanctity of life] has not yet been rejected" (p. 68).

Although quality-of-life proponents claim they wish to enhance everyone's life, many of them are only or primarily concerned with enhancing the lives of people with an "adequate" range of capabilities. Anyone who falls below the minimum standards of acceptability—especially individuals suffering from debilitating illnesses and those whose survival depends upon respirators, feeding tubes, and other life-sustaining aids— is placed in imminent jeopardy of being declared superfluous. Unborn children are sacrificed because they are viewed as only potentially human. Handicapped children are rendered expendable because they do not possess the requisite physical or mental capacities, while the severely afflicted elderly have lost theirs. In the practical order, the quality-of-life imperative too often translates to mean the quality of life for some at the expense of life for others.

A host of other ideologies have similarly furnished the theoretical sparks for igniting scores of inflammatory designations accompanied by aggression on a monumental scale. Marxist-Leninist doctrine was repeatedly invoked to castigate Soviet victims as "enemies" and "oppressors" requiring the most draconian measures. Anti-Semitism—a pernicious form of racism— and the myth of Aryan superiority spawned a nomenclature of defamation for widespread application in the Third Reich. The dogma of reproductive freedom is deployed to conceal the tyranny of killing human lives inside the womb.

All of these ideologies, whatever their idealistic and benevolent guise, share one essential ingredient—they are based on an elitist definition of the human race. And it is this deplorable notion that underlies the explosion of derogatory language directed against vulnerable populations today and in times past.

The Socio-Cultural Context

Dehumanizing language not only encompasses a broad range of victims, it also transcends a variety of societies throughout history and up to the present. A measure of the persistence of this rhetoric is its capacity to become firmly entrenched in totalitarian and democratic societies alike.

Because of their control over so many aspects of thought and behavior, totalitarian social structures provide a fertile soil for the dissemination of degrading semantics. Name-calling was widespread in two of the most tyrannical regimes that ever existed: the Soviet Union and the Third Reich. In these social systems, mass communications were controlled by dictators, tyrants, and their agents. Only their perspectives were circulated to the public. Every societal institution in both countries— law, politics, government, education, and the media—spoke with one voice in socializing the public into assimilating the degrading, threatening images of those deemed expendable.

It is understandable how pejorative rhetoric gains a tenacious toehold in totalitarian societies where extreme censorship and strict control allow only the regime's language and perceptions to be distributed. But how does one account for the large-scale acceptance of degrading semantics and their devastating consequences in democratic societies? How is this possible in cultures founded on an ethos of life, liberty, and justice for all, including and especially the most vulnerable individuals? What is there about modern democratic societies that makes them receptive mediums for the oppression of marginalized humans?

Part of the answer inheres in a socio-cultural structure that encourages the communication of diverse ideas, concepts, philosophies, and values. Within this marketplace of expression, the most bizarre and outlandish notions are not only tolerated but are adopted by large numbers of individuals and groups. What once had been deemed unthinkable becomes normative. The open marketplace of expression, however, often turns out to be more apparent than real. In the United States, for example, instead of a free flow of various points of view, many leading societal institutions—education, the arts, religion, law, philosophy, ethics, medicine, politics—show signs of increasing domination by a politically correct cultural elite bent on imposing its radical agenda onto every facet of American life. Nowhere is this more evident than on the issue of abortion and the nature of human life before birth. The cultural elite promotes unrestricted abortion under the deceptive slogan "pro-choice" and deals with unborn victims by denying their existence altogether.

A prime illustration of how fully the cultural elitist position on abortion has penetrated the political realm is the unrestrained pro-abortion policy of the American Democratic Party, an organization that incessantly proclaims an openness to diverse viewpoints and depicts itself as a champion of society's most downtrodden groups. During the months leading up to the Democratic National Convention in July 1992, the pro-life Democratic governor of Pennsylvania, Robert Casey, made several attempts to confront the contradiction between the Democratic National Platform Committee's abortion-on-demand plank and its commitment to serving the vulnerable. He urged his party "to reexamine its position on abortion in the context of the Democratic Party's historic and noble mission of protecting the powerless." Governor Casey emphasized that "the powerless and the voiceless have been our natural constituency. Let us add to this list the most powerless and voiceless member of the human family: the unborn child" (Andrusko 1992, 13).

Casey's pleas fell on deaf ears. Not only did the Democratic National Committee reject them, but it denied him permission to address the convention on the abortion issue. Here was a snub of the first order. Casey is a two-term governor who is credited with rebuilding the Democratic Party in the nation's fifth largest state. In the 1988 election he swamped a pro-abortion Republican woman by over a million votes. While the Pennsylvania governor was not allowed access to the speaker's podium, six pro-abortion Republican women were showcased to announce their plans to vote Democratic because of President Bush's opposition to abortion. One of them worked for Casey's opponent in the Pennsylvania gubernatorial race. At a press conference during the convention, Governor Casey exposed the totalitarian, anti-democratic nature of the decision preventing him from addressing the delegates. "This convention imposed a gag rule on the most important issue of our time . . . the issue of who lives and who dies, the issue of abortion. It is catering to the far left and to the radical extremists who are not representative of this country" (King 1992, 7).

The Media Elite

Another influential branch of the cultural elite is the media elite, a designation encompassing those who run the institutions of popular culture—major publishing houses; reporters, broadcasters, columnists, editors, bureau chiefs, and executives involved in the collection and construction of the news; and writers, artists, producers, and stars in the television and moviemaking industries. These gatekeepers of information who determine what ideas, perceptions, attitudes, and values are allowed into the public domain are overwhelmingly in favor of the most extreme abortion position—abortion on demand. Studies conducted by Robert Lichter and others reveal that 90 percent of the news media elite have assimilated "right to choose" rhetoric as a prominent tenet of their social gospel. An even greater proportion of those in the world of filmmaking— 97 percent—hold an identical viewpoint.[4]

Not surprising, then, that the media coverage of abortion is so blatantly one-sided. News stories and commentaries on abortion typically make no mention of the existence, let alone humanity, of unborn children. In those few instances when their existence is acknowledged, an array of expressions are employed to trivialize or obscure the significance of human life before birth: protoplasm, tissue, products, contents, egg, ovum, pre-embryo, potential life. The words "kill" and "destroy" are also conspicuously absent from the accounts of abortion constructed by contemporary media gatekeepers. So are pictures of aborted humans. On those rare occasions when members of the media elite report on the act of abortion, they regularly resort to the most abstract, euphemistic terminology: "pregnancy termination," "pregnancy interruption," "removal of the contents of the uterus," "evacuation of the products of conception," "choice," and "selective reduction."

Much of this language is closely in line with two Orwellian statements regarding the indispensable role of semantics in defending the indefensible: "as soon as certain topics are raised, the concrete melts into the abstract" and "such phraseology is needed . . . to name things without calling up mental images of them" (Orwell 1956, 357, 363).

The manner in which today's megapress cosmetizes the killing of the unborn is epitomized by a picture story appearing in the *St. Louis Post-Dispatch* on Missouri's largest abortion facility, the "Reproductive Health Services." The article focuses on scenes of the clinic's roomy and attractive interiors, women decorating one of the rooms, and smiling staff members seated in a beautifully furnished reception room. Also highlighted is a picture of an immaculate "procedure room" equipped with a suction machine. Nowhere are there any graphics of the bodies or mangled parts of aborted babies. The dominant impression projected is a wholly idyllic one of empathetic people offering tender loving care in a pleasant and benevolent environment (Berg 1973, 1–15).

Such characterizations bear a striking resemblance to the German press's euphemistic portrayals of Nazi killing centers as "labor," "resettlement," "rehabilitation," and "concentration" camps. In December 1942 Fritz Fiala, a German newspaper editor, did a picture story on Auschwitz. He wrote about the presence of warm water, a children's kitchen, and an abundant supply of food. Also featured were pictures showing a Jewish coffee shop, a group of smiling nurses, and well-nourished young men. Completely missing was any pictorial evidence of gas chambers, crematoria, and destroyed bodies. This story, with its theme of loving concern, was published by the press throughout Europe (Laqueur 1980, 152–53).

Dehumanizing Language and Its Humanizing Challengers

Historically, one of the main reasons for the decline in or termination of oppression against various people and groups has been the presence of individuals who, even during periods when the discrediting semantics predominated, refused to accept the prevailing norms of name-calling. The success of any genuine human rights movement rests in large part on the capacity of its proponents to forge positive, personalized, and exalted images of the victims as worthwhile human beings whose oppression can no longer be tolerated. Renaming formerly degraded individuals as legitimate human lives deserving of respect and esteem will not necessarily achieve a major change in their treatment. However, given sufficient societal and institutional support, positive labels—like negative labels—can effect a profound change in how people are perceived and therefore treated.

Two major authorities are usually cited to sustain the positive labels designed to counteract linguistic oppression—the natural and supernatural orders of creation. According to the *natural law perspective,* all of the victims covered in this book share one thing in common: a human nature readily demonstrated by appeals to reason, logic, common sense, observation, and scientific findings. The intrinsic value of the victims is based on the democratic, egalitarian principle that all human beings deserve equal protection under the law despite their status, condition, or stage of development. The *divine law tradition* endows human nature with the imprint of spirituality. It portrays all human beings—including the most disabled and defenseless—as individuals of inestimable worth since they are made in the image and likeness of God. References to Holy Scripture and other religious sources furnish the basis for proclaiming the sanctity of every human life.

The secular and sacred foundations of terminology intended to offset massive victimization are often kept separate and distinct. Nonbelievers and individuals who do not wish to impose a religious viewpoint utilize language emphasizing the humanness of the victims. Others prefer to project a more exalted perception by highlighting the divine origin of all human beings. Still others see the human and divine as complementary levels of existence comprising a compelling cornerstone for challenging the dehumanizing rhetoric forged by perpetrators past and present. During the decades preceding the American Civil War many abolitionists invoked both the natural and supernatural law in their efforts to raise public awareness regarding the true nature of black Americans and the unconscionable conditions that slavery imposed upon them. The defenders of other oppressed groups have done and are doing likewise.

A remarkable strain of consistency permeates the language employed to highlight the human and spiritual nature of individuals and groups subjected to massive victimization. The contemporary opponents of abortion and euthanasia rely on the same range of positive expressions to defend the unwanted unborn and born of today that were used to defend Native Americans, African Americans, Soviet people, Jews, women, and other targets of past oppression. Down through the ages and up to the present the advocates of society's most vulnerable groups have thus drawn upon a common core of personalized designations for focusing on the intrinsic value, humanity, and divinity of those being victimized.

A fuller account of this positive, life-affirming language can be found in chapter 18. Table 2, "The Lexicon of Esteem," provides a comparative overview of some of these expressions.

A Lexicon of Esteem

	HUMAN PORTRAYALS	SPIRITUAL PORTRAYALS
Native Americans	"The Indian lives now. . . one of the great races." *(Indian Commissioner John Collier, 1942)*	"[Indians are] intelligent creatures of God." *(Bishop Henry Benjamin Whipple, 1859)*
African Americans	"The Negro was too much of a man to be held a chattel." *(Former slave Frederick Douglass, 1847)*	"God . . . gave them [Africans] life and freedom." *(Petition to New Hampshire legislature, 1779)*
Soviet People	"They [kulaks] are human beings!" *(Former persecutor of kulaks, 1972)*	"[Gulag prisoners are] wise spiritual beings." *(Author Aleksandr Solzhenitsyn, 1973)*
European Jews	"Jews are men and women . . . members of the human race." *(Archbishop Jules-Gerard Saliege's pastoral condemning Nazi persecution)*	"In this household, God's people are always welcome." *(Motivation of Ten Boom family for hiding Jews in Nazi-occupied Holland)*
Women	"[Women are] human beings . . . human fellow-creatures." *(Philosopher John Stuart Mill, 1869)*	"Women [are] in Creation, noble . . . in use, most blessed." *(Esther Sowernan, 1617)*
Unborn Humans	"I will maintain the utmost respect for human life from the time of its conception." *(Declaration of Geneva World Medical Assn., 1948)*	"That unborn child has been carved in the hand of God." *(Nobel Prize speech of Mother Teresa, 1979)*
Dependent and/or Disabled Persons	"A human being who is deserving of food and water as you and I." *(Nurse Jeryl Turco's appeal for patient whose feeding tube was removed, 1987)*	"Immortal beings, children of one Father and heirs with Christ of eternal light." *(Mary Carpenter's defense of poor and neglected children, 1861)*

The Scope of the Study

Massive oppression, however, is too complex a phenomenon to be reduced to language alone. Just why certain groups are singled out for victimization may have little to do with semantics and a lot to do with the availability of economic, social, and psychological resources; power; custom; and population stability, to mention a few factors. A major reason given for the practice of infanticide among the Netsilek Eskimos of the Arctic Circle, for example, was the scarcity of food. In the antebellum American South economics served as a dominant rationalization for enslaving black people. Today, a host of excuses are invoked in defense of abortion and euthanasia: economics, scarcity of resources, lifestyle considerations, overpopulation fears, humanitarianism, and others.

Nevertheless, whatever the utilitarian reasons given to justify oppression, the victims must also be linguistically castigated or consigned to a state of insignificance. Sooner or later, semantic denigration comes into play to ensure the successful implementation of the victimization process. Public health professor Susan C. M. Scrimshaw found that infanticide "is made culturally and personally acceptable in many societies by a definition of life that requires a 'waiting' period after birth before full membership in society is bestowed on an infant" (1984, 460–61). The selection of Jews as scapegoats for the numerous economic, social, and political crises that beset Germany following World War I was preceded by longstanding portrayals of Jews as dangerous, repulsive subhumans. Holocaust scholar Raul Hilberg concludes that Hitler resorted to a centuries-old nomenclature of anti-Semitic stereotypes: "When Hitler spoke about the Jew, he could speak to the Germans in familiar language. When he reviled his victim, he resurrected a medieval conception" (1967, 8).

The main focus of this research, therefore, is centered on derogatory terminology and its impact on a broad spectrum of victims, present and past. The overriding thrust is comparative; it will establish and document a rarely explored and little-known linkage: *the words used against the unwanted unborn and born in contemporary society are, in many instances, the same words constructed to revile some of history's most victimized groups.*

Each chapter in part 1 consists of thumbnail sketches of the various types of oppression directed against a specific group of victims. Highlighted are graphic descriptions of the horrendous nature of the violence perpetrated and its extensiveness. This section underscores the inhumanity of human beings toward other human beings today and in the past.

Chapters 8 through 15 in part 2 focus on the major dehumanizing classifications employed. Every chapter begins with one of the pejorative designations and shows how it is being used against today's most powerless individuals. Each chapter then delineates how the specific disparaging expression was directed against vulnerable individuals in times past. The chapters in this section also include information on the prominence of those responsible for the creation and dissemination of the demeaning language as well as the socio-cultural contexts in which it has been and continues to be embedded.

The chapters in part 3 set forth various ways to combat the dehumanizing rhetoric: chapter 16 exposes the falsity of the degrading designations and includes some suggestions for refuting them; chapter 17 furnishes insights into the disastrous consequences of name-calling both now and long ago, focusing especially on the cause-effect relationship between malevolent words and oppressive actions; chapter 18 emphasizes the power of humanizing and exalted expressions derived from secular and religious sources to overcome the disparaging rhetoric. It shows how the life-affirming terminology cited on behalf of today's most defenseless individuals continues a legacy of discourse employed to defend the rights of the most vulnerable people throughout history.

The postscript considers the current outlook for expanding the boundaries of the human community in light of the growing number of victims before and after birth who have been and are still being defined out of the human race.

Part One

Profiles in Oppression: The Plight of the Victims

1

Global War on the Unwanted Unborn

oday, scores of human lives before birth are proficiently snuffed out in a display of "raw medical power" in radical opposition to the physician-as-healer principle embodied in the doctor's most basic code of ethics, the Hippocratic Oath, an oath containing explicit condemnations of killing, both inside and outside the womb. The uterus—once a private sanctuary suited for growth and development—has been transformed into a deadly environment polluted by the invasion of destructive instruments and poisonous substances. The bodies of the undesired unborn are torn apart, dismembered, obliterated, poisoned, or subjected to lethal injections. Their remains are exploited for research, harvested as tissue and organ transplants, and either incinerated or dumped into the sewage and waste disposal systems.

A Silent Scream in the Womb

On the morning of January 22, 1985—twelve years after the U.S. Supreme Court in its *Roe v. Wade* decision had legalized abortion during all nine months of pregnancy—a movie known as *The Silent Scream* premiered at a press conference in the Senate Office Building. At the core of this film is a seven-minute ultrasound showing an actual abortion being performed on a twelve-week-old preborn human. The packed audience sat stunned as they witnessed the dismemberment of a tiny human being in utero. The film's narrator is Dr. Bernard N. Nathanson, at one time an avowed abortionist, a founding member of the National Association for the Repeal of Abortion Laws (now called the National Abortion Rights and Reproductive Action League), and former director of the largest abortion center in the Western world. His commentary furnishes a rare, noneuphemistic description of the intrauterine destruction process:

> This suction tip, which you can see moving violently back and forth on the bottom of the screen, is the lethal instrument which will ultimately tear apart and destroy the child. . . . We can see the tip moving back and forth as the abortionist seeks the child's body. Once again we see the child's mouth open in a silent scream. . . . This is the silent scream of a child threatened imminently with extinction.
>
> The suction tip has now been firmly clamped to the child's body, and the child is being pulled in a downward direction by the abortionist's suction tip with a negative pressure applied to it, and the body is now being torn systematically from the head. . . .
>
> I am now outlining the child's head. The lower extremities have already been lost. . . . The body is no longer discernible. It has now been torn from the head. . . . The abortionist will attempt to crush the head with this instrument [the polyp forceps], in this manner, and remove the head piecemeal from the uterus. . . . The head is now being locked on by this polyp forceps and the head is being pulled down towards the cervix. Now all we see remaining are simply the shards, the broken fragments, the pieces of tissue which document that there was once a living, defenseless, tiny human being here. (Smith and Tanner 1985, 24, 26)

More Unvarnished Accounts of Feticide

Because Dr. Nathanson has renounced his prior involvement in abortion and is now in the forefront of those opposed to abortion, many abortion advocates have attempted to dismiss his narration as the biased, inflammatory ravings of a newly converted, anti-abortion zealot. But abortion's inherent destructiveness is known to pro- and anti-abortionist alike.

Indeed, comparatively speaking, Dr. Nathanson's descriptions of the unborn's death throes are quite restrained.

Fetal research proponents Dr. Willard Gaylin and Dr. Marc Lappe characterize abortion procedures as "unimaginable acts of violence" that "subject the fetus to dismemberment, salt-osmotic shock, or surgical extirpation" (1975, 66).

An unusually frank description of the destructive impact of saline on the unborn child was furnished by abortionist Dr. William B. Waddill at a preliminary hearing before a California municipal court on April 18, 1977. The purpose of this hearing was to determine whether there was sufficient evidence to bring Dr. Waddill to trial for the strangulation death of a new-born baby girl who survived a saline abortion attempt. Dr. Waddill tried to impress upon the court that it was the saline that killed the baby and not him:

> Hypertonic saline causes tremendous basal dilatation of the blood vessels. In other words, the vessels just dilate and just stay dilated and with the extreme dehydration that occurs throughout the baby through the lungs, the gastrointestinal tract, the kidneys, through the vasculature, the cardiovascular system inside the baby, and the blood vessels of the baby, the brain is, I'm sure, destroyed from lack of blood supply. . . . It is such a caustic and tremen-dously bad and hostile environment for the baby that it just creates an enormous destructive process.[1]

According to an analysis conducted by Columbia University physicians on autopsies from 143 saline abortions, the saline injections led to "acute salt poisoning of the fetus" and "wide-spread vasodilatation, edema, congestion, hemorrhage, shock, and death" (Galen et al. 1974, 354).

A report on 130 Dilatation and Evacuation (D&E) abortions presented at the annual meeting of the Association of Planned Parenthood Physicians in 1977 by Dr. Sadja Goldsmith and col-leagues from the University of California (San Francisco) Medical Center provided the following details regarding this destructive operation: "The fetus was extracted in small pieces to minimize cervical trauma. The fetal head was often the most difficult object to crush and remove because of it size and contour. The operator kept track of each portion of the fetal skeleton in order to be sure of complete evacuation" (pp. 2–3).

Before the same group a year later, abortionist Dr. Warren M. Hern acknowledged how difficult it was for doctors to deny the destructive nature of D&E abortion. "We have reached a point in this particular technology where there is no possibility of denial of an act of destruction by the operator. It is before one's eyes. The sensations of dismemberment flow through the forceps like an electric current" (Hern and Corrigan 1978, 9).

British medical researchers now acknowledge "direct evidence that the fetus has a hormonal stress response" to such invasive procedures as the "termination of pregnancy, especially by surgical techniques involving dismemberment." Their answer to this troubling finding is not to cease performing what is a clearly painful, destructive operation, but to administer pain-relieving medication to the unwanted unborn before dismembering them (Giannakoulopoulos et al. 1994, 80).

Experimental Exploitation of Destruction

In 1974 an American medical journal published the results of an experiment that involved cutting the beating hearts out of aborted babies and placing them in a solution where their contraction rates could be observed. "The hearts survived for many hours without any significant change in their spontaneous contraction rate" (Resch et al. 1974, 73–74).

Fetal researcher Dr. Martti Kekomaki claims he has saved many premature infants by feeding them nutrients from the heads and livers of aborted humans. In 1980 he explained how such an experiment was carried out. "We isolated [cut out] its brain and liver. And then we put those organs through a rinsing machine to examine them for their nutritious substances" (Wade 1980, 20–21).

In January 1984 *Obstetrics and Gynecology* published the findings of an experiment conducted on aborted body parts derived from eighteen hundred D&E abortions. Dr. Warren Hern, the author of this study, subjected the dismembered remains to a series of measurements and statistical analyses. Regarding the assessment of fetal foot size, "sight measurement was taken from the tip of the longest toe (almost always the second) to the tip of the heel." Concerning the distance from the heel to the knee, "the ruler sighted from the bottom of the heel to the top of the flexed knee." The calvarium (the head), due to its crushed condition, presented a formidable obstacle to the achievement of measurement precision. Hern's resolution consisted of filling the "inverted, collapsed fetal calvarium" with water in order to "approximate the natural shape" of the skull (Hern 1984b, 26–32).

A Carnage of Global Proportions

Another alarming facet of abortion, aside from its unmitigated violence and the emotionally detached responses of its practitioners, is its awesome scope. Every year in America alone more than 1.5 million human lives are extinguished inside the womb. Well over 95 percent of these abortions are performed because of social factors, inconvenience, or the fact that the child is not wanted.[2]

The global abortion scene is likewise profoundly distressing. The number of abortions performed on a worldwide scale is estimated at between forty-five and sixty million per year! In the former Soviet Union eleven million abortions were performed each year (Henshaw 1986, 250–51). The "one couple, one child" population policy of the People's Republic of China has resulted in the staggering figure of fifty-three million abortions from 1979 to 1984! (Mosher 1985, 1)

Although the war on the unborn is more blatant in totalitarian regimes, it engulfs millions of victims under democratic and coercive governments alike. As the daily, weekly, and yearly body counts continue to soar, it is easy to lose sight of the immense tragedy inherent in each abortion: the life of a totally unique human being is irretrievably extinguished.

2

Assaults on Dependent and/or Disabled Discards

V iolence against society's most marginal members—the very young, the very old, and those beset with physical and mental afflictions—has been a recurrent phenomenon down through the ages. History is cluttered with barbaric acts visited upon weak, ill, dependent, and "defective" individuals: abuse, abandonment, exposure to the elements, burning, mutilation, suffocation, drowning, strangulation, starvation, and utilization as slave laborers. Oppression against the dependent and disabled is not a fleeting form of behavior confined to a primitive, bygone era or a past event recorded in historical archives. It is also very much a part of the contemporary scene, even in the midst of the many advances made on behalf of those least able to defend themselves.

Infanticide

In ancient Carthage children were sacrificed to wrathful pagan gods during state emergencies and public calamities. Their destruction often took place during special festivals. "Those who were sacrificed to Kronus [the Greek analogue of Moloch] were thrown into the arms of a molten idol . . . with the hands turned upwards, as it were to receive them, yet sloping downwards, so that they dropt into a glowing furnace below" (Wilson 1855, 19).

During the nineteenth century in England and Europe many unwanted newborns were dispatched to wet nurses who did away with their tiny charges by a practice known as "baby farming." In England these "killer nurses" or "angel makers" resorted to imposed starvation, overlaying (smothering the victims by rolling on top of them), extreme neglect, or the administration of opiates (Adamic 1936, 6).

Well into the twentieth century anthropological expeditions conducted among Eskimos residing on the Arctic coast uncovered numerous episodes of infanticide. The techniques of killing usually varied with the seasons. "In winter the newborn infant was placed in the snow porch where its cries could be heard by all visitors. Abandoned on the ice floor, it would rapidly freeze. . . . In summer, a small stone grave was made right by the skin tent and the baby was placed inside, where it cried for many hours until it died" (Balikei 1967, 2:619).

These instances of killing represent just the tip of a massive, age-old iceberg of child victimization. Although the destruction of human infants is commonly believed to be confined to only the most barbaric and primitive societies, it actually transcends the boundaries of savage and civilized cultures alike. This disquieting reality is borne out by a conclusion drawn by anthropologist Laila Williamson: "Infanticide has been practiced on every continent and by people on every level of cultural complexity, from hunters and gatherers to high civilizations, including our ancestors. Rather than being the exception, then, it has been the rule" (1978, 61).

The Denial of Medical Treatment

Dr. Raymond S. Duff and Dr. A. G. M. Campbell disclosed in *The New England Journal of Medicine* (October 25, 1973) that over a thirty-month period forty-three seriously impaired infants at the Yale–New Haven intensive-care nursery died because they were denied life-preserving treatment. The victims included those with Down's syndrome, meningomyelocele (spina bifida), cardiopulmonary disorders, and nervous system difficulties. Duff and Campbell recommended wide latitude in decision making regarding the future of such children, with death as an appropriate "management option" (1973, 890–94).

In May 1977 Phillip Becker, an eleven-year-old child with Down's syndrome living in a small private-care nursery located in San Jose, California, was diagnosed as having a "ventricular septal defect"—a large hole in the wall separating the heart's two pumping chambers. A cardiologist advised that open heart surgery be performed immediately to avert a prolonged, painful death by age thirty. Although Phillip had been institutionalized since birth and had never spent a single minute in his parents' home, they still retained legal custody. The Beckers decided against allowing the surgery.

An extended series of bitter court struggles ensued to determine Phillip's fate. In 1981 California Superior Court Judge William Fernandez granted custody of Phillip to Patsy and Herbert Heath, who had filed for legal guardianship on the grounds that they had become his "psychological, de facto parents." Phillip had spent weekends at their home and called them "mom" and "dad."[1] Unlike the other cases referred to in this chapter, Phillip Becker's ordeal ended happily; he underwent successful heart surgery in 1983, but only because of the herculean legal efforts mustered on his behalf.

The decision not to treat older people when afflicted with ordinary illnesses can have disastrous consequences. A report in *The New England Journal of Medicine* (May 31, 1979) revealed that doctors and nurses decided to withhold treatment (denial of antibiotics and/or hospitalization) from eighty-one febrile residents of nine extended-care facilities in Seattle, Washington. Forty-eight (59 percent) died as a direct result of not being treated for their fevers. Of the thirty-three who survived the lack of treatment, a large proportion did so only temporarily—39 percent died within a month after the febrile episode. The most likely candidates for non-treatment were described as "bedridden," "in pain," "receiving narcotics," "unmarried persons," and "with feeding problems" (Brown and Thompson 1979, 1246–50).

Imposed Starvation

The practice of deliberately starving unwanted handicapped children in prestigious American medical centers was first brought to public attention in 1971 through a film, *Who Should Survive?*, produced by the Joseph P. Kennedy, Jr. Foundation. The movie recreated an actual case in which a child born with Down's syndrome plus duodenal atresia (an intestinal blockage) was allowed to starve to death at Johns Hopkins University Hospital in Baltimore, Maryland, because his parents refused to grant permission for the necessary corrective surgery. A sign—"Nothing by Mouth"—was placed on the bassinet and the child was wheeled into an isolated room. The physician-narrator of the film gave his response to the prolonged death watch. "It took 15 days for the baby to become severely dehydrated enough that he finally died and that was an awful long time."[2]

One of the most highly publicized cases of enforced starvation is that of "Infant Doe," a boy born on April 9, 1982, in a hospital in Bloomington, Indiana. The child had two afflictions: Down's syndrome and a malformed esophagus that prevented food from reaching the stomach. The first could not be altered; the second could have been remedied by low-risk surgery (a 90 percent success rate) that would connect the esophagus to the stomach.

The parents denied permission for the needed surgery *and* for intravenous feeding. A "Do Not Feed" order was taped on Infant Doe's crib. Two days later his stomach acids began corroding his lungs and he started spitting blood. When the hospital nurses threatened to walk out, he was transferred to another part of the hospital and private duty nurses were hired to monitor the situation. It took him six days to expire (Lyon 1985, 31, 35). An attorney involved in trying to save his life revealed that Infant Doe cried uncontrollably during the last four days of life (Bopp 1982, 1, 8). Dr. Anne Bannon, a pediatrician, captures the horrendous ordeal in the following portrayal:

> Baby Doe's shrunken, thin little body, with dry cyanotic skin, extremely dehydrated, breathing shallowly and irregularly, lay passively on fresh hospital linens. Blood was running from a mouth too dry to close. Death by starvation was near. Too late for fluids. Too late for surgery. Too late for justice. (1982, 64)

3

Female Objects of Sexploitation and Violence

S ubjection to countless atrocities has been the plight of many women throughout much of history. The parade of horrors has been virtually endless: female infanticide, enforced prostitution, the burning of women accused of witchcraft, widow burning, the sale of enslaved females, wife battering, pornographic exploitation, rape, incest, and other types of sexual assaults. The persistence of oppression against women is a grim testimony of man's inhumanity toward female members of the human race. Few groups have been exposed to such a broad range of brutalities over such a prolonged duration. And the victimization has not ended; women continue to be abused, exploited, and assaulted on a huge scale in today's world.

Widow Burning

Webster defines *suttee* (widow burning) as "the act or custom of a Hindu woman willingly cremating herself or being cremated on the funeral pyre of her husband as an indication of her devotion to him."

Despite the voluntary and devotional elements in this definition, *suttee* is in actuality a cruel and coercive form of human sacrifice imposed on women against their wills. In Muslim India the reluctant candidate for immolation "was usually surrounded by men armed with sticks who goaded her on to her destination by physical force." Other methods of coercion consisted of tying the hands and legs of the victims as they mounted the pyre, rendering "widows suspected of weakness of will" senseless through drugs or alcohol, and pushing them into the flames of deep, escape-proof pits (Thomas 1964, 263, 295–96).

The lengths to which the perpetrators went to ensure that the unwilling victims be subjected to this destructive ritual is illustrated by an incident that occurred in 1769. A widow escaped from a pyre in the rain. The following day, a search party found her hiding out and dragged her back to the pyre:

> She pleaded to be spared but her own son insisted that she throw herself on the pile as he would lose caste and suffer everlasting humiliation. When she still refused the son with the help of some others present bound her hands and feet and hurled her into the blaze. (Walker 1968, 2:464)

Sexual Assaults

One of the most horrendous atrocities perpetrated against women began on December 13, 1937, when the Japanese army seized China's capital city of Nanking with a vengeance. Besides engaging in widespread looting, arson, and wanton murder, the invading forces committed wholesale sexual assaults against Chinese women. The incidence of rape was so widespread that this outburst became known as "The Rape of Nanking." According to evidence submitted at the International Military Tribunal for the Far East held in Tokyo in 1946, "approximately 20,000 cases of rape occurred within the city during the first month of occupation." The tribunal concluded:

> Death was a frequent penalty for the slightest resistance on the part of a victim or the members of her family who sought to protect her. Even girls of tender years and old women were raped in large numbers through-out the city, and many cases of abnormal or sadistic behavior in connection with the rapings occurred. Many women were killed after the act and their bodies muti-lated. (Brownmiller 1975, 61)

Sexual violence is a stubbornly chronic crime that transcends diverse historical periods and cultures. Down through the ages—in times of war and peace—rape has been employed as a weapon to intimidate, overpower, violate, humiliate, injure, and sometimes kill scores of women. Despite today's legal and social efforts to end this form of sexual terrorism, growing numbers of women face a greater risk of being sexually abused and assaulted. In 1987 just over ninety-one thousand rapes were reported in the United States. This figure represents an increase of 11 percent since 1983. A crime clock compiled by the Federal Bureau of Investigation shows that one rape takes place every six minutes (Dept. of Justice 1988, 6, 13–15).

Battered Wives

In ancient Rome husbands and fathers could put women to death without a public trial. Death was imposed for the most trivial offenses. A Roman husband, Egnatius Metellus, "beat his wife to death because she had drunk some wine; and this murder, far from leading to his being denounced, was not even blamed. People considered that her exemplary punishment had properly expiated her offense against the law of sobriety" (O'Faolain and Martines 1973, 37).

According to the mores prevalent in late thirteenth-century France, "provided he neither kills nor maims her, it is legal for a man to beat his wife when she wrongs him" (ibid., 175). Fifteenth-century England—the so-called Age of Chivalry when knights in shining armor provided damsels in distress with the utmost protection and respect—was also an era in which a popular manual imported from France, "The Knight of the La Tour Landry," furnished a highly unchivalrous prescription for dealing with scolding wives:

He smote her with his fist down to the earth. And then with his foot he struck her in the visage and broke her nose, and all her life after she had her nose crooked that she might not for shame show her visage it was so foul blemished. . . . Therefore the wife ought to suffer and let the husband have the word, and to be master (Trevelyan 1952, 260).

In an article written for *The Contemporary Review* (1878), Frances Power Cobbe disclosed that "over a three-year period in England about six thousand women had been 'brutally assaulted'—that is, maimed, blinded, trampled, burned, and in no inconsiderate number of instances murdered outright" (p. 79). Cobbe identified a pronounced pattern of ever-increasing violence associated with wife beating:

Wife-*beating* in process of time, and in numberless cases, advances to Wife-*torture,* and the Wife-torture usually ends in Wife-maiming, Wife-blinding, or Wife-murder. A man who has "thrashed" his wife with his fists half-a-dozen times, becomes satiated with such enjoyment as that performance brings, and next time he is angry he kicks her with his hob-nailed shoes. When he has kicked her a few times standing or sitting, he kicks her down and stamps on her stomach, her breast, or her face. If he does not wear clogs or hob-nailed shoes, he takes up some other weapon, a knife, a poker, a hammer, a bottle of vitriol, or a lighted lamp, and strikes her with it, or sets her on fire;—and then, and then only, the hopeless creature's sufferings are at an end. (p. 73)

Things did not fare any better for wives in America. The husband's right to "chastise" (a euphemism for beat) his spouse occupied an honored position in American law for a long period of time. This right was granted formal legal approval by the state of Mississippi in 1824. Other states soon followed suit. Not until 1871 did the movement for making wife beating illegal begin to take hold in the system of American jurisprudence. In that year, courts in Alabama and Massachusetts declared: "The privilege, ancient though it be, to beat her with a stick, to pull her hair, choke her, spit in her face or kick her is not now acknowledged by our law" (Dobash and Dobash 1977–78, 430–31).

Despite the removal of legal recognition from wife battering and the improved enforcement of laws against this practice, it still remains deeply embedded in the United States and in other societies throughout the world. As of 1985 in America alone, according to figures furnished by Murray Straus, director of the University of New Hampshire Family Research Laboratory, "more than 1,300,000 wives, out of the nation's 54,000,000 couples, are still being severely assaulted each year." This violence includes "kicking, hitting with a fist, beating up, biting, and using or threatening to use a gun or knife."[1]

Physical, sexual, and other assaults upon women inside and outside the home continue to escalate at such an alarming rate that this appalling situation is often likened to a full-scale "war against women." And the word "femicide" is increasingly employed to highlight the huge proportion of violence perpetrated against women by men.[2]

4

Destruction of European Jews and Others

T he wholesale extermination of Jews and other victims by the Nazis constitutes one of the darkest chapters in the history of inhumanity. During the twelve years of the Third Reich the Holocaust obliterated some six million Jews, approximately 275,000 Germans with disabilities, a quarter of a million Gypsies, millions of Poles and Russians, and untold numbers of miscellaneous "expendables." The Nazis pioneered assembly-line killing in death factories, annihilating human beings quickly and efficiently according to the most advanced methods of destruction: shooting, gassing, burning, and lethal injections, to name a few. The bodies of the victims were also subjected to experimental and commercial exploitation before, during, and after extirpation.

Mobile Killing Units

In the Eastern territories special mobile killing units, called *Einsatzgruppen,* followed upon the heels of the German army in search-and-destroy missions bent on eradicating Jews and individuals not considered up to par with the Aryan standard of perfection. The victims were shot in front of huge ditches and then toppled into the gaping holes. Those who did not expire immediately suffocated as a result of being buried alive.

On October 5, 1942, Hermann Graebe, a German civilian works engineer, witnessed such a scene in the former Volhynian province of Poland. In an affidavit prepared for presentation before the Nuremberg War Crimes Tribunal on July 27, 1946, Graebe wrote about this unnerving experience:

I then walked round the mound and found myself con-
fronted by a tremendous grave. People were closely
wedged together and lying on top of each other so that
only their heads were visible. Nearly all had blood running over their shoulders from their heads. . . . The people—they were completely naked—went down some
steps which were cut in the clay wall of the pit and
clambered over the heads of those who were lying there
to the place to which the SS man directed them. They
lay down in front of the dead and wounded. Some
caressed the living and spoke to them in a low voice.
Then I heard a series of shots. I looked into the pit and
saw that their bodies still twitched or that their heads lay
motionless on top of the other bodies before them.
Blood ran from their necks. (Rietlinger 1961, 205–6)

Death Factories for Genocide

Dying inside the gas chambers of Nazi killing centers was a
painful and prolonged process in which the inmates desper-
ately gasped for life and breath. In their futile efforts to escape
the deadly fumes, the hardiest among them trampled upon
women, children, and the elderly. Body disposal squads developed "special hook-tipped poles," thrust deep into the flesh of
the newly exterminated, to facilitate the task of removing
entangled, bloated, and deformed corpses with blood oozing
from their noses and mouths (Lengyel 1947, 75).

During the height of the killing season at Auschwitz, children were thrown straight into the crematorium furnaces or
into flaming pits, without being gassed first. A witness at the
International Nuremberg Trial speculated as to why this was
done. "It's very difficult to say. We don't know whether they
wanted to economize on gas, or if it was because there was not
enough room in the gas chamber" (Kraus and Kulka 1966, 114).

Testimony presented at Nuremberg on January 7, 1946, disclosed that the Nazis had planned to exterminate over thirty
million Slavic people. Preparations were under way for converting an armament factory into an extermination center that

would "dwarf the gas chambers and crematoria at Auschwitz" (Alexander 1948, 39:311, 318).

Enforced Starvation

The children of foreign workers in countries under Nazi rule were given "racial examinations" to measure their degree of fitness. Those who passed were sent to homes under the auspices of the Lebensborn (fountain of life) to be Germanized. Those who failed were dispatched to special homes where they eventually expired, many due to a policy of enforced starvation. An inspector's report on one such institution revealed that "the home receives only a pint of milk and a piece and a half of sugar per day per baby. With these rations the babies are sure to die of malnutrition in a few months" (Poliakov 1979, 174).

Imposed starvation was a prime weapon against "defective" and emotionally disturbed children languishing in the "children's divisions" of psychiatric and euthanasia hospitals throughout Nazi Germany. Dr. Hermann Pfannmuller, head of the Eglfing-Haar mental hospital, gave a demonstration in 1939 of how the "natural and simple" method of death by starvation operated at his institution. "Food was not withdrawn from the children all at once," he explained, "but by gradual reduction of the rations." According to an eyewitness account, Dr. Pfannmuller picked up one of the children, "a whimpering bundle of skin and bones," and "showed around the child like a dead rabbit." He then said: "This one, for example, may take another two or three days" (Mitscherlich and Mielke 1949, 101).

Experimental Brutalities

The expendables of the Nazi concentration camp at Dachau served as research subjects for a series of scientific monstrosities known as "cooling" or "freezing" experiments designed to develop rewarming techniques for rescuing German aviators or naval personnel forced to abandon their crafts at sea. These experiments consisted of immersing inmates in enormous basins of ice cold water almost to the point of death. After removal from the water, various methods of rewarming were tested on them. Many victims did not survive; they had been either chilled beyond revival or the rewarming method applied did not work.

The following excerpts from a report entitled "On Cooling Experiments on Human Beings," dated October 10, 1942, provide data on the final responses of these terminal human guinea pigs:

> Upon entry into the water a severe cold shuddering appeared. . . . The subject began to groan and made some defensive movements. . . . There followed a progressive rigor, which developed especially strongly in the arm musculature; the arms were strongly flexed and pressed to the body. The rigor increased with the continuation of the cooling, now and then interrupted by tonic-clonic twitchings. . . .
>
> Simultaneous with the rigor a severe *difficulty in breathing* set in. . . . *expiration was prolonged and visibly difficult.* . . . In part this was "normal, much decelerated breathing," in part an agonal form of gasping. . . . Death occurred with a drop in temperature to values between 24.2° and 25.7° C.[1]

Dr. August Hirt, anatomy professor at the Reich University of Strasbourg, displayed a painstaking commitment to proving the inferiority of the Jewish race through skull measurements. The information for this project came from the heads of inmates exterminated in the gas chambers (ibid., 749).

5

Genocide of the Soviet People

A momentous event in Soviet history took place on February 24–25, 1956, at the Twentieth Soviet Party Congress held in Moscow. During a closed session, Nikita S. Khrushchev delivered a devastating report denouncing deceased dictator Joseph Stalin in the most scathing terms. His speech concentrated mainly on the brutal crimes Stalin perpetrated during the 1930s against Party members branded as "enemies of the people." Khrushchev acknowledged that the charges that led to the deaths of "many thousands of honest and innocent Communists" were monstrous fabrications (1962, S32). Khrushchev's revelations, however unprecedented and startling, touched only a small segment of an enormous destruction process. He said nothing about the vastly greater crimes committed against the Soviet people that began during Lenin's reign and continued in massive proportions under Stalin.

The Terror-Famine

Soviet tyranny was directed with incomparable zeal against peasants who resisted the forcible collectivization of agriculture in the late 1920s and early 1930s. During this period a heinous approach toward dealing with uncooperative farmers—artificially induced famine—came of age. This barbaric method of mass extermination hit the Ukraine with unrestrained ferocity. According to figures compiled by Robert Conquest in *The Harvest of Sorrow* (1986), at least seven million Ukrainian peasants—three million of them children—perished during the winter of 1932–33 alone (p. 303). Conquest furnishes a memorable portrayal of the horror produced by this terror-famine:

> Fifty years ago as I write these words, the Ukraine and the Ukrainian, Cossack and other areas to the east—a great stretch of territory with some forty million inhabitants—was like one vast Belsen. A quarter of the rural population, men, women, and children, lay dead or dying, the rest in various stages of debilitation with no strength to bury their families or neighbours. At the same time (as at Belsen), well-fed squads of police or party officials supervised the victims.
>
> This was the climax of the "revolution from above," as Stalin put it, in which he and his associates crushed two elements seen as irremediably hostile to the regime: the peasantry of the USSR as a whole, and the Ukrainian nation. (ibid., 3)

When mass starvation reached its peak, the Soviet Union was exporting large quantities of grain. As one writer put it: "Butter was sent abroad while the Ukrainian infants were dying for lack of milk" (Conquest 1986, 22). Imposed starvation was considered an indispensable weapon against farmers who opposed the regime's agricultural decrees. One highly placed Kremlin official characterized the 1933 "harvest" as "a test of our strength and their endurance. It took a famine to show them who is master here. It has cost millions of lives, but the collective farm system is here to stay. We've won the war" (Kravchenko 1946, 130).

Annihilation in the Gulag

The Gulag Archipelago—"Gulag" is an acronym for the Chief Administration of Corrective Labor Camps and the word "Archipelago" refers to the huge network of these penal camps that dotted the length and breadth of the Soviet Union the way an archipelago dots the sea—served as a vast receptacle for the so-called enemies of the Soviet people (peasants, priests, wreckers, idlers, "deviationists," Communist Party officials out of favor with the regime, intellectuals, engineers, bureaucrats, people who committed the most trivial offenses, and some individuals who did nothing wrong—the sentence for doing nothing wrong was ten years). In this vast tundra, millions were worked to death or died from the effects of beatings, starvation, and contagious diseases.

The most notorious section of the Gulag was the gigantic labor camp complex at Kolyma where some three million people perished due to a fatal combination of executions, inhuman living conditions, impossible labor norms, and virulent epidemics. Robert Conquest's research contains an abundance of horrifying details on the inhumanity of human beings in this deadliest of mass-imprisonment areas. Many instances were reported of prisoners "savagely beheaded with axes in broad daylight or stabbed to death with picks and shovels." At one of the Kolyma camps "prisoners were led with eyes bound to a deep trench and were shot in the ear or the back of the neck" (1978, 84, 57).

The Scope of Oppression

One will never know with certitude how many people were actually exterminated, tortured, exiled, incarcerated, and subjected to other forms of oppression under Soviet totalitarianism. A fully documented appraisal is hard to come by because so many records have been lost, destroyed, concealed, or falsified. A number of estimates, however, provide some indication of the vastness of the evil perpetrated.

In *The Great Terror: A Reassessment,* Robert Conquest places the number killed under the Stalinist regime at twenty million (1990, 486). Soviet historian Anton Antonov-Ovseyenko arrives at the far higher figure of sixty-five million (Methvin 1985, 24). Aleksandr Solzhenitsyn maintains that "internal repression cost us from the beginning of the October Revolution up to 1959, a total of . . . sixty-six million—66,000,000—lives" (1973–74, 2:10). According to historian Roy Medvedev, the total number of victims under Stalin was forty million—at least twenty million deaths and twenty million who suffered severe reprisals.[1] According to historian Alex Nove, "10–11 million perished in the thirties, with the peasants numerically the main victims" (1993, 268). These figures are based on recently declassified Soviet archival material.

None of these estimates includes Soviet deaths incurred in World War II—that figure is commonly believed to be around twenty million. The range of ten to sixty-six million dead refers exclusively to the number of non-war casualties. Nick Eberstadt of the Harvard Center for Population Studies concludes that the Stalin-led Soviet Union waged war on two fronts: "The first was against the invaders; the second was against its own citizenry" (Methvin 1985, 24). The totality of human lives obliterated by the Soviet regime, whether the body count begins with Lenin's or Stalin's dictatorship, is staggering and constitutes one of the most massive slaughters in history.

6

Black Slavery and Kindred Atrocities

The enslavement of black people in the United States—a well-entrenched practice dating from the founding of colonies by Europeans through the Civil War—constituted not only a monstrous iniquity in its own right, but also spawned a legion of barbarities and injustices. Slavery's most basic legacy, the denial of fundamental human rights, continued to run roughshod over black Americans long after the United States abolished involuntary servitude and granted citizenship and attendant rights to blacks in three landmark amendments (thirteenth, fourteenth, and fifteenth) to the United States Constitution enacted between 1865 and 1870. Among the most frequently employed devices to nullify the impact of these major advances were rigid segregation in housing and education, lynching and other forms of violence, denial of voting rights, lack of access to public accommodations, and unequal employment opportunities.

The Travail of the International Slave Trade

During the countless voyages from Africa to the Americas in the heyday of the international slave trade, Africans—bound in chains—were usually forced to spend long periods of time down in the ship's hold, crowded together in a dark, wet, slimy, and stifling environment. When conditions grew unbearable, piercing screams could be heard coming from below deck. Opening the hatches revealed scenes of horror:

> They [the captain and his crew] found a number of them in different stages of suffocation, many of them were

foaming at the mouth, and in the last agonies—many were dead. The tumult they had heard was the frenzy of those suffocating wretches in the last stage of fury and desperation, struggling to extricate themselves. . . . Many destroyed one another, in the hopes of procuring room to breathe; men strangled those next [to] them, and women drove nails into each other's brains. Many unfortunate creatures, on other occasions, took the first opportunity of leaping overboard, and getting rid, in this way of an intolerable life. (Tannenbaum 1947, 25)

According to the best estimates, the number of blacks captured for shipment to the New World, from the sixteenth through the middle of the nineteenth century, ranged from thirteen to twenty million. Of this total, one-third died inland on the way to the African coast, one-third expired crossing the Atlantic Ocean, and one-third reached the New World. When they arrived, "the crowd of purchasers rushed upon the ship and manhandled the frightened Negroes lined up for inspection . . . and the frightened, naked creatures were looked over, measured, felt, and haggled about like cattle at any market" (ibid., 32, 28).

Enslavement American Style

While some masters treated their slaves in a humane manner, a life of bondage, for the most part, was a harsh and grim existence for the great majority of bondsmen. The long hours of backbreaking labor, inadequate nourishment, and the horrendous living conditions exacted a huge toll of human suffering and resulted in drastically shortened life spans. Even minor infractions on the part of slaves could bring forth a multitude of severe punishments, including brutal whippings, torture, and mutilations.

The horrors of slavery are documented in *American Slavery As It Is: Testimony of a Thousand Witnesses* (1839), widely recognized as one of the most devastating indictments of slavery ever recorded:

> We will prove that the slaves in the United States are treated with barbarous inhumanity; that they are over-worked, underfed, wretchedly clad and lodged, and have insufficient sleep; that they are often made to wear round their necks iron chains armed with prongs, to drag heavy chains and weights at their feet while working in the field. . . . that they are often kept confined in the stocks day and night for weeks together, made to wear gags in their mouths for hours or days, have some of their front teeth torn out or broken off, that they may be easily detected when they run away. . . . that they are often sus-pended by the arms and whipped and beaten till they faint, and when revived by restoratives, beaten again till they faint, and sometimes till they die; that their ears are often cut off, their eyes knocked out, their bones broken, their flesh branded with red hot irons; that they are maimed, mutilated and burned to death over slow fires. All these things, and more, and worse, we shall *prove*.[1]

Whatever semblance of family life that existed was torn asunder by such horrendous actions. Economics rather than kin-ship affiliation governed the fate of most slaves. Men, women, and children were sold or auctioned off, not as family units but as separate pieces of property. Not only did the American sys-tem of servitude disrupt and damage so many human lives, it profoundly undermined the black family as well.

The Hunting Down of Escaped Slaves

Such a repressive system could not help but produce a vast number of escape attempts. Reprisals against runaway slaves were exceedingly cruel: castration, flogging, the amputation of a foot, and burning at the stake, to mention but a few. The hiring of trackers with their bloodhounds to hunt down runaway slaves became a flourishing enterprise. The following advertisement is typical of those that appeared in newspapers throughout the South:

> BLOODHOUNDS! The undersigned having a magnificent Pack of hounds, for Trailing and Catching runaway Niggers, takes this method of informing his Friends and the Public, generally, that his prices are as follows: For each day employed in either Hunting or Trailing, $2.50; for catching each slave, $10; for going over ten miles and catching a Slave, $20. If sent for, the above prices will be expected, in Cash. The subscriber lives one mile and a half south of Daudeville.[2]

Mob Violence and Lynching

Lynching—the putting to death by mob action without legal sanction of any individual suspected or convicted of a crime or accused of violating prevailing social customs or mores—claimed the lives of some 3,436 blacks from 1882, when lynchings were first recorded, until the middle of the twentieth century. According to data compiled by the Tuskegee Institute archives, during the 1880s an average of 67 victims were lynched each year; in the 1890s the average annual figure jumped to 111; the first two decades of the twentieth century were characterized by an average lynch rate of 68 annually. In the 1920s and 1930s the yearly average totals tapered off to twenty-eight and twelve respectively.[3] These figures may well understate the actual incidence of lynchings, since they include only those that were recorded. It is likely that many instances of mob violence against blacks were never incorporated into the official statistics.

The methods of lynching were brutal and sadistic. The victims were flogged, dismembered, and tortured unmercifully before being killed by burning, hanging, or shooting. After death their bodies continued to be assaulted, abused, desecrated, and subjected to the most repulsive and destructive rituals. A festive atmosphere sometimes permeated the ghastly executions. Extant photographs show that many onlookers—men, women, and children—did not appear to be bothered by the horrendous spectacles, but seemed as if they were on a Roman holiday or attending a picnic (Harris 1984, 6).

A variety of justifications for lynching were given, ranging from murder and rape to disputing a white man's word, acting "troublesome," using offensive language, and throwing stones. Southern whites defended lynching as a necessary protective measure to stem the alleged tidal wave of sexual assaults perpetrated by black men against white women. This justification turned out to be a fraud—less than 26 percent of those lynched were charged with rape or attempted rape. And many of them had been neither tried nor convicted of this offense (Zangrando 1980, 8).

7

Annihilation of Native Americans

G one are the buffalo. Gone are the numerous and diverse Indian nations that once had depended so completely upon these great beasts for subsistence and survival. The wholesale departure of Native Americans from the landscape of North America was not the inevitable result of a primitive, inferior race naturally wilting before the march of progress and modern civilization. It was due, instead, to a deliberate and pervasive policy of rank exploitation and extermination. The treatment of Native Americans by whites down through the ages is rife with countless atrocities, long trails of broken treaties, dispossession of Indian lands, annihilation of the Indian people and their culture, and enforced confinement to the stifling settings of reservations.

Wounded Knee: Present and Past

On February 28, 1973, activists from the American Indian Movement (AIM) led a takeover of the small village of Wounded Knee, South Dakota, located on the Sioux's Pine Ridge Reservation. They barricaded themselves in a hilltop church for seventy-one days and issued a series of demands pertaining to the failure of the U.S. government to honor rights guaranteed Indians by previously ratified treaties. Russell Means, one of AIM's principal leaders, announced an Indian Declaration of Independence from the United States (Deloria 1974, 77–78).

The occupation at Wounded Knee received extensive television and press coverage. The media displayed a prolonged fascination with how imaginatively and vigorously America's

oldest and most invisible minority had suddenly emerged from
obscurity to assert its concerns. The Indian leaders made use of
this opportunity to highlight the longstanding plight of a people
who had been so thoroughly dispossessed and disenfranchised.

Selection of Wounded Knee as the locale for the 1973
protests against the deplorable governmental treatment of
Indians possessed considerable symbolic significance. It was
on the morning of December 29, 1890, at this same village of
Wounded Knee that soldiers of the United States Seventh
Cavalry ruthlessly massacred over three hundred Sioux Indians.
The soldiers relentlessly pursued the fleeing women and children, shooting them to death and leaving over a two-mile-long
trail of bodies. One of the few survivors, Louise Weasel Bear,
recalled what happened: "We tried to run, but they shot us like
we were a buffalo" (Brown 1970, 417).

A severe blizzard swept over the northern plains late in the
afternoon, preventing burial of the dead Indians. Not until
New Year's Day were the corpses—frozen into the hideous
shapes of violent death—thrown into a mass grave. In his
book on the systematic destruction of Indians of the American
West in the second half of the nineteenth century, *Bury My
Heart at Wounded Knee* (1970), Dee Brown wrote about the
terrible irony of the Wounded Knee massacre during the
Christmas season:

> It was the fourth day after Christmas in the Year of Our
> Lord 1890. When the first torn and bleeding bodies
> were carried into the candlelit church, those who were
> conscious could see Christmas greenery hanging from
> the open rafters. Across the chancel front above the pul-
> pit was strung a crudely lettered banner: PEACE ON
> EARTH, GOOD WILL TO MEN. (ibid., 418)

What happened at Wounded Knee in 1890 does not square
with the predominant image of Indians that many schoolchild-
ren have been brought up to believe. History books and
"Cowboys and Indians" films have long portrayed Indians as

wild savages who wantonly slaughtered innocent white settlers and displayed their scalps as an exhibition of hunting acumen. This, however, is a highly distorted stereotype. In many instances the whites were the real oppressors and the Indians the oppressed. Actually, the Wounded Knee massacre is a far more representative incident in the reprehensible history of Native American victimization by whites.

The Trail of Tears

Among the Indian nations the Cherokee, once occupying the beautiful hill country of northern Georgia and northeastern Alabama plus equally beautiful segments of Tennessee and North Carolina, were far and away the most acculturated group according to white American standards. Many Cherokee lived in the whites' style of housing, wore the same clothes as the whites, switched from hunting to agriculture, became Christian, and adopted the English language as their own. Despite the tremendous strides made in "civilizing" themselves far beyond a level achieved by any Indian nation north of the Rio Grande, and despite the fact that treaties and acts of Congress and two Supreme Court decisions favorable to the Cherokee had secured for them the legal rights to their lands, Georgia and other Southern states pursued an unremitting policy of dispatching all eastern Indians, including the Cherokee, to the territories west of the Mississippi River.

In 1838 Major General Winfield Scott and a party of soldiers forcibly removed the Cherokee from their beloved lands. The task of herding some sixteen thousand reluctant, ill-prepared travelers westward over hundreds of miles of unfamiliar terrain under the most inclement weather conditions proved to be an arduous and disastrous experience. For many, the trek turned out to be a death march—about four thousand individuals, approximately one-fourth of the total, died on what became known as "The Trail of Tears." The following excerpts published in *The New York Observer* furnish an eyewitness report on this tragedy:

The last detachment which we passed on the 7th [comprised nearly] two thousand Indians with horses and mules in proportion. . . . The sick and feeble were carried in wagons—about as comfortable for traveling as a New England ox cart with a covering over it—a great many ride on horseback and multitudes go on foot—even aged females, apparently nearly ready to drop into the grave, were traveling with heavy burdens attached to the back— on the sometimes frozen ground, and sometimes muddy streets, with no covering for the feet except what nature had given them . . . they buried fourteen or fifteen at every stopping place. (Weeks and Gidney 1981, 66–67)

Massacre at Sand Creek

On November 29, 1864, Colonel John Chivington led a contingent of 750 Colorado militia in a surprise and unprovoked attack against a group of peaceful Cheyenne residing in a camp along Sand Creek, Colorado. The Indians had been assured that they were under the protection of the United States Army. Assuming a mistake had been made, Chief Black Kettle raised both a white and an American flag, but to no avail. The troops swept through the camp with unbridled fury, killing 163 Indians, 110 of whom were women and children. Colonel Chivington sent a dispatch from the site of the massacre maintaining that "all did nobly," while *The Rocky Mountain News* reported: "All acquitted themselves well. Colorado soldiers have again covered themselves with glory."[1]

A congressional investigation into the atrocities committed at Sand Creek contains an unvarnished account of what really took place:

And then the scene of murder and barbarity began— men, women, and children were indiscriminately slaughtered. In a few minutes all the Indians were flying over the plain in terror and confusion. A few who endeavored to hide themselves under the bank of the creek were surrounded and shot down in cold blood, offering but feeble resistance. From the sucking babe to the old warrior, all who were overtaken were deliberately murdered. . . .

All manner of depredations were inflicted on their persons; they were scalped, their brains knocked out; the men used their knives, ripped open women, clubbed little children, knocked them in the head with their guns, beat their brains out, mutilated their bodies in every sense of the word. (Joint Committee on the Conduct of War [1864] 1972, 157)

These atrocities represent just a sampling of one of the most unrelenting episodes of mass victimization in history. Beginning with the fateful voyage of Christopher Columbus in 1492, the subjugation, dispossession, and depopulation of the native inhabitants of North America occurred over the better part of four centuries, culminating in the massacre at Wounded Knee in 1890. Such enormous oppression speaks volumes about the ferocity and persistence of white attitudes toward Native Americans.

Part Two
Dehumanizing Stereotypes

8

Deficient Humans: On the Margins of the Human Race

I mposition of the expressions "inferior," "defective," "deficient," "unfit," "potential life," and "lives not worth living"
onto certain classes of human beings has the effect of
consigning them to the margins of the human race. Although
they are acknowledged as official members of the human
species, it is an ambiguous and questionable status subject to
constant scrutiny and endless qualifications. The image persistently projected is that of hopelessly flawed human beings
whose lives are considered so insignificant that they can be
exploited at will, or so devoid of value that their very existence
is placed in severe jeopardy.

Marginalization is an exceedingly expansive process encompassing a wide range of victims. Those at risk include society's
most powerless groups: the genetically afflicted unborn, the
handicapped newborn, the debilitated elderly, and individuals
kept alive on respirators, feeding tubes, and various life-sustaining systems. Others are exiled to the outermost fringes of the
human community, not because they are actually disabled, but
because their main defect involves being too young or too old
or belonging to the wrong gender or wrong racial, ethnic, or
religious group. Who gets marginalized and the criteria for their
relegation to the borders of human existence ultimately varies
according to the prevailing ethic of power. This is the case
today, as it was in the past.

Potential Life before Birth

Only rarely do abortion proponents bother to touch upon the
humanness of the unwanted unborn child. The most they are

willing to grant the preborn is the status of "potential life" or the "potentiality of life." Such an admission is not much of a concession since it consigns the human being before birth to a rudimentary, inferior, and totally expendable form of existence.

One of the most influential expositions of the "potential life" doctrine can be found in the United States Supreme Court's pro-abortion *Roe v. Wade* and *Doe v. Bolton* decisions of 1973. "The fetus, at most," proclaimed the Court majority, "represents only the potentiality of life." Not until the so-called compelling point of viability, wrote Associate Justice Harry Blackmun, the main author of the *Roe* case, does the "potential life" of the unborn begin to approach any worth "because the fetus then presumably has the capability of meaningful life outside the mother's womb." Even then the value of viable "potential life" in utero becomes altogether meaningless because "for the stage subsequent to viability" the Court also sanctioned abortions performed "for the preservation of the life or health of the mother."[1]

Since Blackmun's definition of maternal health ("all factors—physical, emotional, psychological, familial, and the woman's age")[2] is so global, even the most frivolous justifications for abortion late in pregnancy are readily accommodated. Thus in the elitist world of injustice fashioned by Supreme Court justices the "potentiality of life" before birth, even when viable, counts for nothing. Not until after birth does the individual's life become "meaningful" enough to begin to deserve genuine respect and protection.

Many physicians adopted the "potential life" imperative in the wake of the *Roe* case. Two of the most prominent are Dr. H. Tristram Engelhardt, a leading biomedical ethicist, and the late Dr. Alan F. Guttmacher, a giant in the American abortion movement. In June 1973 Dr. Engelhardt maintained that "the potentiality of the fetus, given the right circumstances of developing into a full-blown human" is somewhat akin to a "promissory note." Therefore, he emphasized, "it is hard to see what rights a fetus has aside from potential rights, not having actually secured human existence" (p. 430). Dr. Guttmacher presented his version of "potential life" semantics in the *Reader's Digest* (November 1973): "My own speculations lead me to conclude that life begins only after the birth of a fetus sufficiently mature to survive outside its mother's body. Until then, there is only potential life" (p. 144).

Roe v. Wade and Doe v. Bolton thus paved the way for a radical distortion of perception about the nature of prenatal life from an actual human life with vast potential to a mere potential life with little intrinsic worth.

Postnatal Lives Not Worth Living

Children born with handicaps in contemporary society are particularly susceptible to being devalued by a nomenclature full of references to the "defectiveness" of those considered expendable, often with devastating results. Dr. Raymond Duff and Dr. A. G. M. Campbell employed the phrases "the prognosis for meaningful life was extremely poor or hopeless" and individuals with "little or no hope of achieving meaningful 'humanhood'" (1973, 890–94) to justify the denial of life-sustaining treatment to seriously afflicted infants in the Yale–New Haven Hospital intensive-care nursery.

Quality-of-life rhetoric likewise facilitated the imposed starvation death of Infant Doe, a child born with Down's syndrome and a deformed esophagus. The child's parents "felt that a minimally accepted quality of life was never present for a child suffering from such a condition."[3] The family's obstetrician, Dr. Walter Owens, testified that Infant Doe would never enjoy even "a minimally adequate quality of life" (Lyon 1985, 31). Superior Court Judge John G. Baker—the first jurist to rule in favor of the parents' right to choose starvation as an acceptable medical option—wrote: "Even if the proposed surgery was successful, the possibility of a minimally adequate quality of life was non-existent" (Andrusko 1985, 36–37).

During the numerous court battles over the fate of another disabled child, Phillip Becker, attorney Leonard Edwards called Phillip a minor "who will not lead a 'life worth living.'"

Dr. Harry E. Hartzell, a pediatrician who examined Phillip at the parents' request, asserted that Phillip leads "a life I consider devoid of those qualities which give it human dignity."[4]

Definitions of disabled children as worthless, defective individuals who have no right to life or who would be better off dead are nothing new—they are part of a tradition of denigration that stems from ancient roots. In antiquity the most influential lexicon of defamation aimed at children with disabilities came from the prominent philosophers Aristotle and Plato. As part of the ideal legislation in his *Politics* (book 4, chapter 16), Aristotle proposed: "As to the exposure and rearing of children, let there be a law that no *deformed* child shall live" (1943, 315). Plato, in *The Republic* (book 5), expanded the scope of killing by advocating infanticide for children produced by "inferior parents" and by parents beyond the ideal child-rearing years, as well as for illegitimate children and those born with some type of defect. Plato's antipathy toward the disabled child is reflected in his proposal "to dispose of it as a creature that must not be reared" (1974, 241, 243).

In many infanticidal cultures of the past, unwanted infants—both handicapped and nonhandicapped alike—were considered a deficient brand of humanity that did not become genuinely human until some time after birth. According to Laila Williamson's anthropological survey of these societies, "the killing is made easier by [the] cultural belief that a child is not fully human until accepted as a member of the social group" (1978, 64). In aboriginal New Guinea children were "not regarded as truly human until they had survived for several years" (Langness 1981, 14).

The Inferior Sex

For millennia, women have been persistently portrayed as a subpar gender. The inferiority label was intended to be an all-encompassing notion covering almost every aspect of the woman's being—physical, mental, and emotional.

In England, political reformer John Knox's *The First Blast of the Trumpet Against the Monstrous Regiment of Women* (1558) focused on "the imperfections of women" and "their natural weakness and inordinate appetites." Among its degrading references are "the inferior member" and "weak, frail, impatient, feeble, and foolish" (Breslow 1985, 44–45, 43, 45, 52).

The notorious Marquis de Sade, who in the second half of the eighteenth century terrorized and brutalized scores of female victims to satisfy his insatiable appetite for violent and degrading sex, resorted to the most demeaning terminology when referring to women. He called woman "a puny creature, always inferior to man, infinitely less attractive than he, less ingenious, less wise, constructed in a disgusting manner" (de Sade 1965, 647). These degrading characterizations constituted a major factor in motivating de Sade's abominable behavior.

The phrases "no sense of justice," "defective in the powers of reasoning and deliberation," and "that undersized, narrow-shouldered, broad-hipped, and short-legged race" comprise some of the derogatory descriptions of women in philosopher Arthur Schopenhauer's "Essay on Women" (originally published 1851). These views led him to the conclusion that "they form the *sexus sequior*—the second sex, inferior in every respect to the first" (1951, 65, 68).

A milestone in the war of words against women came in the work of another philosopher, Otto Weininger. His *Sex and Character* (1906) constitutes one of the most extreme defamations of female character ever published—"women are devoid of imagination," "a being whose memory is very slight," "the female must be described as absolutely without the quality of genius," "a woman is without logic," "however degraded a man may be, he is immeasurably above the most superior woman" (1975, 118, 188–89, 195, 196, 252).

Life Unworthy of Life in Nazi Germany

The main victims classified under the "lives not worth living" category in the Third Reich were Germans with physical and mental disabilities. The linguistic assault began long before the Nazi campaign to purge Germany of its "unfit" elements.

During the last half of the nineteenth century Ernst Haeckel, one of Germany's most prominent biologists and philosophers, started propagandizing for eliminating "defectives." In *The Wonders of Life* (1904), he decried "the thousands of cripples, deaf-mutes, idiots, etc. who are born each year with an hereditary burden of incurable disease." Haeckel expressed unrestrained admiration for the ancient Spartan practice of "achieving racial superiority" by putting to death weak, sickly, and deformed babies (pp. 124, 22).

In *Permitting the Destruction of Unworthy Life* (1920), jurist Karl Binding and psychiatrist Alfred Hoche invoked a litany of dehumanizing phrases to disparage the physically and mentally ill as well as those with handicaps and deformities. Binding saw *"no grounds—legally, socially, ethically or religiously"* for not allowing the destruction of "incurable idiots" who are *"the fearsome counter image of true humanity."* He supported extending "the same act of kindness [euthanasia]" to "monstrous births" (pp. 248–49). Hoche's linguistic attacks on the "mentally dead" and the "incurably insane" are laced with demeaning expressions—"complete idiots," "empty human shells," "dead weight existences," "defective people," "wholly worthless," "valueless lives," and "lives not worth living" (pp. 258–63).

The degrading portraits etched of Germany's disabled population shifted into high gear in the early to mid 1930s. At the Congress of the Crimino-Biologic Society held in Hamburg in June 1933, the sacred duty of crimino-biologic science was defined as participation in the "great movement for the regeneration of the people" by helping the state to protect itself from "being overwhelmed by inferior types."[5] In *The Structure of Public Health in the Third Reich* (1935), Dr. Arthur Guett declared that "the ill-conceived 'love of thy neighbor' has to disappear, especially in relation to inferior or asocial creatures."[6]

Eventually the rhetoric of unworthy, inferior life expanded to engulf others in addition to the German handicapped. In 1941 Dr. Otmar von Verschuer, one of Germany's premier racial hygienists, maintained that most Gypsies were "asocial and genetically inferior." Two years later German medical education supervisor Dr. Rudolph Ramm hailed the successful implementation of racial legislation against "the inferior Jewish race" (Proctor 1988, 215, 175). Dr. Leo Alexander, an American medical science consultant to the Nuremberg War Crimes Tribunal, traced the evolution of the notion of worthless life and its capacity to embrace an enormous range of victims:

> Whatever proportions these crimes finally assumed, it became evident to all who investigated them that they had started from small beginnings. The beginnings at first were merely a shift in emphasis in the basic attitude of the physicians. It started with the acceptance of the attitude, basic in the euthanasia movement, that there is such a thing as a life not worthy to be lived. This attitude in its early stages concerned itself merely with the severely and chronically sick. Gradually the sphere of those to be included in this category was enlarged to encompass the socially unproductive, the ideologically unwanted, the racially unwanted and finally all non-Germans. (1949, 44)

Backward Peasants

Of all the groups in Russia, the peasantry constituted one of the greatest obstacles to a Bolshevik takeover. Before, during, and after the October Revolution, Russia remained an overwhelmingly agricultural country with some 80 percent of the population living in the countryside and responsible for more than 50 percent of the national income. Marxist-Leninist policies such as abolition of private property and the assault on traditional family values were abhorrent to the peasantry. Peasants were fiercely attached to the land and placed a high value on independence and family life.

A Marxist remedy was chosen to deal with what became known as "the peasant problem": the fomenting of class warfare among inhabitants of the countryside. Poor and middle-class peasants were told that money-hungry capitalists under the guise of prosperous farmers and traders had invaded the countryside for the purpose of accumulating wealth at the expense of the majority of the peasants. After the Bolsheviks came to power, "Committees of Poor Peasants" were organized to promote "class struggle in the countryside." Marxist propaganda, backed up by the most draconian measures, led to a civil war among the peasants and the eventual forcible collectivization of agriculture on a vast scale.

As was the case with the denigration of other Soviet victims, language played a vital role in discrediting peasants who refused to submit to Marxist-Leninist principles and practices. One of the most common ways employed to impugn recalcitrant peasants was to characterize them as a hopelessly backward, archaic, and ignorant people who were doomed to extinction.

Among the foremost promoters of these degrading images were Karl Marx and his disciples. The Marxists looked upon the peasants and their institutions as a manifestation of "stupidity or blind conservatism," "a remnant of feudal society," and "obsolete from a historical point of view." George V. Plekhanov, the father of Russian Marxism, referred to the Russian peasantry as "barbarian tillers of the soil, cruel and merciless, beasts of burden whose life provided no opportunity for the luxury of thought" (Kingston-Mann 1981, 731, 739, 742). In 1922, Russian author Maxim Gorky wrote that "the uncivilized, stupid, turgid people in the Russian villages will die out . . . and a new race of literate, rational, energetic people will take their place." Vladimir Ilych Lenin, the compulsive revolutionary who transported Marxist polemics and ideology to Russian soil, frequently referred to "the idiocy of rural life," a phrase he appropriated from Marx (Conquest 1986, 20).

In *Marx Against the Peasants: A Study in Social Dogmatism,* David Mitrany concluded that "spurred by these coalesced prejudices and theories Marxism proclaimed a holy war against the peasants . . . an ideological and political war which culminated in the liquidation of the Russian peasantry by the victorious Soviets" (1961, 35).

An Inferior and Subordinate Race

The dogma of inferiority imposed on black people in the antebellum American South was extensive in scope, encompassing physical, intellectual, and personal attributes. Thomas Jefferson's *Notes on the State of Virginia* contains an abundance of references to Negro inferiority:

> Comparing them by their faculties of memory, reason, and imagination, it appears to me, that in memory they are equal to the whites; in reason much inferior, as I think one could scarcely be found capable of tracing and comprehending the investigations of Euclid; and that in imagination they are dull, tasteless, and anomalous. . . . But never yet could I find that a black had uttered a thought above the level of plain narration; never see even an elementary trait of painting or sculpture (1955, 139–40).

Later on Jefferson, himself a slaveowner, "hazarded with diffidence" the opinion that blacks "are inferior in the faculties of reason and imagination." He advanced "it therefore as a suspicion only, that the blacks, whether originally a distinct race, or made distinct by time and circumstances, are inferior to the whites in the endowments both of body and mind" (ibid., 142–43). According to historian Winthrop D. Jordan, Jefferson's "derogation of the Negro revealed the latent possibilities inherent in an accumulated popular tradition of Negro inferiority; it constituted, for all its qualifications, the most intense, extensive, and extreme formulation of anti-Negro 'thought' offered by any American in the thirty years after the Revolution" (1968, 481).

By the 1830s, assertions about the "innate inferiority" of African Americans were openly expressed with increasing fervor. In a message to the South Carolina legislature in 1835, Governor George McDuffie declared blacks to be "utterly unqualified for self-government of any kind" and "in all respects, physical, moral, and political, inferior to millions of the human race" (Hart 1925, 245). Charleston attorney William Drayton continued the semantic assault in *The South Vindicated from the Treason and Fanaticism of the Northern Abolitionists* (1836): "The Negro is constitutionally indolent, voluptuous, and prone to vice; that his mind is heavy, dull, and unambitious; and that the doom which has made the African in all ages and countries, a slave—is the natural consequence of the inferiority of his character" (1969, 232–33).

Numerous references to African Americans as "inferior" beings played an important role in the United States Supreme Court's *Dred Scott v. Sanford* decision of 1857 sanctioning the existence and expansion of slavery. The Court found it compelling that, at the time of ratification of the United States Constitution, Negroes were "considered as a subordinate and inferior class of beings . . . and had no rights or privileges but such as those who held the power and the Government might choose to grant them." The justices also felt reassured about the correctness of their ruling since blacks "had for more than a century been regarded as beings of an inferior order, and altogether unfit to associate with the white race."[7]

A Doomed Inferior Breed

An early proponent of Indians as an inherently defective breed destined for extinction was Bernard Romans. In his *Concise Natural History of East and West Florida* (1775), he called Native Americans "a people not only rude and uncultivated, but incapable of civilization" (Pearce 1965, 47).

As secretary of state in the administration of John Quincy Adams, Henry Clay expressed his opinion regarding the precipitous decline in the Native American population at a cabinet meeting in 1825. "Indians" are "rapidly disappearing" and "destined to extinction," he proclaimed, because they are "essentially inferior to the Anglo-Saxon" (Adams 1874–77, 7:90).

Inferior natives crumbling before the heroics of intrepid frontiersmen comprised a central theme in many frontier romance novels that flourished during the period 1790 to 1860. One of the leading characters in *The Yemassee* (1835) reflected upon "the destiny which awaited his people. He knew that the superior must necessarily be the ruin of the race which is inferior" (Drinnon 1980, 140). James Fenimore Cooper's *The Redskins* (1846) contains a glimmer of regret over the demise of the Indians, but this is offset by the inevitability of the inferior giving way to the superior race: "Like the wheel that rolls along the highway, however, many is the inferior creature that we heedlessly crush in our path. Thus has it been with the red-man, and . . . thus will it continue to be" (1888, 300).

Summary

The similarities in the words constructed to marginalize present and past victims are striking. Those today who relegate the unborn to "only potential life" and reduce handicapped children and adults to "lives not worthy" are invoking the same kinds of expressions employed against some of history's most reviled groups. Down through the ages, women were portrayed as a "defective" and "inferior" sex. Disabled individuals, Jews, and others in the Third Reich were depicted as "defective" and "inferior" lives "not worth living." Peasants in the Soviet Union were portrayed as a "backward" and "stupid" people who were doomed to extinction. Black people in the antebellum American South were regarded as a "subordinate and inferior class of beings" incapable of independent existence and self-governance. Native Americans on the frontier were viewed as an "inferior" breed destined to disappear with the coming of white civilization.

9

Subhuman/Nonhuman Entities: Below the Level of Humanity

I ndividuals and groups exiled to the margins of the human community are always in danger of losing even this most minimal recognition of human status. For some perpetrators, the epithets "defective," "inferior," "potential life," and "life not worth living" are not demeaning enough because they are apt to convey the impression that those labeled with such terms are still, at least implicitly, members of the human race. In the world of massive oppression, acknowledgment of even a semblance of humanity is often considered too risky. Extensive victimization requires stripping away all vestiges of humanity from the victims and reducing them to totally "subhuman" or "nonhuman" creatures existing outside the most remote borders of the human species.

The Subhumanity of Unwanted Fetuses

Of all the designations constructed to dehumanize the unborn, one of the most prevalent is the word "fetus." Fetus is also Latin for unborn child or offspring. This, nevertheless, is the last meaning abortion semanticists wish to project. According to their dictionary of disparagement, "fetus" is defined as a subhuman, nonhuman entity. A semantic strategy for keeping the word "fetus" clear of any human associations was put forth by University of California (Santa Barbara) biologist and abortion proponent, Dr. Garrett Hardin:

Whether the fetus is or is not a human being is a matter
of definition, not fact; and we can define in any way we
wish . . . it would be unwise to define the fetus as
human—(hence tactically unwise ever to refer to the fetus
as an "unborn child"). (1968, 250–51)

The subjectivism underlying the power to make words
mean anything one wishes belies a reckless arbitrariness comparable to Humpty Dumpty's famous oration on linguistic corruption delivered to Alice in Wonderland. When Alice
challenged Humpty Dumpty's definition of glory as "a nice
knock-down argument," he replied:

"When I use a word," Humpty said . . . "it means just
what I choose it to mean—neither more nor less."
"The question is," said Alice, "whether you can
make words mean so many different things."
"The question is," said Humpty Dumpty, "which is
to be master—that's all." (Carroll 1872, 124)

In line with the legacy of semantic gymnastics bequeathed by
Garrett Hardin and Humpty Dumpty, sociologist Amitai Etzioni
contends that most scientists and much of the public view the
"previable fetus" as "not alive, not human, and basically a piece
of tissue." Operating on the basis of this perception, he concludes: "For the first four and one-half months the fetus is subhuman and relatively close to a piece of tissue" (1976, 72).

Other prominent individuals resort to similar terminology in
their efforts to dehumanize human life in the womb. Professor
Joseph Fletcher, an avid abortion proponent and foremost
advocate of situation ethics, refers to the unwanted unborn
throughout all stages of development as "subhuman life in
utero" (1973, 116). Rabbi Wolfe Kelman, executive vice president of the Rabbinical Assembly, flatly denies the humanity of
the unborn. "The thrust of the Jewish tradition for 2,000 years,"
he claims, "has been that a fetus is not a human being."[1]
Abortionist Dr. Howard I. Diamond states that the plight of the
unwanted unborn cannot be compared to the agony of starving

animals and maltreated children because "a fetus is nothing" (Rosen 1977, 75).

Abortion rhetoricians have formulated a schizophrenic rule of thumb to deal with the well-ingrained, centuries-old habit of associating the fetus with a baby: When the occupant in the womb is wanted, *he* or *she* is called "a baby"; when unwanted, *it* is called "a fetus."

A variation on this extreme abuse of language can be found in the testimony of physician-abortionist Dr. Carolyn V. Brown during a deposition hearing held in Anchorage, Alaska, regarding a libel suit she filed against several abortion protesters for calling her a baby killer. Dr. Brown's responses to a series of questions posed by Thomas S. Gingras, attorney for one of the defendants, provide a revealing glimpse into a widely practiced style of discourse:

> Q: Have you ever, in your experience, in a conversation with a doctor of your acquaintance heard the doctor refer to an unborn entity as a baby?
> A: An unborn entity as a baby? Not in the context of abortions, no.
> Q: Have you ever heard it used in that sense in other contexts?
> A: In normal pregnancy in which the woman intends to carry it to term.
> Q: And do you use it yourself?
> A: Not in the context of abortion, no.
> Q: Do you use the term baby in referring to the entity in the context of a pregnancy that's going to be carried to term?
> A: Yes.[2]

The Nonhumanity of Postnatal Discards

Contemporary vulnerables after birth are likewise subjected to a vocabulary replete with nonhuman designations. Nobel Prize–winning scientist Francis H. Crick believes that "no newborn infant should be declared human until it has passed certain tests regarding its genetic endowment and that if it fails these tests it forfeits the right to live" (Schaeffer and Koop 1979, 73). Situation ethics founder Joseph Fletcher considers medical treatment for individuals with Down's syndrome a waste of resources because it would needlessly perpetuate the existence of "a sadly non- or un- or subhuman creature" (1968, 62).

Writing in *The New England Journal of Medicine* (April 8, 1976), philosopher John Lachs called hydrocephalic children "human-looking shapes" and "only human forms." He lamented that too many doctors and nurses treat these "human-looking shapes" as if "they were human, in spite of the fact they lack the least vestige of human behavior, intellectuation or feeling." Lachs proposed "a formalized system of easing death" for them. Such a policy, he reassured, would not be equivalent to condoning murder because "those humanely put to death would not be human beings, only human forms" (1976, 839–40).

Philosopher Michael Tooley, like many colleagues who favor abortion and infanticide, is uncomfortable with the word "human." He avoids using it whenever possible and advises substituting instead "some expression that is more naturally interpreted as referring to a certain type of biological organism characterized in physiological terms, such as 'member of the species Homo sapiens.'" The designation "human," he cautions, should be used "only in contexts where it is not philosophically dangerous" (1972, 43).

For Tooley, apparently, it is philosophically safe to employ the concept "human" only when those so labeled have attained the level of self-consciousness some time after birth. Not until then, according to this orientation, can individuals be considered "legitimate" human beings who are entitled to protection against infanticide. Another advocate of self-consciousness as a requirement for attaining humanhood after birth is biblical literature professor George H. Ball. He asserts that "a newly born infant is not a human being" since "it does not know it is alive; it is not self-conscious" (1981, 286).

Dehumanizing expressions furnished the semantic underpinnings for the 1987 court-sanctioned (New Jersey) starvation death of Nancy Ellen Jobes, a thirty-two-year-old woman who had been kept alive on a feeding tube over a seven-year period. Neurologist Dr. David Carlin stated: "She died as a human being a long time ago" and therefore "should have a funeral." Dr. Joseph Fennelly testified that Nancy's "face is so distorted that you just don't see a normal face. You see the teeth are in every direction. She looks ugly." Dr. Henry Liss referred to her as "this monstrosity of existence" and declared that "we are merely keeping a body alive." Moreover, he added, "she is not a physical entity, a human being."[3]

A Less-than-Human Gender

Professor Otto Weininger's linguistic assaults on the humanity of women descended to rock bottom with the word "nothing." "Women," he wrote, "have no existence and no essence; they are nothing." This declaration was backed up by an excruciating demonstration of philosophic mumbo-jumbo: "All metaphysical, all transcendental existence is logical and moral existence; woman is non-logical and non-moral. . . . She is rather nothing." While the "male is the image of God, the absolute something," Weininger contended, "the female is the symbol of nothing" (1975, 286, 297).

Pornography is a principal medium for depicting women as creatures below the level of humanity. The writings of the Marquis de Sade (1740–1814)—a heavy diet of sex, torture, and killing—are saturated with degrading images of women. While engaging in repeated sexual assaults, de Sade's male perpetrators frequently spout their philosophy of females as contemptible subhuman creatures. In his most demeaning novel, *Justine* (1791), the victimizer takes time out from his brutal attacks against his female victims to express serious doubt whether "this peculiar creature [woman], as distinct from man as is man from the ape, had any reasonable legitimate pretensions to classification as a human" (1965, 647).

Research conducted by leading members of Women Against Violence in Pornography and Media found that even in the most banal and nonviolent pornography "women are not seen as human beings."[4]

In wartime, enemy soldiers are not the only group reduced to a subhuman species; women are likewise prime targets. Vietnam veteran Sergeant Scott Camil recalls a search-and-destroy mission in which a Vietnamese woman who asked for water was subjected to a series of degrading and brutal actions before being shot to death. Camil then described how such acts were justified: "It wasn't like they were humans. You didn't think you were shooting at a human" (Vietnam Veterans Against the War 1972, 14).

Dehumanizing images of women also underlie rape and other acts of sexual violence being perpetrated in contemporary society. "Most acts of rape," according to many studies, are based on "contempt for women." And "to hate someone, you must first dehumanise them, make them sub-human" (Vogelman 1990, 68–69). As one rapist put it: "It was difficult for me to admit that I was dealing with a human being when I was talking to a woman" (Fremont 1984, 249–50).

Subhumans of the Third Reich

From at least the nineteenth century on, controversy raged as to whether European Jews were human or subhuman. To the anti-Semites, the humanity of the Jews was not an indisputable fact, but a question to be resolved by myth, racist ideology, and dehumanizing semantics. German legislator Hermann Ahlwardt delivered a fiery anti-Semitic speech to the *Reichstag* in 1895 containing a typical outburst of dehumanizing verbiage: "If it is now pointed out . . . that the Jew is human too, then I must reject that totally" (Hilberg 1967, 11).

Adolf Hitler's anti-Jewish nomenclature developed during his early adult years spent in Vienna (1907–13). "Wherever I went," he recalled, "I began to see Jews, and the more I saw, the more sharply they became distinguished in my eyes from the rest of humanity" (1971, 56). By 1923, he declared in a speech that "the Jews are undoubtedly a race, but not human" (Aronsfeld 1975, 22).

The claim of the Jew's subhumanity was persistently disseminated by Hitler's chief anti-Semitic propagandist Julius Streicher in his scurrilous weekly newspaper *Der Stuermer*, published without interruption from 1923 to 1945. *Stuermer* cartoons portrayed Jews as evil, repulsive creatures with sinister expressions, dark beady eyes, ugly hooked noses, and protruding lower lips. Streicher and his staff filled their articles with equally disparaging references to Jews as "sub-humans, worse than Negroes" and warned that "the germ of this sub-human" would be permanently implanted in the bloodstream of any non-Jewish woman who had intercourse with a Jew (Varga 1981, 92, 94).

An enormously popular pamphlet published in 1942, *The Subhuman (Der Untermensch)*, epitomized the extreme nature of dehumanizing stereotypes—both printed and pictorial—directed against the Jewish people:

> The sub-human, that biologically seemingly complete creation of nature with hands, feet and a kind of brain, with eyes and mouth, is nevertheless a completely different, dreadful creature. He is only a rough copy of a human being, with human-like facial traits but nonetheless morally and mentally lower than any animal. . . . Sub-human, otherwise nothing. For all that bear a human face are not equal. (Henry and Hillel 1976, 32)

"The Jewish question" functioned as a powerful slogan for raising doubts about and undermining the nature, origins, and humanity of the Jewish people. By 1943, German Foreign Office Press Chief Paul Karl Schmidt conveyed to members of the press how this slogan was to be interpreted to the public: "The Jewish question is no question of humanity, and it is no question of religion; it is solely a question of political hygiene" (Hilberg 1967, 657).

Nonhuman Kulaks

The extermination of "kulaks" (a demeaning designation for peasants who resisted the Soviet collectivization of agriculture) during the 1930s was facilitated by portrayals of them as

subhuman, nonhuman creatures. In his study of the mass starvation imposed on Ukrainian peasants, Robert Conquest
found that the "naming of the kulak" as "a class enemy, a subhuman . . . satisfied the Marxist preconceptions of the Party
activist" by presenting "a flesh-and-blood foe accursed by history" (1986, 120).

A Soviet Party activist in Russian writer Vasily Grossman's
Forever Flowing (1972), looking back on the annihilation of
kulaks, acknowledged the destructive intent underlying the
name-calling and drew an arresting analogy between the
derogatory semantics invoked by the Nazi and Soviet perpetrators alike:

> What I said to myself at the time was "They are not
> human beings, they are kulaks." . . . Just as the Germans
> proclaimed that Jews are not human beings. Thus did
> Lenin and Stalin: kulaks are not human beings. (p. 144)

Similarly, soldiers who herded female prisoners into the baths
of the arctic death camps "no longer thought of them as
human" (Conquest 1978, 184).

Not of the Human Race

In many instances, the humanity of African Americans was
completely obliterated and the victims were lowered to a status far below the threshold of the human species. At a trial
held in New York City in 1741, for instance, blacks con-
demned to death for allegedly starting a series of fires were
called "degenerated and debased below the Dignity of
Humane Species" (Jordan 1968, 119). Although there was
insufficient evidence to link those executed with the acts of
arson, this appeared to be of little importance. The trial functioned as a public display for reinforcing the Negro-as-nonhu-
man contention and for justifying the horrendous punishment
inflicted on the targets of this imagery.

Naturalist Louis Agassiz—a leading nineteenth-century scientist, a professor of zoology and geology at Harvard University,

and founder of the Museum of Natural History—gave a tremendous boost to the process of dehumanizing African Americans. When Agassiz first saw black people in 1846, he wrote to his mother: "The more pity I felt at the sight of this degraded and degenerate race, the more . . . impossible it becomes for me to repress the feeling that they are not of the same blood as we are" (Lurie 1960, 257).

One of the most scathing assaults on the humanity of blacks came in 1867 from the pen of Buckner Payne, a Nashville publisher. Writing under the pseudonym "Ariel," he asserted: "The negro is not a human being." Furthermore, since only the human being possesses a soul, Payne concluded that the Negro "has no soul" and therefore lacks "the endowment of immortality" (pp. 21, 45, 30).

By the turn of the twentieth century, the perceptions of African Americans as repulsive subhuman beings continued to be propagated. Some of the chapter headings in Charles Carroll's *"The Negro A Beast"* (1900) supply typical illustrations of this demeaning rhetoric: "Biblical and Scientific Facts Demonstrating that the Negro is not an Offspring of the Adamic Family"; "Convincing Biblical and Scientific Evidence that the Negro is not of the Human Family"; "The Bible and Divine Revelation, as well as Reason, all Teach that the Negro is not Human" (1969, 45, 105, 339).

Several years later Dr. William T. English attributed the African Americans' lack of "conjugal and maternal affection" to being "subjugated by a wide range of the subhuman." "Bestiality and gratification," he added, were common manifestations of their close affinity to "sub-human ancestors" (1903, 470, 466, 468).

A Human Facade for Concealing Savages

A common variation on the subhuman portrayals consisted of lowering Native Americans to the mere outer shell of a human—just a human "shape" or "form." According to the purveyors of this terminology, underneath the surface manifestation of Indian humanhood lurked a demonic, nonhuman, inhuman creature that posed a substantial danger to civilization in general and the white community in particular.

Hugh Henry Brackenridge, a literary figure associated with the early American frontier, argued that the land belonged to those who cultivated it and not to America's aborigines, whom he described as individuals "sunk beneath the dignity of human nature" although they "bear resemblance and are seen in the shape of men." He concluded that "the life of these is therefore not human" (Marder 1970, 100).

A participant in the massacre of Sac women and children in the woods of Wisconsin in 1832 likened it to "fast getting rid of these demons in human shape" (Elby 1973, 253). David Levy, a resident of Florida, called Native Americans "demons, not men. They have the human form, but nothing of the human heart."[5] During his journey on the Oregon Trail in 1846, historian Francis Parkman maintained that the western Dahcotah tribe possessed "little of humanity except the form" (1925b, 178).

As the stream of settlers, frontiersmen, adventurers, miners, and speculators penetrated westward, the degrading linguistics was concentrated against the Plains Indians. Their manner of life—nomadic, horse-mounted hunters of the buffalo and fierce guardians of the terrain—made them ideally suitable candidates for reduction to the status of dangerous subhuman savages. Plains newspaper editors were particularly scathing in their denunciations. On July 14, 1866, the editor of the *Kearney Herald* (in Nebraska) wrote: "These heartless creatures . . . are destitute of all the promptings of human nature. . . . Their only creed is that which gives them an unrestricted license to use and abuse beings, brutes, and things" (Mardock 1971, 86).

Summary

The designations created to dehumanize vulnerable individuals now and in times past are remarkably similar. Contemporary abortion and euthanasia proponents who denigrate unborn and born humans with the expressions "nonhuman," "subhuman," "only human forms," and "nothing" are echoing the terminology directed against other victims in times past. The expressions "not seen as human beings" and "nothing" comprise mainstays in the longstanding war of words against women. Images of Jews as "not human," "subhuman," and "nothing" provided an omnipresent semantic foundation for racial genocide in Nazi Germany. According to the lexicon of derogation fashioned by Lenin and Stalin, farmers who resisted the excessive Soviet demands made on agriculture were "not human beings." Acceptance of slavery was helped along by perceptions of African Americans as "not human" and "subjected to a wide range of the subhuman." Portrayals of Native Americans as "not human" and just "human forms" furnished a justification for their mass extermination on the frontier.

10

A Species of Lower Animals and Wild Beasts

Demeaning animal metaphors have long served as a popular staple for devaluing human beings. Removal of individuals from membership in the human community and re-classifying them as animals has the effect of consigning them to a lower level of existence where their victimization can be more easily rationalized. Animal analogies are employed to denigrate victims in two fundamental ways: The victims are reduced to the insignificant level of lower, primitive animals whose fate is of no consequence, or they are depicted as dangerous, wild beasts that need to be subdued, hunted down, or destroyed.

Primitive Animals in the Womb

Few victims throughout history have been reduced to a lower level of animality than the unwanted unborn of today. Animalistic stereotypes are likely to be invoked in situations where the plight of the unborn is visible and personalized such as the abortion of a child with life signs or an ultrasound showing the victim being dismembered in utero.

In 1970 nurses in a New York hospital became distraught when they encountered an aborted baby who moved. The attending physician told them not to be bothered since what they witnessed was simply "a reflexive response of a spinal animal" (Kibel 1972, 131).

During a guest appearance on the television program *Nightline* (February 12, 1985), Cornell University neurologist Dr. Hart Peterson tried to neutralize the horror of the abortion shown in the film *The Silent Scream* with a similar reaction.

"What we're seeing here is a primitive response . . . much like that of a primitive animal that's poked with a stick," he emphasized. "It was simply showing a primitive survival response much like that of a lower animal."[1]

Some abortion proponents consider the lowly amoeba to be an especially appropriate form of animal life for use in dehumanizing human life before birth. "The Facts Speak Louder," a booklet produced by Planned Parenthood Federation of America, likens the unborn child's attempt to avoid the suction machine shown in *The Silent Scream* to the "reflex response" of "a one-cell organism such as an amoeba."[2] Before a United States Senate Committee on March 27, 1990, pro-abortion physician Dr. Louis Gerstley attempted to undermine the significance of fetal activity in an ultrasound video with the comment, "an amoeba will retract if touched, too" (U.S. Congress 1990, 92).

Astronomer Carl Sagan and wife Ann Druyan rely upon evolutionary theory to support their thesis that abortion, particularly in the first trimester, represents nothing more significant than removing an entity at the earliest and most repulsive stages of animality. In one of the most dehumanizing portrayals on record (*Parade Magazine,* April 22, 1990), Sagan and Druyan compare the unborn human at different phases of development to a worm, an amphibian, a reptile, and a lower mammal. They indicate that the human embryo resembles "a segmented worm" by the third week and "a newt or tadpole" during the fourth week. Furthermore, they refer to the embryonic face as "reptilian" by the sixth week and "mammalian but somewhat piglike" at the end of the seventh week (pp. 6, 8).

The Animality of Postnatal Discards

Other victims in contemporary society are increasingly at risk of being reduced to primitive animals. "Until a living being can take conscious management of life and its direction," contends biblical studies professor George Ball, "it remains an animal" (1981, 286). Under this classification, he includes newborn infants and comatose adults as well as unborn humans.

In addition to calling the hydrocephalic child only a "human shape" or "human form," philosopher John Lachs stresses that "pigeons have more personality—the indigo bunting more intellect—than this unfortunate mooncalf in our midst" (1976, 839–40).

Animal liberation philosopher Peter Singer likewise favors consigning infants with serious disabilities to a status below that of some animals: "If we compare a severely defective human infant with a nonhuman animal, a dog or a pig, for example, we will find the nonhuman to have superior capacities, both actual and potential, for rationality, self-consciousness, communication, and anything else that can plausibly be considered morally significant" (1983, 129).

Similarly, in the spring of 1992 during a discussion pertaining to the case of Theresa Ann Campo, an anencephalic infant whose parents tried to get declared brain dead so her organs could be donated, Yale University medical professor Robert Levine compared an anencephalic baby's brain "with that of a fish" (Chartrand 1992, 12; Levine 1992, 24).

Female Bestiality

Gross animal references have been frequently utilized to equate women with wild animals that need to be restrained by physical force. They have also functioned to project the image that underneath even the most modest feminine demeanor lurks an insatiable, raging sexual beast that covets every imaginable form of sexual aberration, debauchery, and violence.

Literary works of the past are full of such images. The early satirist Juvenal described a woman filled with sexual desire as "worse than a tigress robbed of its young" (1982, 137). French poet Charles Baudelaire once wrote: "I consider that women are domestic animals which ought to be kept locked up in captivity; they should be well fed and cared for and beaten regularly" (Hays 1964, 201). A popular nineteenth-century English adage states: "The women of Lancashire *are awfully fond* of bad husbands. . . . Our women are like dogs, the more you beat them the more they love you" (Cobbe 1878, 64).

Two modern writers who excel in the practice of debasing women to vulgar, unbridled sexual animals are Henry Miller and Norman Mailer. Their books are replete with passages featuring out-of-control, bestial females who relish being assaulted and ravished by masterful, macho males.

In *Tropic of Capricorn* (1961), Miller depicts sexual conquests as equivalent to "trapping a weasel when night came on" (p. 183). His caricatures of female sexual behavior in *Sexus* (1965) abound with the most degenerate animal analogies:

> She was like a bitch in heat . . . wriggling like a worm on the hook. . . . Mara twisted like an eel. She wasn't even a woman; she was just a mass of indefinable contours wriggling and squirming like a piece of fresh bait. . . . groaning, grunting, squealing like a pig. . . . fornicating with a rabbit. . . . She crouched on all fours like a she animal, quivering and whinnying. . . . She looked like a crazed animal. (pp. 229, 181, 287, 126, 304)

More of the same can be found in Norman Mailer's contributions to the discourse of "rampant female sexual animality." His *Advertisements for Myself* (1959) characterizes women in sexual relations as "the wanton whip-thrash of a wounded snake" and "she thrashed beneath me like a trapped little animal" (1960, 438, 449). Mailer continued these degrading accounts in *An American Dream* (1965): "A carnal transaction with a caged animal," "that smell . . . of the wild boar full of rut" and "she was hungry, like a lean rat" (pp. 34, 43).

In *Pornography and Silence* (1981), Susan Griffin found the ultimate in the animalistic degradation of women—a "secret museum of classic art" portraying women copulating with animals. American, Japanese, Dutch, French, German, and Polish painters have created scenes of women being raped by bulls and coupling with goats, horses, kangaroos, and other animals. In one such painting, a virgin having sexual contact with a monkey is depicted as being "bestialized, devirginized and monkeyfied" (pp. 25–26).

Cartoons published in contemporary pornographic magazines are another principal source for reducing women to the level of sexual beasts who prefer copulating with animals instead of human beings. One of their favorite themes consists of sexual affairs between wives and the family dog. In her analysis of images of debased sexuality (1987) in *Playboy, Hustler,* and *Penthouse,* Dr. Judith A. Reisman includes copies of cartoons depicting female bestiality published in *Playboy* during the 1970s and 1980s.[3]

The Animal Kingdom of the Third Reich

In 1920 German psychiatrist Alfred Hoche invoked animalistic terminology to malign brain-damaged individuals and "idiots." These "mentally dead" individuals, he maintained, stand "far down in the animal kingdom; even their emotional movements do not arise above the level of elementary processes bound to animal life" (Binding and Hoche 1920, 262). Hoche's characterizations established a standard of discourse that helped pave the way for extermination of the physically and mentally handicapped throughout Nazi Germany.

The relegation of Jews to the status of wild animals occupied an honored spot in the nomenclature leading up to the Nazi Holocaust. Before the *Reichstag* in 1895 lawmaker Hermann Ahlwardt called Jews "beasts of prey" and warned that "you'd better exterminate those beasts of prey" (Massing 1949, 303–4). In *Mein Kampf* Adolf Hitler likened Jews to a "pack of wolves which has just fallen on its prey together [but] disintegrates when hunger abates into its individual beasts" (1971, 301).

By the time of the Holocaust, a broad spectrum of victims were caught in the ever-expanding orbit of degrading animal analogies. Dr. Robert Ritter constructed genealogical tables as a basis for "hunting out" Gypsies (Kenrick and Puxson 1972,

175–76). According to an account compiled by Gestapo officials, "Russian prisoners are not prisoners of war in the ordinary sense, but . . . beasts and brutes. They must be primarily treated as such" (Kogon 1950, 186). Nazi medic Dr. August Hirt reminded a colleague at the Nazweiler-Struthof concentration camp that "the prisoners here are animals before all else" (Aziz 1976, 1:232).

Historian George L. Mosse concluded that "likening the so-called inferior races to animals put them low on the chain of being and, by analogy, robbed them of their humanity" (1978, 117).

Imperialist Beasts of Prey

Lenin resorted to wild-animal analogies against a wide range of foes. In the early 1900s he asserted that "the noble landlord is . . . a beast of prey" and referred to the tsar as "the beast on the throne." He maintained that the Russian people were "sharpening their swords" for the upcoming mortal battle against the imperialist government, "a sated beast" (1960–70, 4:406, 16:80, 10:219).

World War I furnished a banner occasion for Lenin to portray Britain, the United States, and France as "wild beasts who have plundered the whole world and are now quarreling over the prey." He considered the vulture—an especially rapacious beast of prey—a perfect metaphor to use against "imperialists" and other enemies:

> The war was started by the British and German vultures who found themselves too cramped living together, and so each of them decided to drown the other in the blood of the workers of the world. . . . Locked in mortal combat, these vultures are on the edge of a precipice. . . . We shall finally hurl the imperialist vultures over the precipice. (ibid., 28:52–53)

Lenin and Stalin showed a partiality toward the use of wolf metaphors as a means of castigating their enemies. Lenin often relied upon the "wolf in sheep's clothing" epithet to sound the alarm about how the Soviet Union was being subverted within by devious, unscrupulous exploiters (ibid., 29:378–79). Stalin charged that South Russia's abundant resources inflamed "the voracious appetites of the imperialist wolves who are trying to wrest this important area from Russia" (1953–55, 4:151).

Black Beasts of Burden and Terror

American slaveholders found "work animal" metaphors to serve as convenient rationalizations for defending the practice of keeping black people in a state of perpetual bondage. In pre-Revolutionary America David Cooper of Burlington, New Jersey, observed that "from the first dawn of reason" children learn "to consider people with a black skin, on a footing with domestic animals, form'd to serve and obey." A leading minister in Newport, Rhode Island, Samuel Hopkins, disclosed that Americans saw Negroes "not as our brethren, or in any degree on a level with us; but as quite another species of animals, made only to serve us and our children" (Jordan 1968, 276).

American Slavery As It Is (1839) contains some noteworthy observations on the scope of the animal parallels used against slaves:

> We have said that slaveowners regard their slaves . . . as mere working animals. . . . The whole vocabulary of slave-holders, their laws, their usages, and their entire treatment of their slaves fully establish this. The same terms are applied to slaves that are given to cattle. They are called "stock." . . . Often the same terms are applied to the different sexes that are applied to males and females among cattle. (1968, 110)

An integral component of the "domestic animal" analogy is the premise that black slaves operated on the strictly instinctual, reflexive level of lower animals. This perception helped many slaveholders remain oblivious to the pain and suffering experienced by those held in bondage. In his defense of slavery (1846), Matthew Estes claimed that the Negro, "as in the case of the mule," could not be overworked because of "a certain hardihood of constitution" (pp. 79–80). Louisiana slaveowner George S. Sawyer mocked the black person's human and familial qualities of "remarkable fidelity and attachment to their masters" as representing merely an "instinctive impulse, possessed even to a higher degree by some of the canine species" (1858, 222, 197).

The staying power of this demeaning terminology is reflected in the comments of Charles Carroll made in 1900, decades after the abolition of slavery. He continued to insist that "the Negro . . . is one of the lower animals" and placed blacks among the creatures "God designed to perform the manual labor" (1969, 102).

After the Civil War more malevolent images of black people as dangerous beasts were propagated with increasing intensity.

In 1867 Nashville publisher Buckner Payne wrote that "a man cannot commit so great an offense against his race, against his country, against his God . . . as to give his daughter in marriage to a negro—*a beast*" (Ariel 1867, 48). South Carolina Senator Benjamin R. Tillman's portrayal of the Negro as "a fiend, a wild beast, seeking whom he may devour" established a nomenclature for widespread emulation (Simkins 1937, 3:166). In 1899 Mrs. L. H. Harris, reflecting "a Southern Woman's View," decried the situation "today in the South" where "every white woman lives next door to a savage . . . negro brute." This "hideous monster," she emphasized, "has the savage nature and murderous instincts of the wild beast and the cunning and lust of a fiend" (pp. 1354–55).

The denigrating imagery erupted with unprecedented fury in conjunction with the spate of lynchings which reached an all-time high of 161 in 1892 and continued at an alarming rate into the early 1900s. Although public segregation and disenfranchisement were defended without resort to the "Negro as beast" stereotype, historian George M. Fredrickson concludes that many Negroes were defined as "literally wild beasts, with uncontrollable sexual passions and criminal natures stamped by heredity. The incredible cruelty and barbarity of lynching thus led to the most extreme defamation of the Negro character that had yet been offered and helped provide the tone and substance for the race-hate literature of the period" (1971, 276).

A Vanishing Breed of Untamable Red Animals

In colonial New England William Bradford, governor of the Massachusetts Bay Colony, called the Indian "a wild Beast in his own Den" (Slotkin 1973, 167). Cotton Mather referred to Native Americans as "Rapacious Wolves" that retreated "into their Inaccessible Dens" (1913, 192–93).

Andrew Jackson of Tennessee, whose fame as an Indian fighter helped him gain the presidency of the United States, invoked similar language to justify wholesale assaults against the Seminole Indians of Florida. "The protection of our citizens," he wrote, "will require that the wolf be struck in his den."[4] Historian Francis Parkman concluded that an "impassable barrier" existed between whites and Indians, a group he dubbed "a troublesome and dangerous species of wild beast" (1925b, 330–31).

The widespread perceptions of Native Americans as wild, primitive animals served to hasten the extinction of Indian lives and alienation of Indian lands in the face of westward expansion. Dr. Charles Caldwell, an influential medical school professor heavily steeped in phrenology, maintained that Native Americans were only "formed, fitted, and intended to inhabit uncultivated forests, and wild prairies." He predicted that "civilization is destined to exterminate them, in common with the wild animals" (1830, 142). Dr. Josiah C. Nott declared: "The Indian . . . is an untamable, carnivorous animal, which is fading away before civilization" (1847, 4:280). Colonel John Gibbon began his prize-winning essay, "Our Indian Question" (1880), with a profile of the Native American as *"a wild animal"* that was *"bound to disappear from this continent"* (Dippie 1982, 131).

Summary

A close kinship exists among the terms manufactured to consign present and past vulnerable groups to an animalistic level. When today's abortion and euthanasia defenders liken their victims to "animals" and "lower animals," they are repeating an enduring legacy of verbal contempt. Down through history women have been depicted as lowly "domestic animals" or unbridled "sexual beasts." The Nazis reduced disabled people to entities "far down in the animal kingdom" and Jews to "animals" and "beasts of prey." Lenin and Stalin employed the designation "beast of prey" to malign anyone suspected of departing from Marxist-Leninist dogma. Slaveholders in the American South viewed African Americans as either "work animals" ordained to serve white civilization or "wild beasts" requiring the most draconian measures. Andrew Jackson and other Indian fighters invoked the phrases "an untamable carnivorous animal" and "wild beasts" to rationalize wholesale assaults against Native Americans.

11

Repulsive Parasitic Creatures

One of the most despicable creatures in nature is the parasite. Within the context of biology, this word includes any organism—plant, insect, or animal—that lives in or on another organism, at whose expense it derives sustenance or protection. Among some of the most typical parasites are lice (small, flat-bodied, wingless, biting or sucking insects parasitic on warm-blooded animals), vermin (small animals or insects that are destructive, annoying, or injurious to health such as cockroaches or rats), and leeches (chiefly aquatic bloodsucking or carnivorous worms).

The relationship between parasite and host is an enforced, asymmetrical state of dependency in which the parasite grows and feeds on a different organism, while contributing nothing to the sustenance and survival of the host. In many instances this relationship of extreme, one-sided dependence is invariably fatal to host and parasite alike.

The parasite metaphor has proven to be an enduring device for devaluing a broad range of human victims, both present and past. The process of denigration has usually involved focusing on various characteristics intrinsic to parasites that, when transferred to the realm of expendable humanity, facilitate oppression on a vast scale. The two most common parasitic qualities attributed to undesired human lives are their total dependence on the host and the threat they pose to the survival of the host. Moreover, the fact that the parasite is an alien organism differing markedly from the host serves as a paradigm for consigning vulnerable human beings to the status of a repugnant species with no rightful claim to membership in the human community.

Fetal Parasites in the Woman's Body

Abortion proponents have transformed the unborn child into an insignificant, nonviable entity that cannot survive on its own or a relentless, harmful, parasitic invader promiscuously ravaging the woman's body, health, and life. These caricatures strike a highly responsive chord in today's world where sheer autonomy has become such a cherished obsession.

Philosopher L. W. Sumner invokes the parasite analogy— "pregnancy is a relation between host and parasite"—in maintaining that the mother has the "right to be rid of the invader" because "the conflict between the fetus and the mother always takes place on her territory, in a body to which she has prior claim." Since "the parasite has invaded the body of the host," Sumner reasons, "the host's property-right over her body includes the right to defend herself against such an invasion." This means, he declares, "she has the right to disconnect the parasite, thereby killing it" (1981, 52, 71, 67).

In *Abortion and Women's Choice* (1984), feminist theoretician Rosalind Pollack Petchesky declares that "on the level of 'biology alone,' the dependence is one-way—the fetus is a parasite." She contends that the fetus contributes nothing to the woman's sustenance, but "only draws from her: nutrients, immunological defenses, hormonal secretions, blood, digestive functions, energy" (p. 346).

Feminist writer Rachel Conrad Wahlberg stresses the same points in her full-scale semantic assault on the humanity of the unwanted unborn penned for the publication *New Women/New Church* in 1987. Once the woman misses her period, asserts Wahlberg, she realizes that "a parasite is living in her . . . is enclosed by her, a being entirely subhuman, entirely dependent upon her." To Wahlberg the unborn child is a "parasitical," "cannibalistic" creature that "feeds on the mother's body without any consideration for her needs" (p. 5).

These degrading characterizations are not confined to radical feminist rhetoric; they have been appropriated by some pro-abortion physicians as well. A typical rendition is evident in the testimony of Dr. Louis Gerstley before a U.S. Senate committee in 1990. Besides comparing the unborn to an amoeba, he resorted to the expression "obligate parasite." When one of the committee members reacted with an expression of disbelief, Dr. Gerstley replied: "It [the fetus] is an obligate parasite. It cannot live on its own. It requires the mother to survive" (U.S. Congress 1990, 91).

Abortionist Dr. Warren Hern has constructed an elaborate portrayal of the fetus as an invasive parasite. He compares the role of the "fetoplacental unit" to the "local invasion" of "a parasite" whose "aggressive mechanisms" can result in compression of the abdominal viscera and vessels, rupture of the uterus, ectopic pregnancy, nutritional deficiency, and maternal hypertension. This sets the stage for the promotion of abortion as an indispensable "defense mechanism" for "the blocking of the deleterious effects of the parasite or its destruction" (1984a, 14–15).

Postnatal Parasites on the Health Care System

Disconnecting rapacious fetal parasites from intrauterine life supports serves as an influential paradigm for disconnecting from respirators and feeding tubes those patients viewed as parasitic entities insatiably depleting the health care system of valuable medical resources and services. Although modern-day euthanasia proponents are strongly inclined to emphasize a humanitarian motivation (to spare the person the prolonged agony of painful dying) in support of their proposals, they occasionally, nonetheless, construct designations that—short of using the actual word "parasite"—depict the chronically dependent patient as unmistakably parasitic in character. In *The Hastings Center Report* of October 1983 ethicist Daniel Callahan wrote that "a denial of nutrition may in the long run become the only effective way to make certain that a large number of biologically tenacious patients actually die" (p. 22). This expression conveys the image of the patient as a relentlessly grasping species that clings as tenaciously to life and life-support technology as would a parasite to its host.

Some of those who have day-to-day experience with "bothersome" patients are prone to express their contempt in more direct and deeply degrading language. A nurse with twenty years' experience in intensive care reports that the word "parasite" is being used to dehumanize debilitated, comatose, and elderly patients at a medical center located in Middle America:

> A nurse involved in the process of placing a comatose man in a chair remarked: "This parasite is draining me and everyone else."
>
> When a seriously debilitated patient—newly transferred from a nursing home—is encountered in the emergency room, it is a common practice for the staff to say: "That's a real parasite."[1]

Gardens of Unconscious Vegetables

A pervasive manifestation of the parasite analogy today is the depiction of vulnerable chronic patients as "vegetables" or individuals existing in a "persistent vegetative state" (PVS). Both expressions often project images of mindless creatures involved in the useless process of merely "vegetating" or voraciously depleting scarce resources. Yale University pediatrician Dr. Raymond Duff calls severely disabled infants "vegetated individuals who have no human potential."[2] Philosopher John Lachs decries "the 'gardens' that flourish in our major hospitals—of the thousands of human vegetables we sustain on life-preserving machines." "I cannot make myself believe," he declares, "that the unconscious vegetables in our hospitals are in any sense human" (1976, 839–40). Bioethics professor Joseph Fletcher likewise laments the situation in which an "incorrigible human vegetable" is "constantly eating up private or public financial resources in violation of the distributive justice owed to others" (1973, 119).

Dr. R. Lamerton, a medical officer at St. Joseph's Hospice in London, exposes the real purpose underlying the widespread use of the terms "vegetable" and "vegetative"—to mentally demote patients by inventing "a name we can despise." Whatever "subhuman name" is chosen, he stresses, "its effect is to alter our attitude to the persons concerned. They become disposable." Moreover, Lamerton explains, applying this disparaging nomenclature "to humans whose bodies are damaged or unconscious can change our whole willingness to care for and give to them of our best" (1974, 1184–85).

A return to the Nazi era reveals that similar terminology was applied on a vast scale to justify ridding Germany of its physically and mentally disabled people. The semantic foundation was established in the last decade of the nineteenth century when biologist-philosopher Ernst Haeckel, a major forerunner of Nazi ideology, campaigned in favor of capital punishment for "incorrigible criminals," a position he equated with "a careful rooting out of weeds" for the benefit of "good and useful plants" in a "well-cultivated garden" (1892, 1:178).

In 1936 the word "vegetate" appeared in *Mission and Conscience,* a propaganda novel advocating euthanasia for a woman with multiple sclerosis. The book's main message came through in the question "Would you, if you were a cripple, want to vegetate forever?" (Proctor 1988, 183). During the darkest days of the Third Reich Hitler's SS director Heinrich Himmler likened the Holocaust perpetrator to "the plant breeding specialist who, when he wants to breed a pure new strain from a well-tried species that has been exhausted by too much crossbreeding, first goes over the field to cull the unwanted plants" (Lifton 1986, 16–17).

Sexual Parasites

Women constitute another perennial victim of parasitic labeling. Like the parasite, the woman is commonly depicted as an innately clinging creature who cannot subsist on her own, an entity with an insatiable impulse to attach herself to a host (the man) in order to survive. She is frequently dubbed a "sexual parasite" whose success in maintaining herself in the state of parasitism is attributed to sexual seduction, guile, and female artifice.

Rene Guyon's unabashed proclamation of sexual license, *Sexual Freedom* (1950), asserts that women in general "regard parasitism on the male as their ideal, and if possible parasitism upon one 'host,' a man able to provide a stable position . . . that guarantee of permanence which is most congenial to a parasite." Guyon maintains that "average women" are unlikely "to welcome social or legal changes which will interfere with their parasitic role" since "there are many advantages in being a parasite." His conclusions are repeatedly reinforced with parasitic expressions: "Woman is almost universally parasitic"; "parasitism . . . is woman's intrinsic nature"; "her parasitic instinct"; "woman's sexual parasitism is innate" (1958, 207, 263, 214, xi, 208, 212, 198).

The lowering of women to "parasites" is not the exclusive domain of men with an axe to grind against females. More of the same can be found in Simone de Beauvoir's *The Second Sex* (1952). De Beauvoir, a prolific French author and leading figure in modern-day feminism, reserves her most vitriolic language for married women who do not work outside the home. She castigates marriage as "obscene in principle," "a surviving relic of dead ways," and "a form of servitude" that transforms women into "praying mantises" and "leeches" (1974, 496, 509, 211, 539). De Beauvoir calls the housewife "subordinate, secondary, parasitic" because her "work within the home gives her no autonomy," "is not directly useful to society," and "produces nothing." She is particularly exasperated with women who willingly choose to "live as parasites" even when they have the wherewithal to do otherwise. These "parasitic" women, she laments, are "extremely demoralizing for the woman who aims at self-sufficiency" (ibid., 510, 777).

Although de Beauvoir and other feminists claim to be simply in support of the woman's right to perform any kind of work she chooses—whether it be exercised inside or outside the home—their litmus test of nonparasitism, independence, and fulfillment is full-time gainful employment in the labor force. Such claims notwithstanding, feminist rhetoric is replete with images of homemakers as "parasites" on husband, home, or hearth, and almost entirely devoid of any references to working women as "parasites" on either the employer or the job.

Parasites on the Body of Europe

Consignment of Jews and others to the status of grasping, unscrupulous, and dangerous parasites intent on exploiting and annihilating the people and institutions of Germany proved to be one of the most ubiquitous forms of dehumanization before and during the Nazi Holocaust. The name-calling started early from reputable intellectual circles. In 1818 Christoph Heinrich Pfaff, a scientist "of high intellectual standards and genuine liberal convictions," compared the Jew to "a rapidly growing parasitic plant that winds round the still healthy tree to suck up the life juice until the trunk, emaciated and eaten up from within, falls moldering into decay" (Katz 1980, 149, 150). Hermann Ahlwardt's anti-Semitic diatribe of 1895 referred to Jews as "parasites, exploiters" and concluded that "these parasites must be made harmless by a special law" (Massing 1949, 302, 304).

Hitler repeatedly warned about the ominous threat presented to nations, states, and people by the invasion of "Jewish parasites":

> He [the Jew] was never a nomad, but only and always a *parasite* in the body of other peoples. . . . His spreading is a typical phenomenon for all parasites; he always seeks a new feeding ground for his race. . . . He is and remains the typical parasite, a sponger who like a noxious bacillus keeps spreading as soon as a favorable medium invites him. . . . Wherever he appears, the host people dies out after a shorter or longer period. (1971, 304–5)

Holocaust perpetrators resorted extensively to hostile semantics about parasites. By 1942 Nazi propagandist Julius Streicher was publishing articles calling for "the elimination of these parasites" (Varga 1981, 291). A booklet—*The Jew as Global Parasite*

(1944)—served as an important source of propaganda for those charged with implementing "the final solution." It emphasized that "the Jew is a parasite" that "leads an uprooted existence at the expense of its host nations." According to the booklet's most fundamental theme, "the Jewish global parasite knows only one aim: complete annihilation" and is therefore engaged in a never-ending search "for new hosts" to exploit, consume, and destroy.[3]

European Gypsies, long considered a subhuman species living a parasitical existence, became another main target of the menacing terminology. A memorandum drawn up in Austria during the Nazi era referred to Gypsies as "parasites within the body of our people, causing immense damage" and proposed "a National Socialist solution for the Gypsy question" (Poliakov 1979, 265).

Soviet Parasites

During the heyday of Soviet tyranny those who expressed the slightest qualms about Communism or lacked sufficient revolutionary fervor were in danger of being branded "parasites." This designation originated with Karl Marx, who depicted the French state bureaucracy spawned by capitalism as an "appalling parasitic growth, which enmeshes the body of French society like a net and chokes all its pores" (1965, 107).

Lenin drew directly from Marx's vocabulary of parasitism and applied it to a wide assortment of social systems, institutions, and individuals. Regarding the fate of bureaucratic officials, idlers, and those sponging off the masses, Lenin called for ousting "this parasitic stratum from their posts" (1960–70, 21:356). The "bureaucratic stratum" he spoke of included the bourgeoisie, intellectuals, the labor aristocracy, and others.

Farmers who harbored reservations about yielding to the Soviet collectivization of agriculture were subjected to an unremitting barrage of parasitic expressions. The most common designation constructed to impugn recalcitrant peasants was the word "kulak." This disparaging term—derived from the Russian word for fist—originally referred to miserly, unscrupulous rural traders or middlemen who became rich by exploiting the labor of less fortunate villagers. Its meaning was expanded enormously to engulf not only peasants who were well off, but also nonprosperous farmers who dared express an aversion to joining the collective state farms or voiced a negative attitude toward the Soviet regime.

The "kulak" epithet was primarily equated with such loathsome creatures as "parasites," "leeches," and "vermin." This association functioned to reinforce the prevailing negative images and accentuated the revolting traits attributed to an abominable foe with a ravenous appetite for unlimited exploitation. In the Soviet lexicon the words "kulak" and "parasite" became synonymous.

Lenin referred to kulaks as "the most brutal, callous and savage exploiters" and charged that "our state grain monopoly" was being subverted by "the rural rich, the kulak, the parasite who has been robbing the neighborhood for decades." He called for "a great *'crusade'*" against "the grain profiteers, the kulaks, the parasites" (ibid., 28:56; 27:393, 396).

Stalin carried Lenin's vitriolic vocabulary to its most disastrous outcome on December 27, 1929, when he announced: "To launch an offensive against the kulaks means that we must smash the kulaks, eliminate them as a class" (1953–55, 12:174). This order served as a prelude to the terror-famine, which resulted in the starvation deaths of over seven million Ukrainian farmers in one winter alone! Communist Party officials responsible for implementing the policy of enforced starvation ridiculed those who made desperate efforts to survive on acorns and potato peelings: "Look at the parasites! They went digging for acorns in the snow with their bare hands—They'll do anything to get out of working" (Conquest 1986, 235).

During the 1960s and later, the "parasite" epithet continued to persist, especially against individuals suspected of not working hard enough or of harboring anti-Soviet sentiments. In 1965 Joseph Brodsky, an outstanding young Soviet poet, was sentenced to five years of forced labor for the act of "parasitism" since his works did not produce what the state authorities considered an adequate income (Shatz 1980,

117–18). In 1973 the prominent dissident writer Andrei Amalrik was sent to a labor camp because, according to prosecutor Milhail Malyarov, "he contributed nothing to the state. He was a parasite" (Sakharov 1974, 185).

A Parasitic Race

Slaveholders in the antebellum American South exploited the parasite tag to justify black bondage. They glorified slavery as "a positive good," not only because it was seen as vital to the economy of the South, but also because it was considered the best and only appropriate condition for the blacks themselves. The slaveowner presented himself as a benevolent master who furnished the essential sustenance and environment (the "plantation community") for a race that could only survive in a subservient state. Emancipation, according to this doctrine, was one of the worst possible calamities that could befall a group so incapable of sustaining an autonomous existence. Thus the Negro liberated from servitude—like the parasite without a host—was depicted as a creature doomed to extinction.

An avid proponent of the notion that black people were a parasitic type of species was Dr. Daniel Drake, a physician and scientist from Cincinnati. Drake wrote a letter to Dr. John C. Warren of Boston on April 5, 1851, in which he stressed that the Africans "are, in every part of the United States, a serving people, parasitic to the white man in propensity, and devoted to his menial employments" (1940, 31).

In John Pendleton Kennedy's *Swallow Barn* (1822), a novel containing a highly romanticized portrayal of life on the plantation, Southern aristocrats defend slavery as imperative for the survival of the black race. The Negro is described as "essentially parasitic, dependent upon guidance for his most indispensable necessaries, without foresight or thrift of any kind" (Brown 1937, 19).

Portrayals of African Americans as parasites continued to persist long after the end of the Civil War. These later versions convey more deeply degrading images of black people as soulless entities lacking the most rudimentary qualities of cognition, awareness, and moral development. Writing in the *Transactions* of the Medical Society of Virginia (1909), Dr. E. T. Brady furnishes a prime example of this demeaning rhetoric:

> The negro question, in my mind, must be treated as a parasite. They have been educated by the North and by some of the Southern people, until some of our intelligent people really believe they have a soul. They have not. They are just as devoid of ethical sentiment or consciousness as the fly and the maggot. They are parasites. (Murrell 1909, 173)

Cinnamon-Colored Vermin and Lice

Vermin and lice were the terms most often invoked to portray Indians as dangerous, parasitic invaders that had to be eradicated.

Colonel Henry Bouquet, an American calvary officer charged with exterminating Indians in colonial North America, wrote about his task in the following manner: "to extirpate that vermin from a country they have forfeited, and, with it, all claim to the rights of humanity" and "clear the country of that vermin" (Parkman 1897–98, 2:42). In 1854 Dr. Henry Patterson of Philadelphia referred to Native Americans as "the cinnamon-colored vermin west of the Mississippi" (Nott and Gliddon 1954, xxxviii).

A variation on the repulsive parasite analogy—"nits make lice"—was called upon to justify the killing of Indian children. In the Indian-hating frontier novel *Tom Quick, the Indian Slayer* (1851), Tom contemplated sparing a baby's life, but then the recognition that "the child would in a few years become an Indian . . . so enraged him that he instantly dashed out its brains." Whenever questioned about his reason for killing Indian children, he responded: "Nits make lice" (Barnett 1975, 131).

The same dictum stood at the heart of Colonel John Chivington's instructions to his regiment for massacring Cheyenne encamped alongside Sand Creek, Colorado, on November 29, 1864: "Kill and scalp all, big and little; nits make lice" (Andrist 1964, 89).

Blood-Sucking Parasites

One of the most fearsome traits associated with parasites is their blood-sucking proclivities. The leech and vampire bat are prime representatives of this type of parasite. The threat to one's blood supply by a parasitic aggressor represents the gravest of assaults, since blood is such a basic substance of life itself. The blood-draining propensity of parasitic creatures transforms them into the most revolting and threatening entities imaginable.

By extension, labeling unwanted human beings as blood-sucking parasites conveys the ultimate in repugnant and malevolent characterizations. Such portrayals cry out for nothing less than the most draconian measures against those upon whom the labels are imposed.

Human beings in utero comprise a readily accessible target for the blood-extracting epithets. Writing in *Parade Magazine* (April 22, 1990), astronomer Carl Sagan and his wife, scientist Ann Druyan, furnish an ominous reference to the unborn as "a kind of parasite on the walls of the uterus," an entity that "destroys tissue in its path" and "sucks blood from capillaries" (p. 6).

Seriously ill hospitalized patients constitute another vulnerable target for the blood-siphoning images. An intensive care nurse recalls an incident in which laboratory technicians called upon to draw blood from a patient in the Intensive Care Unit responded with sarcastic irony: "This is a switch. Instead of this parasite taking our blood, we're taking its."[4]

The repulsive, blood-sucking expressions aimed at the unborn and born of today are in the same league with the blood-sucking imagery directed against history's most victimized groups.

Hitler's universe of Jewish parasites is saturated with such phrases as the Jew is "the eternal blood-sucker" whose exploitative behavior constitutes a "blood-sucking tyranny." He stressed "how greatly" the Jew "has sinned against the masses" and "has squeezed and sucked their blood again and again." Hitler accused Jews of exploiting the financial problems of others, acting like "a true blood-sucker that attaches himself to the body of the unhappy people and cannot be picked off." He also expressed alarm about "contamination of our blood" by "these black parasites of the nation" (1971, 310, 309, 313, 562).

Lenin and Stalin made extensive use of blood-sucking terminology, particularly against the kulaks. Lenin charged that "these blood-suckers have grown rich on the want suffered by people in the war" and "these leeches have sucked the blood of the working people and grown richer as the workers in the cities and factories have starved" (1960–70, 28:56–58). In 1934, after millions of peasants had been eradicated under the guise of a campaign against dangerous, ruthless, blood-sucking parasitic kulaks, Stalin announced: "The elimination of the parasitic classes has led to the disappearance of . . . the kulak-exploiters, the blood-sucking usurer" (1953–55, 13:340, 342).

North American Indians were regularly stereotyped as "bloodthirsty" savages that not only derived the greatest pleasure out of spilling the blood of white settlers, but also—like an insatiable parasite—climaxed their orgy by feeding off the blood of their victims. In *The History of the Discovery of America* (1810), an anthology of Indian war narratives, author-editor Henry Trumbull claimed that the Puritan conquest consisted of destroying or dispersing "a horde of fierce and blood thirsty *savages*" (Slotkin 1973, 433). Frontier literature is rife with blood-drinking traits attributed to Native Americans. In *The Last of the Mohicans* (1821), James Fenimore Cooper describes thousands of "raving savages" who, after massacring a group of pioneers, are so aroused by the "flow of blood" that they "kneeled to the earth and drank freely, exultantly, hellishly, of the crimson tide" (1951, 208). Robert Montgomery Bird's Indian-hating novel *Nick of the Woods* (1837) bristles with contemptible portrayals of Native Americans as "bloodthirsty creatures." The story's main villain is an Indian "that has drunk the blood of women and children" (1967, 228).

Summary

Relegation of humans today and in the past to voracious, repulsive creatures is replete with a repetitive litany of parasitic metaphors. Those intent on characterizing the unborn as a "parasite" ravaging the life and health of the mother by "suck[ing] blood" and nutrients from her body and the debilitated patient as a vegetative "parasite" depleting the health care system are replicating a line of discourse deeply rooted in the annals of infamy. Feminist writer Simone de Beauvoir castigated homemakers as "subordinate, secondary, parasitic" individuals who contribute nothing to society. Hitler and his followers portrayed the Jew as a "global parasite" and an "eternal blood-sucker" that repeatedly "squeezed and sucked . . . blood" from the masses. Lenin and Stalin depicted independent farmers as "blood-sucking parasitic kulaks" that "sucked the blood of the working people." Slaveowners viewed African Americans as an "essentially parasitic" race in need of bondage for survival. Indian-hating literature is full of references to Native Americans as "vermin," "lice," and "blood-thirsty savages" who fed on the blood of their victims.

12

Diseases of
Epidemic Proportions

Disease metaphors occupy a central position in the semantic war against the most defenseless human lives. In many instances, people suffering from real illnesses have borne an enormous brunt of the disease-infested rhetoric. For the most part, however, the malignant metaphors have nothing to do with real diseases; they are aimed at perfectly healthy human beings whose main deficiency is being unwanted. In "Disease As Political Metaphor" Susan Sontag's observations about the purpose underlying the use of the cancer concept can also be applied to other illness analogies, including those explored in this chapter. "To describe a phenomenon as a cancer is an incitement to violence," she writes. "And it is, in most cases, a justification . . . of harsh measures, including, usually, violence" (1978, 33).

Diseased Entities

Linguistic reduction of individuals and groups to diseased entities ranks among the most degrading uses of metaphor. The words "illness," "sickness," and "disease" are often fraught with the grim imagery of abnormality, pathology, infirmity, deformity, retardation, and revulsion.

An Illness of Nine Months' Duration

The most prominent use of the disease analogy by contemporary abortion proponents is the consignment of pregnancy, particularly when unwanted, and along with it, the unborn child, to the status of an illness, with abortion as the preferred method of "treatment." This is a manifestation of the medicalization of destruction, a process of semantic alchemy involving the redefinition of human beings as diseases and the reconceptualization of their extermination as a legitimate medical procedure.

An early expression of the pregnancy-as-disease concept appeared in *Time* magazine (September 17, 1967) under the title "Disease of Unwanted Pregnancy." Obstetrics professor Dr. Kenneth J. Ryan was quoted as saying "the 'disease' of an unwanted pregnancy is not usually fatal, but living with it is so onerous that many women risk death via criminal abortion rather than suffer its far-reaching effects" (p. 84).

In an address before the American Anthropological Association in 1970, leading abortion advocate Dr. Warren Hern called pregnancy an essentially "pathological condition" and emphasized that "this 'illness' is not just biological but social and economic." Hern cited a litany of symptoms that, he contended, demonstrate the abnormality of the pregnant state (1971, 5–10). Since then he has continued to espouse his disease-filled perception of pregnancy with increasing vehemence. In *Abortion Practice* (1984), Hern repeats a full-scale semantic assault on the "outmoded" view of pregnancy as normal and concludes that "'unwantedness' may be regarded as a major complication of pregnancy, with surgical intervention in the form of abortion as the indicated treatment" (pp. 6, 8).

Planned Parenthood Federation of America and its affiliates are among the most avid supporters of the pregnancy-as-disease doctrine. In 1975 Planned Parenthood of New York declared: "Ending a pregnancy that threatens everything that makes a woman's life worth living is no more unnatural than treating an illness that can cripple her" (p. 40). The following year Planned Parenthood board member Dr. James Irwin asserted that "in a girl under 18 we consider pregnancy a disease" (Lake 1976, 153).

Patients As Pathology

Contemporary hospitals and nursing homes serve as prime settings for defining vulnerable groups after birth—seriously disabled patients and the elderly—as "illnesses" rather than human beings who happen to be suffering from physical and/or mental impairments. Sociologist Terry Mizrahi's analysis of dehumanizing language employed against patients by house staff physicians at a leading Southern university medical center includes many references to patients as diseases. Interns complained about getting "stuck" with "dehydrated UTIs [patients with urinary tract infections]." Both faculty and house staff members referred to patients suffering from strokes as "the stroke is over there." The designation "look at those 'sicklers'" was used to denigrate individuals with sickle cell anemia (1986, 73, 101).

Mizrahi found that patients in ERs (Emergency Rooms) and ICUs (Intensive Care Units) were prime targets of this kind of verbal abuse. A junior resident declared loudly: "You can see some great 'pathology' coming in the ER and then there are the patients!" This comment evoked laughter and joking among his peers. A senior resident said to colleagues in the ICU: "I'd like a 'triple-lobe pneumonia' to come in tonight with a touch of edema, just enough to put the 'wire' (a Swan-Gaiz catheter) in" (ibid., 101).

In today's youth-oriented culture the aging process itself is often viewed as a "disease" and old people are looked upon as nonfunctional entities in a stage of hopeless decline. A classic illustration of this stereotype is the practice of equating the confused elderly with the disease of senile dementia. It is commonly believed that the disoriented and sometimes delusional behavior manifested by aged persons is a sure sign of senility—an unalterable condition of inevitable deterioration intrinsic to growing old—rather than the result of reversible medical and psychological conditions such as anemia, malnutrition, depression, reactions to medication, hypothyroidism, and congestive heart failure (Glassman 1980, 138–44).

The Disabled Sex

Throughout history linguistic attacks on women have been regularly laden with sickness imagery. The female anatomical

makeup, in particular, has been persistently equated with illness, infirmities, contaminated wounds, and disabilities.

The assaults began early. Aristotle wrote: "We should look
upon the female state as being as it were a deformity" (1953,
459, 461). In 1851 E. J. Tilt called the woman's life cycle "a long
chain of never-ending infirmities" (Jalland and Hooper 1986,
33). Gagliani, a writer during this same period, referred to
women as "invalids" who "only have intervals of health in the
course of a continual disease" (Ellis 1914, 283).

According to Freudian dogma, the woman typically equates
the absence of the male sex organ with a severe biological
defect—a permanent wound and visible scar—that carries over
into the social, psychological, and cognitive spheres as well.
"After a woman has become aware of the wound to her narcis-
sism," Freud taught, "she develops, like a scar, a sense of inferiority" (1959, 192).

In a paper presented before the Anthropological Society of
London in 1869, J. McGregor Allan stressed the "severe disabling
impact" of menstruation, which he termed the "periodic illness."
"At such times," he maintained, "women are unfit for any great
mental or physical labour." Moreover, he found it "extremely
doubtful how far they can be considered responsible beings
while the crisis lasts" (7:cxcix, cxcviii).

The woman-hating world of Henry Miller's *Tropic of Cancer*
(1961) is populated with men who repeatedly defile female
sexual anatomy by resorting to the expressions "it's disgusting,"
"an ugly gash," and "the wound that never heals" (140, 249).

The Affliction of Blackness

For centuries, the imposition of disease epithets on black people focused on skin color. Having black skin was widely interpreted as representing an aberration, a precipitous decline
from what was considered to be the norm of health, purity,
goodness, and attractiveness—the color white. As early as
1578, English geographer George Best wrote that the blackness of Negroes "proceedeth of some naturall infection of the
first inhabitants of that Countrey [Ethiopia], and so all the

whole progenie of them descended, are still polluted with the same blot of infection" (Hakluyt 1965, 7:262–63).

Even Dr. Benjamin Rush, a slavery opponent, set forth before the American Philosophical Society on July 14, 1792, a "scientific" explanation of blackness as a disease in a thesis: "Observations Intended to Favour a Supposition That the Black Color (As It Is Called) of the Negroes Is Derived from the Leprosy." Rush concluded by proposing that a cure be found for the "disease" of Negro blackness. "Is the color of the negroes a disease?" he asked. "Then let science and humanity combine their efforts, and endeavor to discover a remedy for it." Encouraging "attempts to cure this disease of the skin of negroes," he predicted, "shall produce a large portion of happiness in the world" (1799, 289–97).

In 1798 pamphleteer John Morgan Rhees considered the links forged between the Negro's color and "a leprous disease" compelling enough to express the hope that doctors would "exert their skills in pointing out a remedy" (Jordan 1968, 521n).

Virulent Maladies

When combined with the expressions "infection," "contagion," "epidemic," "plague," and "pestilence," disease analogies are intended to project a more ominous image of undesired, vulnerable humans as dangerous, infectious epidemic diseases that threaten the health and life of those who count—the wanted segments of the human race.

An Epidemic of Unwanted Pregnancies

Not only is unintended pregnancy defined as a pathological condition in its own right; it is often portrayed as a contagion that threatens to contaminate and destroy the pregnant woman's health and life. On the broader societal level, unwanted pregnancy is likened to a kind of plague that is rapidly spreading throughout the globe.

Abortion advocate and psychiatrist Natalie Shainess relies upon disease concepts to characterize unwelcome pregnancy as a sinister, contagious malady. She compares unwanted pregnancy to an "alien germ" and "unseen infection deep in the body[;] it insists on expression through one symptom or another" (1970, 20).

Dr. Warren Hern furnishes a litany of "illness parameters of the condition of pregnancy": increased venous pressure, elevated basal metabolism rate, sodium and water retention, hypercoagulability of blood, nausea and vomiting, urinary disturbances, fatigue, increased irritability, marked fluctuations in libido, leg cramps, abdominal pain, backache, anemia, uterine rupture, diabetes, urinary tract infection, ectopic pregnancy, hemorrhage, puerperal psychosis, amniotic fluid embolism, puerperal infection, and uterine dysfunction (1984a, 10–14).

Hern also presents pregnancy as a life-threatening illness when compared to abortion. Maternal deaths from term pregnancy, he claims, are much higher than maternal deaths from abortion. Hern places "the risk of death due to pregnancy untreated by abortion" at "16 times greater than the risk of death due to abortion." Undoubtedly, such a totally negative and terror-inducing depiction of pregnancy provides a compelling justification for Hern and other abortionists to continue performing abortions as "the indicated treatment of choice for pregnancy" (ibid., 24, 8).

A booklet put out by Planned Parenthood's Alan Guttmacher Institute in 1976 warned about the "epidemic of adolescent pregnancies" (Planned Parenthood Federation of America 1976). During the same year Dr. Willard Cates of the Centers for Disease Control called unwanted pregnancies "epidemic" (Cates, Grimes, and Smith 1978, 115, 120). The word "epidemic" is meant to project the menacing image of a virulent contagion calling for drastic action. It is within the context of such a dire emergency that abortion is defined as a public health measure.

Contagious Infections

People with disabilities in today's society are still treated as if their handicap poses a threat to others because of the infectious qualities ascribed to it. The consequences of tagging people with handicaps as equivalent to contagious diseases is recounted by the wife of a husband with a disability. "He told me many times when he first began to walk with the cane, he noticed how people would step back in order to avoid any contact with him. He said the expressions on their face and their actions of trying to avoid him gave the impression that his handicap was some kind of disease that was contagious."[1]

Such terms echo the designations invoked against institutionalized physically and mentally handicapped patients in early twentieth-century America. Before the New York Conference of Charities and Corrections in 1900, Dr. John F. Fitzgerald, superintendent of the Rome State Custodial Asylum, described the "idiotic child" as "a source of moral contagion to the other children which is far reaching in its results" (1901, 129). A year later Dr. W. Duncan McKim, a New York physician, said that "feeble-minded" individuals, as well as epileptics, alcoholics, and the chronically insane, "contaminate posterity, in an ever-widening reach, until whole nations have partaken of the infection" (1901, 184–85, 193). In 1913 mental deficiency expert Dr. Martin W. Barr referred to "imbeciles" as "festering sores in the life of society" (p. 190).

A Plague of Females

During classical antiquity and later, women were regularly labeled "plagues." The Greek writer Hesiod dubbed Pandora the first of "the damnable race of women—a plague which men must live with."[2] An identical view was expressed in a satirical poem written by the Greek poet Semonides. "Yes, this is the worst plague Zeus has made—women" (Lloyd-Jones 1975, 54). In his tirade against females in positions of power and leadership—*The First Blast of the Trumpet Against the Monstrous Regiment of Women* (1558)—John Knox contended that God "hath raised up these Jezebels to be the uttermost of his plagues" (Breslow 1985, 66).

Much of the plague-saturated imagery emanated from the "highly infectious" quality attributed to the menstrual cycle. The Roman scholar Pliny (A.D. 61–113) accused the menstruating woman of ruining crops, destroying gardens, and killing bees. The peasants of Eastern Europe held that food was especially susceptible to "the deadly contagion." All would go wrong, they warned, if a woman were allowed to bake bread, make pickles, or churn butter during her period (de Beauvoir 1974, 168).

Furthermore, menstruation has been blamed for inducing a host of afflictions, ranging from epilepsy to that condition habitually associated with females—hysteria. In the leading British medical journal *The Lancet* (April 12, 1873), Dr. Robert Barnes wrote: "It is a matter of frequent observation that the first attack of hysteria or epilepsy coincides with the first effort at menstruation, and that a fit is liable to recur at successive menstrual epochs" (pp. 514–15).

Many women have thus suffered from a severe case of double jeopardy: not only were they declared to be a bleeding, disgusting, and disabled gender, but also a dangerous source of uncleanness and contagion.

Jewish Germ Carriers

Adolf Hitler's anti-Semitic diatribe *Mein Kampf* includes numerous references to Jews as "the foreign virus" that spreads infection throughout the world; in short, a "world plague." Hitler even utilized this terminology to malign the Jewish influence in Germany's cultural life: "A pestilence, spiritual pestilence, worse than the Black Death of olden times" and "germ-carriers of the worse sort" that "poison men's souls" (1971, 339, 78, 58).

Holocaust perpetrators found germ analogies to be an invaluable device for justifying their destructive actions. "Jews are injurious and carriers of many sicknesses," asserted Julius Streicher. "They cause the same reaction as a virus to a human body." Streicher likened the enactment of anti-Jewish legislation to an attempt by the human body "to fight off a virus" (Varga 1981, 232).

Heinrich Himmler invoked a similar characterization for warning his SS generals against stealing property from dead Jews: "We don't want in the end, just because we have exterminated a germ, to be infected by that germ and die from it" (Hilberg 1967, 647).

Soviet Ideology on Infections

Many Bolshevik tirades featured dire warnings about the infectious, epidemic nature of various religions and ideological movements at variance with Marxist-Leninist revolutionary dogma.

Lenin stated that "every religious idea, every idea of God, even flirting with the idea of God, is unutterable vileness . . . of the most dangerous kind, 'contagion' of the most abominable kind" (Conquest 1986, 199).

In addition, Lenin characterized liquidationism and otzovism-ultimatumism as "abscesses" that "contaminate" the organism of the Party and dubbed reformism "a dangerous disease." He expressed outrage against the masses who had succumbed to "the defencist epidemic." Lenin also called revolutionary phrase-making "the vile itch . . . a catching disease" and reminded his followers that throughout history revolutionary parties "became infected with revolutionary phrase-making and perished as a result."[3]

Stalin was preoccupied with preventing Leon Trotsky's "non-Bolshevik teaching from infecting those sections of our Party which it reckons to capture, namely, our youth" (1953–55, 9:150).

"A Pestilence of Blacks"

Slaveowners and like-minded groups made extensive use of malignant metaphors in their defense of Negro servitude. Freeing slaves, they argued, would be tantamount to spreading virulent epidemics among members of the white community. Long after the end of slavery the same imagery continued to be deployed to justify the segregation of blacks.

From 1815 to the 1830s the American Colonization Society, a proponent of dispatching blacks to Africa, concluded: "The free blacks in our country are . . . a contagion wherever they reside" (Garrison 1968, 125). Attorney William Drayton warned that the abolition of slavery would result in releasing more than two million slaves "to sweep the fair South like a pestilence" (1969, 247). William J. Grayson's poem, *The Hireling and the Slave* (1856), depicted blacks in the North as constituting "a moral pestilence" (Brown 1939, 281). Thomas Dixon's racist novel, *The Leopard's Spots* (1902), described them as a "menace . . . throwing the blight of its shadow over future generations, a veritable Black Death for the land and its people" (1967, 33).

Physicians conferred medical respectability on the terminology of infection. In 1843 Dr. Josiah C. Nott published an article entitled "The Mulatto a Hybrid—Probable Extermination of the Two Races if the Whites and Blacks are Allowed to Intermarry." Dr. Nott concluded that the "hybrid mulatto" was "a degenerate, unnatural offspring, doomed by nature to work out its own destruction" (p. 255).

Disease-Ridden Tribes

In the battles between Indians and whites on the frontier, North America's original inhabitants were invariably cast as the villains, even in those numerous situations where whites were the aggressors. The threat of Indian aggression was overwhelmingly compared to a dangerous contagion that, once unleashed, was capable of spreading in a wild and impulsive manner. Thus when Native Americans fought against the settlers, it was typically portrayed not as a justifiable defense, but as the irrational, purely instinctual response of a dangerous mob whose uncontrollable outbursts were analogous to the spread of a virulent epidemic.

This bias is reflected throughout historian Francis Parkman's accounts of the role of Indians in North America: "the contagion of the war" afflicted the Cherokee and "they perpetrated numerous murders"; the Ottawa warriors "caught the fierce contagion" and startled "the distant garrison with unearthly yells"; "the warlike contagion spread to the Indians of Nova Scotia"; "the Iroquois had proved more deadly enemies than the pestilence" (1897–98, 2:123, 1:243; 1902a, 1:244; 1902b, 2:224).

An Epidemic of Venereal Diseases

A variation on the presentation of unwanted people as raging epidemics is to associate them with venereal diseases such as gonorrhea and syphilis. This portrayal typically assumes two forms: equating the victims with sexually transmitted diseases or vilifying them for being foremost carriers and spreaders of these diseases.

The Sexually Transmitted Condition of Unwanted Pregnancy

The leading proponents of the depiction of unwanted pregnancy as a venereal disease that can be best combatted by abortion are Dr. Willard Cates and colleagues associated with the Centers for Disease Control in Atlanta, Georgia. Their 1978 article, "Abortion as a Treatment for Unwanted Pregnancy: The Number Two Sexually-Transmitted Condition," features an elaborate rationale for classifying unintended pregnancy as a venereal disease: "Unwanted pregnancy is transmitted sexually, is socially and emotionally pathologic, and has many other characteristics of the conventional venereal diseases." It concludes on a predictable note: "Unwanted pregnancy should be considered a sexually-transmitted condition of epidemic proportion; moreover, legal abortion is an effective, safe, curative treatment for that condition" (pp. 115–16, 120).

Another proponent of the notion of unwelcome pregnancy as a "venereal disease" is medical ethics professor Joseph Fletcher. In *Humanhood: Essays in Biomedical Ethics* (1979), he writes: "Pregnancy when wanted is a healthy process, *pregnancy when not wanted is a disease*—in fact, a venereal disease" (p. 138).

The "Jewification" of Syphilis

Blaming Jews for spreading venereal diseases—especially syphilis—and contaminating racial purity comprised a major component of anti-Semitic polemics in the Third Reich.

The links alleged between Jews and syphilis in *Mein Kampf* established a mode of discourse for widespread emulation during the Nazi era. Hitler not only placed the lion's share of responsibility on Jews for "the spreading contamination of our sexual life" and "the syphilization of our people" but also called syphilis "the Jewish disease." Furthermore, he referred to the moral degeneracy accompanying venereal disease as the "Jewification of our spiritual life" (pp. 248–49, 253, 247).

In 1933 Wilhelm Reich identified the "fear of syphilis" as "one of the major sources of National Socialism's political views and its anti-Semitism" (1970, 82).

Syphilitic Indians

One of the diseases most commonly attributed to Indians was syphilis. Frequent appearances of the word "syphilis" alongside references to Native Americans were intended to give the impression of a profoundly contagious and degenerate race.

During the 1790s and early 1800s the California Indians were repeatedly portrayed as being overwhelmed with venereal disease. Some of the designations disseminated in publications of that time included: "Permeated to the marrow of their bones with venereal disease," "syphilitic Indian," "very much contaminated and this malady syphilis is incurable," and "venereal diseases are devouring them" (Cook 1976, 26–27).

A renewal of these images took hold in the period 1848–70, an era when California was invaded by gold seekers, adventurers, and land speculators. The phrases "of a syphilitic character" and "tainted and poisoned with venereal disease" were circulated with great regularity. According to historian Sherburne Cook, the Indian reservation agents listed so many references to syphilis that "reading their reports becomes monotonous" (ibid., 270).

Ironically, although syphilis and other venereal diseases were characterized as being intrinsic to the Native American culture and Indians were blamed for their spread, it was the Spanish and then the Anglo-American invaders who were largely responsible for infecting the native population. Cook concludes that by the advent of the Anglo-Americans, California's "mission Indians" had been "very heavily infected" by Spanish soldiers. "The effect of the American influx," he found, "was merely to extend and intensify the existing condi-

tion by bringing in fresh sources of infection and spreading it
. . . to tribes which had previously escaped" (ibid., 268).

Summary

The repugnant disease metaphors concocted to devalue individuals today and in the past share a close affinity. Today's
definers of unwanted pregnancy as a "disease," "venereal disease," "infection," "germ," and "epidemic," and of undesired
patients as "diseases" and "pathology" are repeating a rhetoric
of vilification directed against a host of diverse victims down
through the ages. For millennia, women have been depicted as
"diseases," "deadly contaminations," and "plagues." The Nazi
nomenclature associated Jews with a "germ," "world plague,"
"pestilence," and "syphilis." Soviet semanticists reviled their victims with such standbys as "diseased condition," "disorder,"
"epidemic," and "contagion." Images of black people as a "contagion" and a "pestilence" were widely circulated in the
American South before and after the Civil War. North American
Indians were frequently linked with the spread of "syphilis,"
"contagions," and "pestilences."

13

Inanimate Objects for Exploitation

The semantic transformation of undesired human beings into inanimate objects—mere things with no semblance of personality, humanity, consciousness, life, or vitality—constitutes one of the most radical and pervasive forms of denigration. In this process of objectification people are reduced to the level of insignificant matter that can be used, moved, manipulated, and disposed of with impunity.

Objectification also involves an extreme asymmetrical relationship in which power plays an all-encompassing role. The definition of the powerless or those with little power as "property," "possessions," "merchandise," and "commodities" endows some individuals with the ultimate power of ownership over others. Those who perceive themselves as owners believe they can do anything they want to others because they view them as their rightful personal possessions.

A Universe of Inanimate Objects and Expendable Material

Whenever the words "object" and "material" are employed to denigrate human lives, two images are likely to predominate: the sheer insignificance of those saddled with these labels and their utilization as items for rank exploitation ranging from slave labor to experimental atrocities.

Fetal Material

Portrayals of abortion as merely the removal of insignificant "material" abound in the rhetoric of abortion proponents.

Abortion: A Woman's Guide, a book published by Planned Parenthood of New York City in the 1970s, characterizes the "embryo, amniotic fluid, and placenta" between the sixth and tenth week as merely a "bulk of material . . . about the size of a plum." It indicates, furthermore, that in saline abortions performed between the sixteenth and twentieth week of pregnancy "the uterus pushes out the fetal and placental material." The Planned Parenthood guide offers assurance that aborted women do not have "to see the material that has been removed" (1975, 36, 67).

A typical example of how this terminology is incorporated in leading medical journals is a report on fifty first-trimester abortions published in *Obstetrics & Gynecology* (July 1985). The authors never refer to what was aborted as the remains of obliterated human beings, but simply as "material," "suctioned or curetted material," "cellular material," and "abortion material" (Jacobson and Goetsch, 124–26).

In an article entitled "A New Attack on Abortion" (February 2, 1987), *Newsweek* describes the dismembered body extracted in the D&E abortion shown in Dr. Bernard Nathanson's film, *The Eclipse of Reason,* as "fetal material being pulled from a woman's vagina" (p. 32).

Medical scientists have appropriated the notion of aborted humans as "fetal material" in order to justify expanding the boundaries of fetal experimentation. On March 13, 1987, a panel of medical, ethical, and legal experts published a statement in *Science* magazine favoring the transplantation of brain tissue from aborted humans to benefit people suffering from serious neurological disorders. Mary Mahowald, co-director of the Center for Biomedical Ethics at Case Western Reserve Medical School, maintained that the proposal simply involved removing "fetal material" from "dead fetuses that have been legally aborted."[1]

Nursing Home Work Objects

Another group in contemporary society at great risk of being labeled "objects" for physical manipulation and abuse are the elderly in nursing homes, particularly seriously debilitated and noncommunicative patients. However, even hospital patients who are not profoundly impaired are still treated as if they were "objects" instead of human beings, especially when their behavior is viewed as disruptive to the daily institutional routines.

In his 1975 study of the Murray Manor nursing home, sociologist Jaber Gubrium found that many patients were treated "like an object" since "the only thing considered relevant is the work routine." He compared the floor staff's attitude toward patients to "what it is toward, for example, a stuck door or a jammed siderail on a bed." Gubrium lists some of the ways in which the residents were "physically manipulated" like inanimate objects: "They may be shoved aside. If they are in wheel chairs, they may simply be wheeled to one corner of a room. They may be lifted bodily and placed somewhere" (pp. 151–52). When the residents protested about being left alone in an isolated spot for long periods of time, their protests were simply ignored by the staff.

A similar atmosphere of patient dehumanization prevailed during the late 1970s at the Sunny Hill Convalescent Center. "I came to see the patients as 'work objects'" was a common expression among staff who performed their duties according to the rigid dictates of a busy work schedule. This type of bureaucratic setup had no room for focusing on patients as human beings. "The rush imposed by a heavy work load," sociologist Andrea Fontana discovered, led aides to engage in a persistent process of patient objectification:

> It becomes legitimate to stuff food down their throats because the goal has become serving the meal, not nourishing the patient, or to lift them in and out of bed as if they were inanimate dummies because the goal is bed making[,] not making the patient comfortable. . . . What is suffering here is not a car malfunctioning from shoddy workmanship, but human beings who by being treated as inanimate objects end up becoming inanimate objects. (1974, 144, 155–56)

Female Objects of Pornography

Some of the most demeaning images of women as objects can be found in the vast contemporary pornographic industry of books, films, videotapes, music, magazines, photographs, and sadomasochistic paraphernalia. Pornographic fare thrives on graphic images of promiscuous sex combined with unadorned violence—females being whipped, punched, raped, sodomized, tied up, hung upside down, dismembered, humiliated, and physically annihilated. There is no such thing as true rape in these depraved tales, since, according to the tenets of pornographic dogma, every woman deep down—her outward demeanor notwithstanding—possesses a craving to be sexually molested, assaulted, and debauched.

Pornography carries the objectification of women to new depths of debasement with an obsessive focus on the female body—the body projected is devoid of essence, will, spirit, soul, and integrity. It comprises pieces of sheer "material" and "matter"—legs, sex organs, breasts, buttocks—upon which the male acts out his lust and aggression. The pornography manufactured by Henry Miller is replete with accounts of sexual conquests over women depicted as "impersonal matter, mindless tissue endlessly compliant" (Millett 1970, 313). Susan Griffin refers to pornography as a "sadistic act" that "reduces a woman to a mere thing, to an entirely material object without a soul." "Pornography's revenge against nature," she emphasizes, "is precisely to deprive matter of spirit. And so in one act, pornography humiliates woman's body, by reducing her soul" (1981, 3, 49).

Playboy magazine—a pioneer in the creation of sophisticated, sexist pornography—peddles another dehumanized object: women as "sexual toys" for manipulation and consumption by avant-garde playboys. Or, as Susan Brownmiller aptly portrays this version of pornographic fare, "females as anonymous objects to be used, abused, broken and discarded" (1975, 394). The playboy inevitably tires of his expendable "plaything"—especially when it begins to show the slightest signs of age—and opts for a younger model.

In her autobiography, *Ordeal* (1980), former pornographic film star Linda Lovelace revealed that she was treated like "an inflatable plastic doll, a puppet. They picked me up and moved me here and there; they spread my legs this way and that; they shoved their things at me and into me." She described herself as "not a person anymore. I was a robot . . . a wind-up toy. . . . I had become someone's else's thing" (pp. 45, 91).

Transport Material for Auschwitz

Jews dispatched from the transit camps of Nazi-occupied countries to the death camps in the eastern territories were commonly classified as "transport material." Upon arrival at the extermination centers the victims were immediately defined as "material" for work exploitation, terminal medical experiments, and disintegration.

Filip Muller, a Czech Jew who was compelled to labor in a "special work detail" charged with burning the bodies of gas chamber victims in the Auschwitz crematorium, recounted that the designation "pieces" was used to describe those scheduled for incineration. One night around midnight, with a large backlog of bodies awaiting incineration, an SS officer burst into the crematorium and asked: "How many pieces are left?" He was told: "Around five hundred pieces." To this, he replied: "By morning those five hundred pieces must be reduced to ashes" (Lanzmann 1975, 158).

The same kind of degrading terminology is included in a memorandum dated June 5, 1942, regarding "technical changes" needed to improve the "load space" of "special vehicles" used to gas Jews:

> The merchandise abroad displays during the operation a natural tendency to rush to the rear doors. . . . When the doors are shut, the load always presses hard against them as soon as darkness sets in. This is because the load naturally rushes toward the light when darkness sets in, which makes closing the doors difficult. . . . It would

therefore be useful to light the lamp before and during the first moments of the operation. (ibid., 103–4)

The giant I. G. Farben Chemical Corporation exploited concentration camp inmates as "work material" for constructing its huge rubber and oil installations located at Auschwitz. Joseph Borkin's study of Farben's substantial role in the Holocaust—*The Crime and Punishment of I. G. Farben* (1978)— traces the increasingly harsh phases of a savage salvage operation in which human beings were viewed as strictly "consumable raw material":

> I. G. reduced slave labor to a consumable raw material, a human ore from which the mineral of life was systematically extracted. When no usable energy remained, the living dross was shipped to the gassing chambers and cremation furnaces where the S.S. recycled it into the German war economy—gold teeth for the Reichsbank, hair for mattresses, and fat for soap. (p. 126)

Nazi medics earmarked the bodies and organs of death camp inmates as choice "material" for research manipulation and mutilation. Dr. Sigmund Rascher called Jews highly suitable "experimental material" for the death-inducing high altitude experiments.[2] Anatomy professor Dr. August Hirt gave precise instructions on "the collection of the material" [severed heads] after "the subsequently induced death of the Jew" (ibid., 749). Neurologist Dr. Julius Hallervorden reasoned: "If you are going to kill all these people, at least take the brains out so that the material could be utilized." When the severed brains were delivered to him in batches of 150–250 at a time, he responded with unbounded enthusiasm: "There was wonderful material among those brains, beautiful mental defectives, malformations and early infantile diseases" (Schreiber n.d., 56).

Raw Material for Soviet Slave Labor

The Soviet preoccupation with reducing individuals to "raw material" for molding by the state is one of the main themes in

Boris Pasternak's novel *Doctor Zhivago* (1958). Zhivago initially welcomed the Bolshevik Revolution, but in time grew disenchanted with a regime that brutalized so many people. At one point in the story, Zhivago exposes the basic attitude of the revolutionary leaders toward the people: They view the human being as simply "a lump of raw material that needs to be processed by them" (p. 338).

Influential ideologues devised a plan for applying the "raw material" concept to justify the working to death of individuals in the Soviet slave labor camps. Jurist I. L. Averbakh identified the goal of Soviet "corrective labor" as "this transformation of the *nastiest human material* into worthwhile, fully useful, active, and conscientious builders of socialism." Although writer Maxim Gorky cautioned that *"human raw material* is immeasurably more difficult to work than wood," he nonetheless supported and even glorified the utilization of Gulag slave laborers for gigantic building projects such as a canal intended to unite the White and Baltic Seas (Solzhenitsyn 1973–74, 2:104, 86).

A widely accepted formula for transforming this "nastiest human material" in the Gulag was supplied by a leading proponent of the "corrective labor" doctrine, Naftaly Frenkel: "We have to squeeze everything out of a prisoner in the first three months—after that we don't need him anymore" (ibid., 49).

Forest Objects

Besides being equated with "wild animals" belonging to the wilderness, Native Americans were frequently lowered to the state of the inanimate objects in their surroundings. Their personalities, physical makeup, and culture were engulfed by this extreme process of objectification.

An early example of an object metaphor used against Native Americans came from the pen of Cotton Mather. In his history of New England during the period 1620–98, *Magnalia Christi Americana,* he wrote that Indians were "the veriest *ruines of mankind,* which were to be found anywhere on the face of the earth" (1967, 1:558).

Stereotypes of Indians as "things" abounded in the writings of historian Francis Parkman. He likened their "savage" nature to "a volcano covered with snow; and no man can say when or where the wild-fire will burst forth." Similarly, "each savage countenance," Parkman asserted, "seemed carved in wood, and none could have detected the ferocious passions hidden beneath that immovable mask" (1897–98, 1:46, 210). He also compared Indian character to "a rock" that, due to its extreme rigidity, was doomed to extinction:

> Some races, like some metals, combine the greatest flexibility with the greatest strength. But the Indian is hewn out of a rock. You can rarely change the form without destruction of the substance. . . . And it is this fixed and rigid quality which has proved his ruin. He will not learn the arts of civilization, and he and his forest must perish together. (ibid., 48)

The Ownership and Disposal of Property

Viewing individuals as strictly property to be used and disposed of at the owner's whim is made to order for today's consumer-oriented, throwaway society where built-in obsolescence leads to a cycle of consuming and discarding short-lived products. It likewise flourished in times past.

Possessions of the Woman's Body

The oft-repeated contention that abortion involves nothing other than the woman's right to control her body has spawned a perception of the preborn human as a piece of "personal property" to be dealt with in any way the owner—the pregnant woman—sees fit. Abortion defender Rachel Conrad Wahlberg contends that the woman literally owns the fetus. "It is hers. It is her *possession*" (1987, 5). Human life in utero is thus deprived of its uniqueness, integrity, and indivisibility, and relegated to the insignificant, morally neutral status of just another body part.

Such imagery serves to enhance acceptance of the rapidly expanding biomedical industry of reproductive technology. In its "Ethical Statement on In Vitro Fertilization" (1984), the American Fertility Society classified human embryos as "property of the donors" and declared that "the donors therefore have the right to decide at their sole discretion the disposition of these items" (p. 12).

Attorney Lori B. Andrews, in an article with the revealing title "My Body, My Property" (1986), categorizes human embryos as "body parts" and argues that women should "have the autonomy to treat their own parts as property, particularly their regenerative parts." Moreover, operating on the premise "that people's body parts are their personal property," Andrews believes women should be allowed "to transfer and sell their own body parts" (p. 37).

Female Property for Male Consumption

From early times, men acted upon the notion that women were licit "pieces of property" to take and possess, often by violent means. One of the earliest laws pertaining to marriage gave husbands the authority "to rule their wives as necessary and inseparable possessions" (O'Faolain and Martines 1973, 34–35). For many centuries rape was consistently defined in law, not as a violent attack on the woman, but as simply the "robbing of" or "trespass against" another man's "property" (Brownmiller 1975, 17–18, 163). Today's rapists hold to "the cultural view of women as sexual commodities, dehumanized and devoid of autonomy and dignity" (Scully and Marolla 1984, 542). As one sex offender put it in a study of convicted rapists conducted in the early 1980s, "I had no feelings at all, she was like an object" (Scully 1988, 209).

In a similar manner, Frances Power Cobbe's nineteenth-century study, "Wife-Torture in England," reveals that consignment of women to the status of "property" has long furnished a major justification for wife beating:

> The special depreciation of wives is more directly responsible for the outrages they endure. The notion that a man's wife is his PROPERTY . . . is the fatal root of

incalculable evil and misery. Every brutal-minded man, and many a man who in other relations of life is not brutal, entertains more or less vaguely the notion that his wife is his *thing,* and is ready to ask with indignation (as we read again and again in the police reports) of any one who interferes with his treatment of her: "May I not do what I will *with my own?"* (1878, 62)

Wife battering still exists today on an alarming scale, and one of its main justifications continues to be a perception of wives as "possessions" that can be used and abused according to the whim of the husband owner. In a study of battered wives carried out in the mid 1970s, a woman disclosed that when she cried and protested after being beaten on her honeymoon, her husband responded: "I married you so I own you" (Dobash and Dobash 1979, 55). In 1989 former wife batterer Chuck Switzer acknowledged: "I considered my wife when I married her to become my property, and I wanted absolute and total control."[3] Lee Grant, the director of a documentary film on battered women, stresses that wife beating is part of a well-entrenched tradition that says, "I own this woman. I can do whatever I want to this woman" (ibid., 7).

A Species of Black Property and Merchandise

George Washington, like other distinguished figures of his time, looked upon slaves as "a very troublesome species of property" from which he desired to free himself and his state (Davis 1975, 171). Yet, despite the troublesome nature of this "property," he still continued to reap profits from it.

The merchandising of slaves as property was discussed with as much consuming interest as cotton and tobacco prices. In 1853 a South Carolina editor observed: "Boys sold for about five hundred dollars." A North Carolina editor reported: "This species of property is at least 30 per cent higher now, (in the dull season of the year), than it was last January. . . . What negroes will bring next January, it is impossible for mortal man to say" (Stampp 1968, 204).

In the *Dred Scott* decision of 1857, the U.S. Supreme Court relied upon the longstanding, fixed, and widely held perception of black people as "articles of property and merchandise." The Court majority cited a piece of slavery history to bolster their ruling: "A negro of the African race was regarded by them [the English] as an article of property, and held, and bought and sold as such, in every one of the thirteen colonies which united in the Declaration of Independence, and afterwards formed the Constitution of the United States."[4]

Chief Justice Roger Brooke Taney and his judicial brethren continually emphasized that no member of the Negro race "had ever migrated to the United States voluntarily; all of them had been brought here as articles of merchandise." Since "the right of property in a slave is distinctly and expressly affirmed in the Constitution, the right to traffic in it like an ordinary article of merchandise and property," they reasoned, "was guaranteed to the citizens of the United States, in every state that might desire it."[5]

Anthropological Specimens from a Bygone Era

Native Americans have been habitually banished to the status of mere "relics," "artifacts," and "specimens" belonging to the past. As far back as 1845, Ralph Waldo Emerson stated that "we in Massachusetts see the Indians only as a picturesque antiquity" (Emerson and Forbes 1912, 7:23).

A journalist who covered the display of Indian skills and handicrafts at The World Columbian Exposition held in Chicago in 1893 referred to them as "living specimens." Chicago resident Emma Sickles waged an unsuccessful campaign against the presentation of Indians as "helpless specimens of science or schoolwork" (Hoxie 1979, 333–34).

At the Louisiana Purchase Exposition in St. Louis (1904), the Smithsonian Institution's W. J. McGee called Indians selected for inclusion in a "Congress of the Races" exhibit "least removed from the sub-human or quadrume form." St. Louis newspapers found the encampment of "primitives" so amusing that they ran satirical stories on them. These and other incidents led historian

Frederick E. Hoxie to conclude: "Traditional natives were accepted as anthropological specimens: harmless objects that could be ridiculed without fear or embarrassment." He identified the Indian as being "positioned in the center of a bizarre anthropological curiosity shop" (ibid., 336–38).

As recently as 1971, a cultural historian charged that "solemn social anthropologists and scientific folklorists" still view the Indian, not as a human being, but "as a living artifact to be described, measured, classified, and motif-indexed" (McDermott 1971, 45). Historian Donald A. Kaufmann highlighted the significant role of the media in typecasting the Indian as "a historical relic," "a total cardboard figure," and "a museum piece" (1975, 489, 498, 503).

Summary

The degrading words invoked to objectify human beings now and long ago have much in common. Contemporary portrayals of the unborn as female "property" or "material" for fetal research, nursing home patients as expendable "inanimate objects," and women as male "property" for sexploitation and violence bear a startling kinship with the demeaning language directed against diverse victims in times past. For centuries rape was defined as "trespass against another man's property." The targets of Nazi genocide were processed as "merchandise" and "material" for shipment to the death camps where they were exploited as "research material" in terminal experiments and "raw material" in the I. G. Farben factories at Auschwitz. Prisoners in the Soviet Gulag became expendable "raw material" for death-inducing work projects. Slaveowners in the antebellum American South regarded African Americans as "a species of property" for slave labor and "articles of merchandise" for public sale. "Anthropological specimen" and "museum piece" have long served as prime expressions for devaluing the character and culture of Native Americans.

14

Waste Products:
At the Bottom of the
Subhuman Scrap Pile

The semantic consignment of humans to the status of noxious waste products places them at the lowermost depths of the subhuman rubbish heap. This loathsome nomenclature spans many eras from ancient times to the present. It has engulfed and continues to engulf victims at all phases of the human life cycle.

Garbage and trash metaphors are considered apt designations by the perpetrators because many victims, both current and past, share the same ultimate fate as waste matter: disintegration through incineration.

Fetal Wastage

Waste analogies function as invaluable semantic aids for offsetting the repulsive task of removing aborted bodies and body parts. An article in *Obstetrics & Gynecology* (July 1967) describes the "products" of suction abortion as "debris from the conceptus." A noteworthy feature is a chart estimating the "amount of debris withdrawn" according to when (in weeks of gestation) the abortions were performed (Kerslake and Casey 1967, 37, 43).

Waste metaphors likewise help combat the unsavory details associated with the disposal of dead fetuses. In February 1982, 16,500 aborted bodies were found in a huge metal storage container outside Los Angeles, each submerged in formaldehyde inside a plastic container. To Assistant Coroner Richard Wilson, this unnerving discovery did not constitute "evidence of foul play," but only the possibility of "health code" violations "covering the disposal of medical waste" (Thimmesch 1982, 5B). The following year, Wichita, Kansas, public health affairs director Mary Ellen Conlee was shown graphic pictures of aborted bodies slated for burning in the city-owned incinerator along with dead cats and dogs. She assured the press that the employee responsible for allowing the pictures to be taken of "the pathological waste" would be disciplined (Effron and Floerchinger 1983, 2A).

The linguistic reduction of aborted humans to waste material is increasingly invoked to justify fetal research and the harvesting of fetal organs for transplantation. In 1980 Finnish fetal researcher Dr. Martti Kekomaki defended cutting off the heads of fifty-two babies aborted alive:

> The fetuses are fully alive when we cut their heads off, but anesthetics are definitely unnecessary. An aborted baby is just garbage and that's where it ends up. Why not make use of it for society. . . . You must see it like this: these fetuses are just refuse. (Wade 1980, 20–21)

At a forum on genetic engineering convened by *Harper's Magazine* in 1987, Harper's editor Lewis H. Lapham gave the following rationale in support of using fetal brain implants for Alzheimer's patients: "We're talking about a waste product here: thousands of fetuses are discarded every day."[1]

Dumping Grounds for Postnatal Rubbish

Children and adults with serious disabilities are being subjected to a barrage of repugnant waste analogies by health care professionals. Nursing homes, Veterans Administration hospitals, and city medical centers serve as prime "dumping grounds" for society's throwaway people.

Sociologist Terry Mizrahi found that the word "garbage" was frequently employed to castigate "troublesome" patients in a major southern university medical center (1986, 66). At a hospital in the midwestern part of the United States it is a standard practice to label the seriously debilitated and comatose patient a POG, an acronym for "piece of garbage."[2] Among the glossary of slang expressions used by house physicians at the Harvard University Medical School is the entry *"garbageman* a baby born with serious defects" (Konner 1987, 383). In her study of the social organization of a nursing home (1981), Jackie Howsden charges that "our throw-away society" exploits this institution "as a collection of what may as well be called 'human garbage'" (p. 36).

According to the findings of sociologist Roger Jeffrey, medical staff members working in the accident and emergency departments of three English hospitals view many of their patients as "rubbish." The following comments typified the staff's attitude toward these "undesirable" patients:

> If there's anything interesting we'll stop, but there's a lot of rubbish this morning. . . . We have the usual rubbish, but also a subdural hemorrhage. . . . It's a thankless task, seeing all the rubbish, as we call it, coming through. . . . We get our share of rubbish. (1979, 92, 94)

A Dead Weight of Human Refuse and Waste

Waste epithets have likewise served as a perennial weapon for degrading some of history's most powerless victims—children and the handicapped.

In the late 1800s the Canadian press called the shipment of children from Britain to Canada "a wholesale dumping of moral refuse on its shores." The Hamilton (Ontario) *Palladium of Labor* castigated Maria Rye, a leader in the child emigration movement, for "dumping the refuse of British jails, slums, and workhouses" onto Canada (Rooke and Schnell 1981, 399, 401–2).

Dr. E. E. Southard, director of the Psychopathic Hospital in Boston, presented a paper in 1915 at the National Conference of

Charities and Corrections in which he referred to "the feeble-minded" as "waste materials" and expressed concern about "what to do with these waste materials." The answer, he believed, could be found in "the modern doctrine of efficiency in economics," a major goal of which "is to make use of all such waste materials" just as "all the great firms" develop methods for "the disposal of their by-products." "Let us," Southard concluded, "look upon the feeble-minded as in some sense by-products of society" (p. 316).

In *The Pivot of Civilization* (1922), Planned Parenthood founder Margaret Sanger called physically and mentally handicapped people in institutions "a dead weight of human waste." In one of the book's chapters—with the revealing title "The Cruelty of Charity"—Sanger bemoaned the money "squandered" by the state of New York on the upkeep of "this dead weight of human waste"—namely, "inmates . . . in alms-houses, reformatories, schools for the blind, deaf and mute, in insane asylums, in homes for the feeble-minded and epileptic" (pp. 116, 112).

Female Sewers

Occasionally women have felt the brunt of the waste analogies by being compared to sewers. Prostitutes have been the most frequent target. A well-known adage spanning many centuries reads: "Prostitutes are to a city what sewers are to a palace" (de Beauvoir 1974, 115).

The sewer epithet is not confined to prostitutes of a bygone era, but is also meant to denigrate contemporary women. This is evident in the compulsive obscenity conjured up by such modern authors as Henry Miller. To Miller, the woman's body is a proper object for the ventilation of male contempt as well as equivalent to a "sewer" for the disposal of "refuse." His attitude toward female sexual anatomy is summed up in the comment: "One crack is as good as another and over every sewer there's a grating" (1963, 144).

Miller's version of the typical sexual conquest consists of dumping waste into its natural disposal site, the woman's body: "During intercourse they passed out of me, as though I were emptying refuse in a sewer" (1978, 110).

Products for the Trash Can of Europe

Poland, the major setting for the systematic execution and disposal of millions, was dubbed the "trashcan of Europe" by Nazi rhetoricians (Poliakov 1979, 115). After touring the Warsaw ghetto in 1939, Nazi Propaganda Minister Joseph Goebbels reported to Hitler that "the Jew is a waste product" (Hochhuth 1980, 18). Regarding the task of body disposal at Treblinka—one of Poland's largest killing centers—extermination specialist Christian Wirth peered into the huge pits of blue-black corpses and posed the question: "What shall we do with this garbage?" (Sereny 1974, 201).

At another killing site located in Poland an SS guard referred to a massive grave containing the bodies of newly destroyed Jews as a ditch "filled up with rubbish" (Wyman 1984, 4). A police officer in charge of exterminating Jews and others in the eastern territories wrote about the targets of his destructive activities in the following manner: "There are four kinds of action a week. Sometimes Jews, sometimes Bohemians, partisans, and all kinds of trash" (Poliakov 1979, 128).

The perception of Holocaust victims as "waste matter" to be disposed of in the most technically efficient manner also carried over to the task of burning bodies in the crematory ovens. A physician who conducted death selections at Auschwitz revealed that "the problem of the crematorium and its capacity" was viewed as equivalent to "the ordinary problem of sewerage" (Lifton 1986, 179).

The Soviet Rubbish Heap

Long before Bolshevik perpetrators began imposing waste metaphors on individuals and movements considered inimical to Soviet totalitarianism, Karl Marx had already established the groundwork. He charged that the capitalist state was "clogged by all manner of medieval rubbish." Since Marxist doctrine declared the ownership of property one of the worst vices, the individual who aspired to own a plot of land was ridiculed for hemming "himself in against all society on his own dung-heap" (Lenin 1960–70, 12:467).

Marx's expressions found a receptive purveyor in Lenin, whose language belied an extreme intolerance toward other points of view: Petty-bourgeois socialism was portrayed as "medieval rubbish"; capitalism, "debris" and "historical rubbish"; opportunism, "old anarchistic rubbish"; physical idealism and related philosophies, "refuse fit only for the garbage-heap"; and speeches favoring democracy, "utterly worthless rubbish" (ibid., 1:289, 353; 26:480; 7:286; 14:313; 26:473).

Stalin pursued the rubbish analogy with a vengeance. Throughout his quest for and attainment of power, he called upon his comrades to rebuff "the attempts of certain 'writers' and 'historians' to smuggle disguised Trotskyite rubbish into our literature." In 1929, when Nicholas Bukharin and the Right Opposition protested against the rapid, enforced collectivization of agriculture, Stalin dismissed them as the last vestiges of "old bourgeois-liberal rubbish" that had "collapsed and crumbled into dust" (1953–55, 13:102, 12:137). At the Great Purge Trial, where Bukharin and other leaders paid the supreme penalty, prosecutor Andrei Vyshinsky called the defendants "a foul-smelling heap of human garbage" (Tucker and Cohen 1965, 520).

Black Trash

American merchants of the pre–Civil War era placed a premium on deriving lucrative profits from the slave trade, and those slaves who did not measure up to the prevailing norms for profitable property owing to physical and other afflictions became known as "the refuse." On June 19, 1681, Virginia planter-industrialist William Fitzhugh sent a letter to attorney Ralph Wormly in England to purchase slaves for him from an anticipated shipment. "I am so remote," Fitzhugh wrote, "that . . . they'll be all disposed of or at least none left but the refuse."[3]

The slave narrative of William Wells Brown (1847) includes an account of how the perception of blacks as "trash" was translated into practice. The incident involved the drowning of a black man by a gang of whites one evening in New Orleans. The next morning Brown saw the body of the victim on the shore:

I watched to see what they would do with it. It was left there until between eight and nine o'clock, when a cart, which takes up the trash out of the streets, came along, and the body was thrown in, and in a few minutes more was covered over with dirt which they were removing from the streets. During the whole time, I did not see more than six or seven persons around it, who, from their manner, evidently regarded it as no uncommon occurrence. (1968, 61)

Such defamatory expressions were also invoked to disparage the unique cultural contributions made to American society by the black race. Before the South Carolina Medical Society (1903), Dr. William English stated that "the negro race is . . . a heritage of organic and psychic debris" (p. 469).

Red Wastes

Native Americans were often cast in the role of promiscuous plunderers of the land—a repugnant species of subhumanity relentlessly ravaging the earth and leaving in its wake a huge wasteland. In his essay on "The Indians of Eastern Massachusetts," written in the 1620s, George E. Ellis stated: "The Indians simply wasted everything within their reach. . . . They required enormous spaces of wilderness for their mode of existence" (Jennings 1975, 82).

The association of Native Americans with the worst wastelands was a persistent theme in Francis Parkman's *The Conspiracy of Pontiac*. He depicted "the wastes . . . of nature" as the "congenial home" of Indians and identified the "Indian buffalo hunter" as one of the few tenants still inhabiting "the dreary wastes." To Parkman, "all Kentucky was a vacant waste, a mere skirmishing ground for the hostile war-parties" (1897–98, 1:3, 75, 154).

According to Theodore Roosevelt, one of the most important aspects of westward expansion included the task of liberating territories that had degenerated into "game preserves" and "red wastes" from savages hopelessly mired in squalor

(1889, 1:90). He proclaimed that the "mighty civilized races" were "gradually bringing peace into the red wastes where the barbarian peoples of the world hold sway" (1902, 38).

For some Indian haters, the portrayal of natives as mindless, rapacious exploiters who turned the earth into a gigantic wasteland was not sufficiently demeaning. Plunging lower down the scale of subhumanity, they relegated Native Americans to the very "waste" they were so often accused of producing. William Hubbard wrote about the Pequot Indians as "the Dregs and Lees of the Earth, and Dross of Mankind" (Drinnon 1980, 40). Christopher Brooke's poem of 1622 demeans Indians as "the very dregs, garbage, and spanne of Earth" (Berkhofer 1978, 20).

Summary

The repulsive designations invented to reduce present and prior victims to waste products are extraordinarily alike. Those currently involved in consigning preborn humans to "protoplasmic rubbish," "pathological waste," "garbage," "debris," and "refuse," and troublesome patients to "rubbish" and "refuse," have resurrected a style of semantic degradation from bygone eras. Women's bodies have been regularly referred to as "sewers" for the emptying of "refuse." Nazi propagandists labeled Jews "rubbish," "trash," "garbage," and "waste products" for disposal in crematory ovens. People, groups, and ideas viewed with disfavor by the Soviet regime were relegated to "rubbish," "garbage," "refuse," and "debris" on history's "garbage heap." Physically and mentally disabled patients in American institutions of the past were commonly dubbed "waste material" and "a dead weight of human waste." African-American culture was once characterized as "a heritage of organic and psychic debris" and severely exploited slaves as "refuse." In times past, North American Indians were equated with "garbage" and accused of reducing the environment to a vast "red wasteland."

15

Legal Nonpersons: Nonexistence before the Law

Of the numerous expressions created to denigrate human beings, "nonperson" may well rank as the most devastating of all. Although words such as "parasite," "venereal disease," and "garbage" are more patently offensive, the unique perniciousness of "nonperson" derives not from its capacity to offend, but from the fact that it alone has been explicitly enshrined into law. And a "legal nonperson" is an entity devoid of basic rights, including in many instances the most fundamental right of all, life itself.

Today's Nonpersons

"Nonperson" is fast becoming the designation of choice for denigrating unborn and born contemporary expendables. In some instances, it is employed as just another synonym for "subhuman" and "nonhuman." In a growing number of other contexts, "nonperson" has been endowed with the awesome authority of the law. Further, the nonperson epithet has inaugurated a new litmus test for survival: no longer is one's humanity a sufficient basis for meriting the right to life; one must also be a "person." The definition of personhood required to qualify for existence is an increasingly elitist one whereby expanding numbers of individuals are declared expendable and consigned to the rightless category of "legal nonpersons."

Fetal Nonpersons

On January 22, 1973, the United States Supreme Court in its *Roe v. Wade* decision ushered in the modern era of legal nonpersonhood by maintaining that "the unborn have never been recognized in the law as persons in the whole sense." With this as a semantic foundation, a majority of the justices (7-2) ruled that "the word 'person,' as used in the Fourteenth Amendment, does not include the unborn."[1] This decision represents the most radical of transformations: what once had been a pejorative label confined to the private realm of personal prejudice was catapulted to the public domain of full-fledged legality.

Since 1973 an endless flow of policy statements enacted by influential groups, articles in professional journals, prestigious conferences, and court rulings have invoked the legal nonpersonhood doctrine as a basis for upholding the abortion liberty.[2] Members of the abortion establishment have exercised the utmost vigilance to ensure that unborn children remain legal nonpersons. They know full well that keeping the unborn in the rightless status of nonpersonhood perpetuates as well as expands their massive program of killing and associated forms of exploitation. They are acutely mindful of the highly persuasive teaching role of the law and how quickly the legal definition of the unborn as an insignificant creature not worthy of protection invades the realm of psychology, where it becomes deeply embedded in the psyches of many people.

Philosophy professor Michael Tooley has exhibited a dogged persistence in formulating a philosophical model of nonpersonhood for unborn as well as newborn children. He equates the word "person" with an organism that has "a serious right to life." The only way for "an organism" to qualify as a legitimate person under Tooley's definition is "if it possesses the concept of a self as a continuing subject of experiences and other mental states, and believes that it is itself such a continuing entity" (1972, 44). The upshot of this self-conscious requirement is that the unborn are not persons because they are not self-conscious beings.

In her oft-quoted article, "On the Moral and Legal Status of Abortion" (January 1973), Mary Ann Warren asserts that "a fetus . . . is not a person" and "whatever its stage of development, satisfies none of the basic criteria of personhood." She maintains that "even a fully developed fetus" in the final months of pregnancy is "considerably less personlike than is the average mature mammal" or "the average fish" and therefore "cannot be said to have any more right to life than, let us say, a newborn guppy" (pp. 47, 58). Warren's reduction of unborn humans to a level lower than mammals and fish belies an unabashed commitment to thoroughly depersonalizing the occupant in the womb.

A meeting held on March 11–13, 1982, in Houston, Texas, entitled *Human Life Symposium: An Interdisciplinary Approach to the Concept of Person* typifies how the dogma of legal personhood is employed to protect the abortion liberty (Shaw and Doudera 1983). The title alone is an outlandish misnomer. It was anything but a human life symposium. A far more accurate designation would have been *An Anti-Life Symposium: A Pro-Abortion Approach to Maintaining a Severely Constricted Concept of Person*.

Despite the trappings of objectivity surrounding the conference—its sponsors consisted of the American Society of Law and Medicine and the Institute for the Interprofessional Study of Health Law—it was actually convened to offset attempts by the United States Congress to restore legal personhood to all human beings "from conception, without regard to race, sex, age, health, defect, or condition of dependence." An overwhelming majority of those who presented papers are among America's most vociferous abortion proponents. Harriet F. Pilpel, general counsel to the Planned Parenthood Federation of America and a tireless, voluble defender of civil liberties for just about everyone except the unborn, talked about "Personhood, Abortion, and the Right to Privacy." Dr. George M. Ryan, one of the most vocal pro-abortion physicians ever to serve as president of the American College of Obstetricians and Gynecologists (1981–82), spoke on "Medical Implications of Bestowing Personhood" (ibid., 149–60, 84–89).

Experimental Exploitation of Fetal Nonpersons

True to its expansionist nature, the nonperson epithet functions as a useful device for widening the frontiers of fetal research. Other pejorative terms ordinarily directed against the unborn such as "subhuman" and "nonhuman" are not as appropriate here because fetal experimentation is commonly classified under the heading of "human experimentation." The federal commission established in 1973 to examine the ethics of research on the fetus and other vulnerable groups, for instance, was called "The National Commission for the Protection of Human Subjects of Biomedical and Behavioral Research."

Mary Anne Warren also ranks in the forefront of academics who employ "nonpersonhood" as a foundation for support of fetal research. In the influential ethics journal *The Hastings Center Report* (October 1978), she expressed approval for utilizing the kidneys of aborted babies for transplantation. The morality of harvesting an organ farm of spare fetal parts intended for the wanted members of society rests on Warren's perception of the unborn as "an entity far below the threshold of personhood" (pp. 23–24).

Many others in the philosophic and medical establishments find "nonperson" to be an indispensable concept upon which to build a consensus for enlarging the sphere of research on the unborn slated for abortion. An attempt to forge such a consensus was a major thrust of the Trans-Disciplinary Symposium on Philosophy and Medicine held at the University of Missouri-Columbia in 1980. This conference, entitled *The Concept of Person and Its Implications for the Use of the Fetus in Biomedicine,* was funded by the National Endowment for the Humanities, the Education and Research Foundation of the American Medical Association, and the University of Missouri Graduate School. The title alone is a dead giveaway regarding what the participants were up to: the denial of personhood as a rationalization for fetal experimentation.

Among the conference participants, physician-ethicist Dr. H. Tristram Engelhardt proved to be one of the most ardent advocates of nonpersonhood as a basis for support of fetal research. Proceeding from a definition of persons as "entities that are self-conscious, rational, and self-determining," he declared that "fetuses, even viable fetuses, are not persons" because "there is no evidence" that they possess these capabilities" (1983, 184, 192).

For him, the key concepts "person," "nonperson," and "viability" comprise a semantic framework for subjecting "fetuses to dangerous and harmful research as long as those fetuses will be aborted prior to viability." One of the permissible experiments he envisions is *"developing* fetuses *in vitro* to early stages of gestation in order to do adequate research on fetal physiology." Since "fetuses are not persons" and important scientific information is likely to be derived from such research, then, according to Engelhardt, "the moral presumption would be that scientists may generate fetuses for research, and perform experiments upon them as long as they are not brought to term, do research upon non-viable fetuses *ex utero,* and expedite the death of fetuses prior to viability" (ibid., 197–98).

Engelhardt does recognize that the public's sensitivity toward children could become seriously debased by allowing odious experiments on the unborn too much visibility, no matter how noble their stated purpose. One way of preventing this from happening, he suggests, would be "to discourage such research from being displayed openly (thus, for example, we no longer have public executions, even in states approving such executions)." This suggestion is meant to strike the type of balance he considers reasonable: "Namely, the concern to acquire better knowledge in order to assume better health for the future persons we will bring into existence, while avoiding practices that might brutalize us as a civilization" (ibid., 198).

It is consoling that Engelhardt realizes the potentially brutalizing impact resulting from public exposure to the sight of harmful experiments being performed on society's preborn "nonpersons." He fails to consider, however, that a far more likely reaction to the open spectacle of morbidly curious scientists inflicting all sorts of barbaric procedures on the bodies of human guinea pigs destined for abortion extirpation, or already extirpated, is one of public outrage. Even subjects in the so-called nonviable stage look decidedly human despite the depersonalizing names foisted upon them. Unless this kind of research is concealed from public view, the days of nonpersonhood for the unborn would be numbered. If enough people ever got wind of the true nature of such scientific atrocities, not only would they likely identify with the unborn child as a genuine member of the human community, they would also more readily see through the charade of nonpersonhood in the womb and insist that both the killing and the experimental manipulation be ended by restoring unborn children to their rightful position as legal persons.

Contemporary Postnatal Nonpersons

It was inevitable that the nonpersonhood creed would invade the intensive care nursery and other health care settings to engulf individuals after birth who lack the prescribed physical, cognitive, and psychological capabilities due to genetic afflictions, illness, or accidents. Although handicapped people and other vulnerable groups have not yet been officially defined as "nonpersons" under the law, there are ominous signs, nevertheless, that some sectors of the legal system are doing just that in practice. Leading intellectuals, philosophers, and physicians are hard at work paving the way for this eventuality.

In *Abortion and Infanticide* (1983), Michael Tooley builds a case for justifying the killing of infants as well as unborn humans on the contention that they lack the most basic attributes of personhood, especially self-consciousness. As an adjunct to his preoccupation with developing an intellectualized rationalization for depersonalizing certain classes of human beings, Tooley introduces the term "quasi-person." This expression is supposed to allow for consideration of the developmental principle that the attainment of personhood by "nonpersons" is a matter of gradations—a gradual process of unfolding—instead of something that happens at a fixed point in time. Tooley defines a "quasi-person" as an entity that possesses the property of personhood "to some extent, but not to the extent character-istic of full-fledged persons, such as normal adult human beings" (p. 420).

When, then, do human "nonpersons" become bona fide per-sons? Tooley's answer is inconclusive at best. Only around three months past birth is he willing to consider granting the status of a "quasi-person" to the infant. Just how long it takes a "quasi-person" to become a real person on a moral par with normal adults is left up in the air. In Tooley's words:

> The general picture that emerges is as follows. New-born humans are neither persons nor even quasi-persons, and their destruction is in no way intrinsically morally wrong. At about the age of three months, however, they proba-bly acquire properties that are morally significant, and that make it to some extent intrinsically wrong to destroy them. As they develop further, their destruction becomes more and more seriously wrong, until eventually it is comparable in seriousness to the destruction of a normal adult human being. (ibid., 411–12)

Tooley conjectures further that humans may "not become per-sons until, say, about the age of one" (ibid., 424).

Such qualifying phrases as "probably acquire," "to some extent intrinsically wrong," and "about the age of one" reveal a great deal of ambiguity. Tooley admits that "any serious attempt to determine the point at which a human being becomes a per-son, or a quasi-person" is "highly tentative" (ibid., 421). Although his book is supposed to represent a model of impec-cable logic and precise reasoning, the concepts "nonperson" and its pseudo-derivative "quasi-person" are exceedingly slip-pery creations whose vague boundaries contain wide latitude for ensnaring a huge variety of victims at all phases of the human life continuum.

Philosopher John Lachs possesses a mindset similar to that of Michael Tooley. One of Lachs's leading candidates for nonpersonhood is hydrocephalic children. His proposal for "humanely" putting these individuals to death is predicated on a thoroughly depersonalized portrait of them as "nonpersons" as well as "creatures," "human-looking shapes," and "only human forms." To Lachs, hydrocephalic children cannot become persons because they lack the most basic attribute of personhood: a functioning brain. He identifies what he believes to be a common mistake in perception made by those who care for these infants:

> The child itself (and to make the point more forcefully, I should not even call it a "child") is not a person, and the fundamental error of our ways consists in thinking that it is one (1976, 839).

Another foremost proponent of nonpersonhood as a foundation for infanticide is Baylor University ethics professor Earl E. Shelp. In *Born to Die?* (1986), he comes down strongly on the side of the parents' absolute right to determine the fate of their handicapped newborn children. Entrance into the "moral community" of persons identified by Shelp requires the attainment of such capacities as rationality, self-consciousness, and self-determination. "All newborn human infants," he declares, "fail the test for personhood" because they do not possess "the relevant properties" (pp. 114, 115).

Although Shelp gives the impression that only the most severely and hopelessly disabled infants would be sacrificed on the altar of nonpersonhood, he considers a decision to let die or kill reasonable in cases "where there is less than a high probability that the result of treatment will be a normal or near normal life." Among the list of victims covered under his nonpersonhood classification are children with Down's syndrome, spina bifida, blindness, paralysis, or any handicap that "would impose upon others an unreasonable, grave, disproportionate, or incommensurate burden" (ibid., 17, 175).

Shelp's pronouncements on nonpersonhood lead to the formulation of a distorted "principle of justice" for dealing with "defective" infants—"equals may be treated unequally." Within this context, "the life of nonpersons can have value, but no value of the sort that cannot be overridden by the needs and interests of others." Despite the plenitude of past injustices wrought by "a tyranny of the powerful over the impotent," Shelp claims that giving priority to "the interests and needs of others" over "the limited but absorbing prospects of the neonate, does not constitute an abuse of the strong over the weak." Shelp is much more concerned about "a tyranny of the dependent in which the production of able persons is consumed by the almost limitless needs of dependent beings" (ibid., 23, 114, 115, 119, 137).

The boundaries of nonpersonhood forged by Tooley, Lachs, and Shelp have been expanded considerably by psychiatrist-anthropologist Virginia Abernethy. *Newsweek* quotes her as saying: "As long as an individual is completely dependent upon the mother, it's not a person." More specifically, this means that personhood is not acquired until the individual becomes a moral agent at three or four years after birth. *Newsweek* admits this is not an atypical view, but one shared by other "pro-choice theorists" (Woodward with Uehling 1985, 29).

Another group at imminent risk of being crushed by the nonpersonhood juggernaut are the unconscious victims of strokes and other afflictions. An article in *Seminars in Neurology* (March 1984) asserts that patients in "a persistent vegetative state" have "ceased to be persons and are merely living organisms." The authors of this article are perfectly clear about the intent underlying such terminology: "When a patient is no longer a person, he may not necessarily have the protection of the moral rules in the same way that rational persons do" (Gert and Culver 1984, 14). Neurologist Ronald Cranford envisions a time when PVS (persistent vegetative state) will be equated with "nonpersonhood" (Lippman 1991, 66).

A special report on the teaching of ethics in the medical school curriculum published in *The New England Journal of Medicine* on January 24, 1985, contains an indication of how much further the nonperson doctrine threatens to reach. Several members in the group of physicians and philosophers who prepared the report recommended that the question about when a dying patient ceases to be a person should be incorporated into the basic medical ethics curriculum. This, they acknowledged, represented a natural extension of a closely related question at the other end of the life span: When does a fetus become a person? (Culver et al. 1985, 253–56).

Historical Perspectives on the Dark Side of Nonpersonhood

Contemporary abortion and euthanasia proponents place the most positive gloss on their consignment of individuals to the category of "nonpersons." Studiously avoided are any connections between this terminology and the language used against some of history's most oppressed groups. Yet there are some remarkable semantic and legal associations that require closer exploration.

Female Nonpersons

For much of history and throughout a variety of cultures, women as a class have been treated as if they were "nonpersons" before the law. Whatever the form of oppression—enforced marriage, sexual slavery, denial of voting rights, discrimination in employment, rape, wife beating, sexual harassment—women, often dubbed the inferior sex, have long suffered in the status of second class citizenship. True equality before the law—a cornerstone of legal personhood—with respect to women is an ideal fraught with marked ambivalence and implacable opposition.

Several court decisions rendered in England as late as after the turn of the twentieth century defined women as "nonpersons," particularly in cases concerning voting rights and the right to hold office. In *Nairn v. University of St. Andrews* (1909) the court ruled that female graduates of Saint Andrews University could not vote since only legal persons possessed this right and "the statutory word 'person' did not in these circumstances include women." It was held in *Viscountess*

Rhondda's Claim (1922) that "the word 'person' as used in the act [an act of Parliament] could not rightly be interpreted to include women in those entitled to sit in the House of Lords."[3]

One would think that after enactment of the Nineteenth Amendment to the U.S. Constitution in 1920 granting women the right to vote, their personhood had been decisively and unequivocally established in the fabric of American law. This, however, proves to be an unwarranted assumption. In *Commonwealth v. Walosky* (1931) the Massachusetts Supreme Court decided that women could not serve on juries because they were not persons according to state law. In the words of Judge C. J. Rugg, who authored this decision: "The intent of the Legislature must have been, in using the word 'person' in statutes concerning jurors and jury lists, to confine its meaning to men." Moreover, he declared: "It is unthinkable that those who first framed and selected the words for the statute . . . had any design that it should ever include women within its scope" (ibid., 660–61).

Although great strides have been made in advancing women to a position of equality under the law, depersonalized images of females as "nonpersons" continue to abound, particularly in contemporary pornographic materials. The devastating impact of this degrading imagery is evident in the words of a rapist who justified what he had done with the comment: "She wasn't like a person" (Scully and Marolla 1985, 260).

Nonpersons of the Third Reich

Removing Jews from the lawfully protected status of legal personhood was accomplished in Nazi Germany by defining them as "non-Aryans." Such a classification supplied the semantic foundation for the passage of over four hundred laws, ordinances, and decrees against Jews leading up to the "final solution." The significance of this concept is attested to by Holocaust scholar Raul Hilberg: "When in the early days of 1933 the first civil servant wrote the first definition of a 'non-Aryan' into a civil service ordinance, the fate of European Jewry was sealed" (1967, 669).

A milestone on the road to genocide under legal auspices occurred in 1936 when the highest court of Germany, the *Reichsgericht,* deprived Jews of civil rights by equating them with sickness and death. According to an analysis of this decision by legal scholar Ernst Fraenkel, "the *Reichsgericht* itself refused to recognize Jews living in Germany as 'persons' in the legal sense" (1941, 95). Historian George L. Mosse concludes that the process of extirpating Jews from the position of "legal personalities" occurred on March 22, 1938, with a law depriving religious congregations of legal protection (1978, 210).

In *The Origins of Totalitarianism* (1973), political scientist Hannah Arendt found that the hallmark of a totalitarian society such as Nazi Germany is the exclusion of those deemed stateless from the protected ranks of "legal persons" (p. 290).

Soviet Unpersons

"Unperson"—a close cousin to "nonperson"—is an apt expression to describe those unwanted individuals who were extinguished during the height of Soviet tyranny. George Orwell endowed this designation with enduring notoriety. In his novel *1984,* vaporized (destroyed) victims quickly became "unpersons." Such was the fate of Comrade Withers, a member of the Inner Party who had fallen out of favor. Although he had once existed in the fullest extent as a leading Party official, the "refs unpersons" provided the basis for his physical annihilation as well as the deletion of all references to him in newspapers and other printed material. Thus Withers had been declared "an *unperson.* He did not exist; he had never existed" (1949, 46).

The practice of erasing purged "unpersons" from historical and public records was elevated to an art form in the Soviet Union. The case of Soviet Secret Police Chief Lavrenti Beria serves as a prime example. Soon after Stalin died in 1953, Beria was charged with treason and summarily executed. The publishers of *The Soviet Encyclopedia* immediately instructed their subscribers to remove an extensive article on Beria and replace it with one pertaining to the Bering Sea. Suddenly a once powerful, well-known figure was reduced to an "unperson" who had never existed.[4]

Although many Communist Party dignitaries suffered a fate identical to that of Beria, the huge bulk of victims exterminated first under the iron rule of Lenin, and then Stalin, were ordinary citizens. Getting rid of these victims turned out to be a relatively simple task; there was no need to expunge their names from the records, since most of them never reached the hallowed heights of public recognition. Individuals, families, and entire villages in droves were wiped off the face of the earth, never to be heard of again.

No group experienced the impact of unpersonhood more totally and brutally than the Ukrainian peasants who were intentionally starved to death for refusing to cooperate with the Soviet collectivization of agriculture. As mass starvation raged through the Ukraine in the early 1930s, the Soviet government denied the existence of this terror-famine and the enormous number of victims consumed by it. No references to the huge death toll could be found either in the Soviet or Ukrainian press. Arthur Koestler observed firsthand the famine-ravished areas and reported that the local press was full of highly positive stories about competitions between factory shock brigades, smiling young people carrying banners, giant combines in the Urals, but "not one word about the local famine, epidemics, the dying out of whole villages. . . . The enormous land was covered with a blanket of silence." Whenever the reality of the genocidal famine was brought up, Soviet officials dismissed it as "lies circulated by the counter-revolutionary organizations abroad" (Conquest 1986, 311–12).

Today, more than sixty years after the holocaust of Ukrainian farmers, Soviet leaders have yet to acknowledge what actually happened. This atrocity has been thoroughly obliterated from public consciousness and its victims remain at the invisible level of "unpersons."

Black Nonpersons in the Antebellum American South

In *Dred Scott v. Sanford* (1857) the United States Supreme Court—drawing upon the concepts "nonpeople" and "noncitizens"—reaffirmed the denial of fundamental rights to black people and sanctioned the expansion of the slave system westward. Chief Justice Roger Brooke Taney asserted that Negroes are not "constituent members" of the "sovereign people" and "are not included, and were not intended to be included, under the word 'citizen' in the Constitution, and can therefore claim none of the rights and privileges which that instrument provides for and secures to citizens of the United States."[5]

Throughout the opinion rendered in *Dred Scott,* the terms "people" and "citizens" are "synonymous terms, and mean the same thing" and therefore often appear together. Taney highlighted those clauses in the Constitution that, he maintained, indicated that members of "the negro race" were "not regarded as a portion of the people or citizens of the Government." He added that "it is too plain for argument, that they have never been regarded as part of the people or citizens of the State" (ibid., 404, 411, 412).

There is a striking resemblance between the above constructs and the "person" and "nonperson" designations that operate to deny legal rights to today's unborn victims. The *Roe v. Wade* assertion that "the word 'person,' as used in the Fourteenth Amendment, does not include the unborn" is closely related to the *Dred Scott* declaration that blacks are excluded from membership in the "sovereign people" and "are not included, or were not intended to be included, under the word 'citizen' in the Constitution." Just as exclusion of unborn children from the constitutionally protected category of "person" relegates them to the rightless state of "nonperson," the exclusion of blacks from the constitutionally secure classification of "sovereign people" or "citizens" reduced them to the rightless status of "nonpeople" or "noncitizens."

Borrowing a page directly from *Roe* ("the unborn have never been recognized in the law as a person in the whole sense"), federal circuit court judge and former law professor John T. Noonan characterized the plight of blacks under the *Dred Scott* ruling in the following manner: "Nowhere henceforth could a black in the United States be protected by federal law as a person in the whole sense of the term" (1979, 81).

Only one year after *Dred Scott* did the expression "not a person"—instead of "not people" or "not citizens"—begin appearing in cases pertaining to slavery. In *Bailey & als. v. Poindexter's Ex'or* (1858), the highest court of Virginia ruled that slaves had no legal capacity to choose between emancipation and public sale because they were not "persons" before the law. According to the court:

> In the eyes of the law, so far certainly as civil rights and relations are concerned, the slave is not a person, but a thing. The investiture of a chattel with civil rights is indeed a legal solecism and absurdity. The attribution of legal personality to a chattel slave . . . implies a palpable contradiction in terms.[6]

Although United States Supreme Court Justice Harry Blackmun, main author of *Roe,* did not cite *Bailey* in his opinion, he certainly could have, since the language he employed to depersonalize unborn children is almost an exact replica of the terminology used in *Bailey* to depersonalize black slaves. The *Roe* contention that "the unborn have never been recognized in the law as persons" repeats both in style and substance the *Bailey* assertion that "in the eyes of the law . . . the slave is not a person." Moreover, those today who believe it would be ludicrous to grant legal personhood to the unborn are echoing the sentiments expressed in *Bailey;* that is, "the attribution of legal personality to a chattel slave" was considered "a legal solecism and absurdity" and implied "a palpable contradiction in terms."

Native American Nonpersons

Robbing Indians of their lands and lives started soon after the white settlers arrived on the shores of North America. The assault on Native American culture, property, and lives continued unabated until the late 1880s, a period when the Indians had been largely subdued and confined to a stifling existence on reservations. The unrelenting dispossession of Indian territory was overwhelmingly justified according to a pervasive perception of Native Americans as legal nonpersons—insignificant entities possessing few rights or safeguards under the law.

For much of their history, the original inhabitants of North America were treated as less than persons in the legal sense. It is on this basis that the state and federal governments saw fit to disregard and violate a total of 371 treaties legally promulgated with various Indian tribes and nations.

Writing in *The American Law Review* (1881), legal scholar George F. Canfield identified an indispensable connection between the concept of "nonperson" and the longstanding congressional treatment of Native Americans. Although proclaiming the Indian's humanhood ("Hath not an Indian eyes? Tickle him, will he not laugh? Yes."), Canfield concluded that "an Indian is not a person within the meaning of the Constitution." Therefore, he maintained, "the power of Congress over him is supreme and absolute." According to Canfield:

> Congress may prevent an Indian leaving his reservation, and while he is on a reservation it may deprive him of his liberty, his property, his life. . . . Congress may break its treaties with him as it may repeal a statute. (pp. 28, 33)

A Modern Paradox: Objects and Animals As Persons; Human Beings as Nonpersons

While the quota of human beings deemed eligible for personhood is rapidly dwindling, the pool of nonhumans and things considered appropriate candidates for personhood is on the increase. The spectrum of acceptable nonhuman aspirants is exceedingly wide. It incorporates almost every conceivable object or entity, ranging all the way from ships, trees, forests, and rivers to animals, advanced computers, and aliens from other planets. Ironically, those who experience the greatest difficulty perceiving unborn and newborn humans as persons are often the same individuals who entertain no reservations whatsoever in expressing approval of legal personhood for objects and animals. This surely rates as a contradiction of far-reaching proportions.

The Personification of Ships and Corporations

Ships have long enjoyed the protected legal status of "persons" in American law. An example of how vessels are personified comes from a decision rendered by the United States Supreme Court in *Tucker v. Alexandroff* (1901):

> A ship is born when she is launched, and lives so long as her identity is preserved. Prior to her launching she is a mere congeries of wood and iron. . . . In the baptism of launching she receives her name, and from the moment her keel touches the water she is transformed. . . . She acquires a personality of her own.[7]

In the late nineteenth century the Supreme Court also handed down a series of rulings defining corporations as "persons" under various provisions of the United States Constitution. Among the provisions specified were the equal protection and due process clauses of the Fourteenth Amendment, the amendment that secured the rights of black people. The Court extended such protective coverage to all types of corporations as well.

One of the beneficiaries of the Court's generosity was the Southern Pacific Railroad. In 1885 Santa Clara County sued Southern Pacific for recovery of unpaid taxes. The Supreme Court decided in favor of the railroad company and ruled that such an assessment was invalid. The attorneys representing Southern Pacific argued that railroad corporations should be defined as "persons within the meaning of the Fourteenth Amendment of the Constitution." The Court found this interpretation persuasive enough to declare unanimously that "the defendant Corporations are persons within the intent clause in Section 1 of the Fourteenth Amendment to the Constitution of the United States, which forbids a State to deny to any person within its jurisdiction the equal protection of the laws."[8]

Personhood for the Natural Environment

Law professor Christopher D. Stone describes the world of the lawyer as "peopled with inanimate right-holders: trusts, corporations, joint ventures, municipalities . . . partnerships, and nation-states, to mention just a few." In an article, "Should Trees Have Legal Standing?—Toward Legal Rights for Natural Objects," published in the *Southern California Law Review* (spring 1972), he recommends extending the rights encompassed under legal personhood still further to include "forests, oceans, rivers, and other so-called 'natural objects' in the environment as a whole" (pp. 452, 456).

Stone anticipates the resistance his proposal may encounter. Under the heading "Thinking the Unthinkable," he looks back into legal history to find similar obstacles against the conferral of legal personhood on blacks as well as ships and corporations. He is consoled by the highly successful efforts of pathfinding attorneys to transform what was once considered unthinkable into a perfectly acceptable legal principle. "To urge a court that an endangered river is 'a person,'" Stone asserts, "will call for lawyers as bold and imaginative as those who convinced the Supreme Court that a railroad corporation was a 'person' under the fourteenth amendment, a constitutional provision theretofore generally thought of as designed to secure the rights of the freedman" (ibid., 465). Stone views his advocacy of legal rights for natural objects as wholly consistent with such a "progressive" trend.

Justice Douglas's Sanctity-of-Environmental-Life Ethic

The Sierra Club—an organization with a special interest in the conservation of national parks, game refuges, and forests—was concerned about the detrimental impact of a project involving the construction of a ski resort and summer recreational facilities in an area of great natural beauty located in northern California.

In June 1969 the Sierra Club filed a suit to prevent any construction on the land. On April 19, 1972, the United States Supreme Court, in *Sierra Club v. Morton,* ruled against the Sierra Club on the grounds that it lacked the legal standing to sue.

Justice William O. Douglas, the most stalwart environmentalist ever to serve on the Supreme Court, took strong exception to this decision. His extensive dissenting opinion features a proposal to confer legal personhood on "valleys, alpine meadows, rivers, lakes, estuaries, beaches, ridges, groves of trees, swampland, or even the air that feels the destructive pressures of modern technology and modern life." As documentation to justify "the conferral of standing upon environmental objects to sue for their own preservation," Douglas cites three sources: the law journal article authored by Christopher Stone, the definition of ships as "persons," and the bestowal of personhood onto corporations. He notes with full accord that "a ship has a legal personality, a fiction found useful for maritime purposes" and "the ordinary corporation is a 'person' for purposes of the adjudicatory processes." From this, Douglas draws the conclusion that "so it should be as respects valleys, meadows" and all segments of the natural environment.[9]

The importance of granting legal standing to those most intimately involved with the environment to enable them to testify on behalf of preserving all of nature's wonders constitutes a major thrust of Douglas's dissent. He repeatedly returns to it, often in a particularly eloquent manner:

> Then there will be assurances that all of the forms of life which it represents will stand before the court—the pileated woodpecker as well as the coyote and bear, the lemmings as well as the trout in the stream. Those inarticulate members of the ecological group cannot speak. But those people who have so frequented the place as to know its values and wonders will be able to speak for the entire ecological community. (ibid., 752)

During his prime, Justice Douglas spent a good bit of time trudging through the wilderness. His love of the outdoors was deep and abiding. He never failed to champion the glories and virtues of nature in numerous speeches, magazine articles, and well-received books. To Douglas, the trees, forests, mountains, and rivers comprised a sacred, mystical terrain in dire need of protection from the invasion of mindless technology, rampant commercialization, and insensitive destroyers of the ecological balance.

This sanctity-of-environmental-life orientation likewise permeated Douglas's dissent. The following passage reflects his sentiments about the earth and its abundant harvest of miracles:

> A teaspoonful of living earth contains 5 million bacteria, 20 million fungi, 1 million protozoa, and 200,000 algae. No living human can predict what vital miracles may be locked in this dab of life, this stupendous reservoir of genetic materials that have evolved continuously since the dawn of the earth. For example, molds have existed on earth for about 2 billion years. But only in this century did we unlock the secret of penicillins, tetracyclines, and other antibiotics from the lowly molds, and thus fashion the most powerful and effective medicines ever discovered by man. (ibid., 750)

For Douglas, the ecological community is an all-embracing entity encompassing within its expansive orbit water, land, and air, as well as all sorts of animal and plant life. Thus, according to Douglas, the environment in its broadest sense should be classified as "legal persons" and members of the Sierra Club and others who have direct contact with and appreciation of the outdoors should possess legitimate authority to serve as prime advocates of the ecological community before courts and agencies.

A Non-Ecological Approach
toward the Intrauterine Environment

It is supremely ironic that Douglas's concern for nature and all its creatures did not extend to unborn children. In *Roe v. Wade* and its companion case, *Doe v. Bolton,* he joined the 7-2 majority that denied legal personhood to human beings in utero and created a private right to kill the unborn throughout all stages of prenatal development. His slavish conformity in this case to the slogans and shibboleths manufactured by pro-abortion ideologues is completely out of character for a man who prided himself on rugged individualism and a longstanding reputation as "a great dissenter." It is extremely paradoxical that Justice Douglas, a self-proclaimed progressive and inveterate explorer of the globe's most breathtaking sights, turned out to be, in *Roe* and *Doe,* a steadfast reactionary, unwilling to explore, let alone probe in depth, the world and ecology of human life before birth.

Justice Douglas's concurring opinion is rife with specious ambiguities about the nature of prenatal life. "The protection of the fetus when it has acquired life is a legitimate concern of the State," he wrote. However, "when life is present is a question we do not try to resolve." Douglas embellishes his exercises in obscurantism with quotations from former Supreme Court Justice Tom Clark: "To say that life is present at conception is to give recognition to the potential, rather than the actual. . . . When sperm meets egg, life may eventually form, but quite often it does not, and until it is actually present, it cannot be destroyed."[10]

The Douglas of *Sierra Club* is a marked contrast to the Douglas of *Roe* and *Doe.* The bold visionary who wished to endow rivers, valleys, mountains, and animals with legal personhood found it impossible to do likewise for unborn children. While Douglas expressed absolute certitude about the existence and intrinsic worth of natural objects and members of the animal kingdom, he relegated the onset and value of human life before birth to the insignificant status of an unresolvable question best left in the highly subjective realm of personal opinion or something to be controverted by experts. He saw the most wondrous marvels in "a teaspoon of living earth," and yet trivialized conception as merely the union of sperm and egg rather than hailing it as a momentous event in which the life of a totally unique human being is initiated. He expressed alarm about how insecticides, pollutants, and crass commercial exploitation threatened to destroy the very fabric of the *extrauterine environment,* but was abysmally silent about how abortion transforms the *intrauterine environment* into a deadly habitat polluted beyond belief by the invasion of lethal instruments and poisonous substances. He presented himself as a spokesman for "those inarticulate members of the ecological group" but remained oblivious to the plight of the voiceless unwanted unborn.

The Expanding Universe of Nonhuman Persons

The schizophrenic cast of mind prevalent in Justice Douglas's opinions is far from an atypical phenomenon. It reflects, instead, a common pattern, especially among intellectuals who perceive "nonperson" as an apt construct for justifying abortion, infanticide, and euthanasia, while simultaneously agonizing over the lack of personhood for animals and other nonhuman entities.

In his "groundbreaking" essay, "Abortion and Infanticide," first published in *Philosophy and Public Affairs* (fall 1972), philosopher Michael Tooley is not particularly concerned about knowing "the exact point at which a human infant acquires a right to life," since "in the vast majority of cases in which infanticide is desirable, its desirability will be apparent within a short time after birth." A more "deeply disturbing" and "troubling worry" for him "is whether adult animals belonging to species other than Homo sapiens may not also possess a serious right to life." And "once one reflects upon the question of the basic moral principles involved in the ascription of a right to life of organisms," Tooley declares, "one may find himself driven to conclude that our everyday treatment of animals is morally indefensible, and that we are in fact murdering innocent persons" (pp. 64–65).

In *Abortion and Infanticide* (1983), Tooley continues to build a philosophical rationale for protecting animals by defining them as "persons" besides elaborating additional criteria for sustaining his defense of nonpersonhood for the unborn and for infants up until at least three months after birth. His plan of personhood for animals admits of degrees and would operate in the following manner:

> Members of some species would not even be quasi-persons, and hence their destruction would be in no way intrinsically wrong. Members of other species would be quasi-persons, and their destruction therefore wrong to a greater or lesser degree. Finally, normal adult members of some species—such as, perhaps, chimpanzees, whales, and dolphins—might be persons, so that their destruction would be comparable to the destruction of normal adult human beings. (p. 412)

At this point it would be reasonable to conclude that the waterfront of nonhuman candidates for personhood has been fully covered. One would be hard put to come up with a more exhaustive list than the ships and corporations of American law; the forests, mountains, rivers, and valleys of attorney Christopher Stone and Justice William O. Douglas; and the chimpanzees, whales, and dolphins of philosopher Michael Tooley. What other entities could possibly be included? Has not the concept of nonhuman personhood been extended beyond its outermost limits?

Endowed with a futuristic vision that outstrips even the most fertile imaginations of his fellow colleagues, Tooley also envisions the inclusion of robots, advanced computers, and sophisticated machines among the already bloated gallery of proposed nonhuman persons. He does not believe it farfetched to classify as a person a robot that would possess psychological, intellectual, and behavioral capabilities "indistinguishable from those of human beings." His computer-person scenario consists of the following:

> The idea of there being an immaterial mental substance connected in certain ways with a complex electronic computer is in itself logically no more problematic than the idea of such a substance's being associated with

certain biological entities. On any theory, then, it is at least logically possible that there should be electronic persons. (ibid., 180)

In Tooley's "brave new world" where the boundaries between science and science fiction are hopelessly obscured, "if electronic persons are possible, then so are potential electronic persons." An example of this would be "an electronic device that, although it did not possess those properties that make something a person, was so programmed that it would alter its own circuitry in such a way that it could come to have those (possibly emergent) properties that make something a person." Furthermore, reasons Tooley, "if electronic persons are logically possible, so are mechanical ones, and the potentiality principle will have to be extended to cover potential mechanical persons" (ibid., 180–81).

Another individual straight out of Tooley's "twilight zone" of philosophy is professor Mary Anne Warren. Ever ready to search for nontraditional recipients for the benefits of personhood, she finds hope in the high-tech developments of the future. "Citizens of the next century," she advises, "should be prepared to recognize highly advanced, self-aware robots or computers, should such be developed, and intelligent inhabitants of other worlds, should such be found, as people in the fullest sense, and to respect their moral rights" (1973, 56–57).

That there are individuals—and the numbers are increasing—who seriously believe legal personhood should be conferred upon forests, rivers, valleys, animals, computers, machines, and aliens, but not on growing categories of human beings, may seem bizarre and shocking to many people. Yet, from another vantage point, it may not be that strange after all, but an all-too-accurate reflection of today's throwaway society where pet rocks and cabbage patch dolls have been successfully promoted as replacements for human beings and human relationships. The movement to personalize a broad range of nonhuman beings and objects may also serve to divert attention away from the destructive energy directed against the enormous number of human beings defined as "nonpersons." In addition, the love and compassion ordinarily channeled toward the care of human lives may well have been displaced onto nonhuman objects in order to compensate for the large-scale killing perpetrated. If the current trend of excluding growing numbers of humans from the ranks of personhood continues, it is likely that the number of nonhuman objects proposed as serious candidates for personhood will likewise continue to escalate.

Summary

Reduction of human lives to the nonexistent status of legal nonpersons reflects a persistence transcending contemporary and historical periods. Today's promoters of the "nonperson" epithet as a device for justifying the legalization of abortion, fetal research, and euthanasia are resorting to the same tactic employed to legitimize violence against a variety of groups long ago. Through much of history women as a class have been treated as "less than persons" before the law. Legal scholar Ernst Fraenkel found that a 1936 German high court ruling "refused to recognize Jews living in Germany as 'persons' in the legal sense." The designation "unperson" served as a convenient weapon for rationalizing the annihilation of Soviet people and erasing evidence of their existence from public records. "In the eyes of the law," according to a Virginia Supreme Court decision in 1858, "the slave is not a person." The longstanding assaults on Native American culture, territories, and lives by federal agencies and state governments prompted George Canfield to conclude in the *American Law Review* of 1881 that "an Indian is not a person within the meaning of the Constitution."

Part Three

Challenges to
Dehumanizing Rhetoric

16

The Reality Test: Refuting the Validity of Disparaging Designations

T he degrading expressions directed against today's unwanted unborn and born constitute pernicious stereotypes at odds with the intrinsic humanity of those who are being dehumanized and physically impacted by the demeaning rhetoric. An urgent need exists to expose and challenge the rank duplicity underlying this terminology.

Semantic Gymnastics

One way of discrediting the semantic assaults on contemporary victims is to quote those who admit that the derogatory vocabulary they have constructed is based on outlandish falsehoods. The prime source that should be cited in regard to this is the 1970 *California Medicine* editorial discussed in chapter 1. This article acknowledges that "very considerable semantic gymnastics" are required to avoid "the scientific fact which everyone really knows that human life begins at conception" and "to rationalize abortion as anything but taking a human life." Such "a schizophrenic sort of subterfuge is necessary," the editorial emphasizes, in order to obtain acceptance of abortion as "moral, right and even necessary" and "because while a new ethic [the quality of life] is being accepted the old one [the sanctity of life] has not yet been rejected."[1]

It should also be underscored that semantic gymnastics are envisioned as an indispensable tool for facilitating the oppression of the unwanted after birth: "One may anticipate further development of these roles as the problems of birth control and birth selection are extended inevitably to death selection and death control" (ibid.).

The editorial thus actually admits that lying in a way that is comparable to a psychiatric disorder is essential for sanctioning abortion and euthanasia. In an unusually candid manner, the statement identifies and advocates an approach based on subterfuge, an approach that has helped spawn the abundance of terms invoked to devalue undesired human beings before and after birth. Although other anti-life proponents are not apt to be so forthright, the same strategy of semantic gymnastics is basic to their nomenclature of denigration as well.

The Potential Life Fallacy

Another way of challenging the war of words against today's vulnerable victims is to show that the expressions concocted are in direct opposition to the true nature of prenatal life. Take, for example, the phrases "potential life," "potential human life," and "at best only the potentiality of life." These designations comprise cornerstones of semantic derision employed by the United States Supreme Court in *Roe v. Wade* to devalue the significance of human life before birth.[2]

What exists inside the womb, to the contrary, is not potential life but an actual, uniquely human life. This remains so during the entire human life cycle. The individual at fertilization is not a potential life, but an actual human life in the first stage of existence. Throughout pregnancy the fetus is not a potential life, but an actual human being living and growing during the prenatal stages of development. The child at six months after birth is not a potential life, but an actual human life in the infancy phase. The seventy-year-old person is not a potential life, but an actual human life proceeding through the later adult stage of the human life span.

Although the sperm and egg are alive, neither qualifies as an actual human life. Each possesses some of the characteristics that go into creating a human being. Both are potentially human ingredients. But not until they unite at fertilization does the major transformation take place from the stage of potential life to that of an actual human being who is so distinct that he or she will never again be duplicated in the history of the world.

From conception throughout each phase of intra- and extrauterine existence the person remains totally and indivisibly human. He or she is *never a potential human being* but *always an actual human being with vast potentials.* Whatever potentials an individual is conceived with are encoded in the person's genetic makeup. These traits, capacities, and qualities unfold gradually. Each has its special time of ascendance. It takes many years beyond conception and birth for them to develop anywhere near their optimal level. Some potentials are never actualized. The extent to which the potentials the human being possesses at fertilization are ever brought to fruition depends largely on the benevolence of the environment encountered inside and outside the womb. A warm, secure, and stable environment populated by loving parents and significant others who furnish the child with a diverse range of opportunities for growth and development is an excellent milieu for enhancing the advancement of the individual's innate talents.

Furthermore, to say that only potential life exists before birth or at any other stage is to arbitrarily single out certain phases of development as less important than other phases. To say that at one phase the person is only potential life and at another phase is actual human life is to flirt with absurdity. This contention flies in the face of the widely accepted principle of the essentially interdependent relationship of all stages of the human life continuum. No one phase is irrelevant or insignificant. All are important. The more advanced stages of human development owe their existence to the successful unfolding of previous phases of growth. All stages of life are inextricably bound together.

An enormous amount of scientific evidence supports the reality that the person from the beginning of intrauterine existence is an actual and not a potential human life. Leading medical textbooks such as Keith L. Moore's *Before We Are*

Born (1989) state unequivocally that "development can be divided into *prenatal* and *postnatal* periods, but it is important to understand that *human development is a continuous process that begins at fertilization* [italics in original]" (p. 1). Dr. Jerome Lejeune, professor of fundamental genetics at the University of Rene Descartes in Paris and discoverer of the chromosomal disease causing Down's syndrome, testified before a U.S. Senate subcommittee: "To accept the fact that, after fertilization has taken place, a new human has come into being is no longer a matter of taste or of opinion. The human nature of the human being from conception to old age is not a metaphysical contention, it is a plain experimental evidence" (1981, 64). An article in *The New York Times* (October 8, 1991) on Nobel Prize winners includes the following admission: "The Nobel committee noted that life begins with the activation of ion channels as the sperm merges with the egg at fertilization" (Altman 1991, C3).

Federal circuit court judge and former University of California (Berkeley) law professor John T. Noonan refers to the "potential life" classification imposed on the unborn by the United States Supreme Court in *Roe v. Wade* as an "oxymoron." "If the being was life," Noonan asks, "how was it potential? What is living is alive. It is not potentially alive" (1979, 147).

Windows on the Womb

One of the greatest threats to the dehumanizing images of the unborn manufactured by the abortion establishment comes from the miracle technologies of ultrasound and fetoscopy and revolutionary advances in fetal therapy and surgery that reveal in a graphic and compelling manner that the tiny passenger within the womb is nothing less than a bona fide human being from the very onset of pregnancy.

The power of ultrasound is attested to by Dr. John C. Fletcher and Dr. Mark I. Evans, who, in *The New England Journal of Medicine* (February 17, 1983), reported on the cases of two pregnant women who decided against abortion after seeing ultrasonic films of their unborn children early in pregnancy. The authors concluded that such an experience precipitated maternal bonding—the propensity of the mother to form a close emotional attachment with her baby. When one of the women was asked about her reaction to seeing "the small, visibly moving fetal form on the screen," she said: "I feel that it is human. . . . I couldn't have an abortion now." The other woman replied: "It really made a difference to see that it was alive. I am going all the way with the baby. I believe it is human" (pp. 392–93).

An inevitable consequence of fetologists and surgeons pioneering radical new methods of treating unborn humans is the increase in personalized images of the fetus as a patient deserving the best possible care and treatment. The leading medical textbook *Williams Obstetrics* (1985) states that "the fetus is no longer dealt with as a maternal appendage" but as "a patient who should be given the same meticulous care by the physician that we long have given the pregnant woman" (Pritchard, MacDonald, and Grant 1985, 267, 139).

Abortion proponents are acutely aware of what a formidable challenge such portrayals present to the depersonalized, anachronistic perceptions of the unborn they have constructed. At a National Abortion Federation meeting in 1982 Planned Parenthood executive Alfred F. Moran warned that "we are going to find ourselves isolated" unless "we are prepared to begin to recognize that technology and medical sciences and perceptions of fetal viability are radically changing in our society." He was especially horrified by the potential of the new life-promoting fetal therapy for jeopardizing the right to abortion. "We begin to see the fetus as a patient; which tends to personalize it," he emphasized.[3]

Advocates of abortion are also intimidated by medical advances in treating premature infants. After staff reporter Susan Oakie wrote in *The Washington Post* about how a more positive view of the fetus emerging from these advances could undermine the pro-abortion movement, a member of the movement criticized her for "hurting the cause" (1989, 1, 4, 5). From this, Oakie acknowledged the pervasive expectation that reporters, particularly female reporters, were supposed to write "only stories that support abortion rights" (Shaw 1990, A1).

The life-enhancing thrust of fetal surgery stands in stark opposition to the life-denying essence of abortion technology. Each advance in fetal therapy crystallizes the inherent contradiction between the therapeutic medicine of fetologists and the exterminative procedures of abortionists. The powerful images of the fetus emanating from medical science possess an incomparable capacity for exposing the fraudulent and horrendous nature of dehumanizing rhetoric imposed on the unborn. The ramifications of these images are far-reaching: it is but a short step from the view of the fetus as a legitimate patient to the perception of the fetus as a legal person with constitutional rights. All the more reason that these images be communicated extensively.

The Lower Animal Canard

Likening the unwelcome unborn to a form of "lower animal" life represents another assault on the truth. At no time in pregnancy does the child in the womb go through various animal stages before reaching the human stage. At all phases of prenatal development the preborn child is a human and never an animal.

Such an erroneous portrayal is part of a longstanding tradition, particularly among believers in evolution, of regarding the unborn human as proceeding through a series of nonhuman and animal phases before reaching the human stage sometime late in pregnancy or not until birth. This perspective is at the core of ancestral recapitulation, a theory based on the contention that fetal development rapidly recapitulates the entire evolutionary history of the species. This theory, however, like the derogatory images of the unborn it has spawned, has been proven to be erroneous. Even avid evolutionist Stephen Jay Gould in *Ever Since Darwin* (1977) declared that by the end of the 1920s recapitulation theory "had utterly collapsed" (p. 216). In a 1988 article in *American Scientist,* Yale biology professor Dr. Keith Thompson called it "dead as a doornail" (p. 273).

Although this theory and its degrading semantic progeny have been thoroughly disproved, their remnants linger on in the rhetoric of some contemporary abortion defenders. A prominent example is the article penned by scientists Carl Sagan and wife Ann Druyan *(Parade,* April 22, 1990) comparing the human fetus, at various stages of development, to a worm, a tadpole, a fish, an amphibian, a reptile, a pig, a primate, and finally, a human being. They even maintain that at one point in fetal development "there is a pronounced tail" (pp. 5–7).

To the contrary, modern science has demonstrated that every step in fetal development is uniquely human and does not repeat nonhuman and then human evolution. Nevertheless, Sagan and Druyan have chosen to resuscitate the suppositions of a long-discarded theory that has no scientific credibility. Their defense of abortion, like the theory and semantics they invoke to back it up, is morally and scientifically bankrupt.

Similarly, the reduction of the preborn human to a dangerous parasite—a repulsive entity that invades the woman's body and threatens to destroy her autonomy, health, and life—is false and absurd from a logical and scientific perspective, as well as a blatant distortion of the real relationship between the mother and her unborn child. A parasite is an organism of one species that invades the organism of a different species from an outside source and associates with the host in a negative, unhealthy, and detrimental manner. An unborn child, on the other hand, is an individual of one species *(Homo sapiens)* who develops from an inner source and lives inside the uterine cavity of an individual of the same species *(Homo sapiens).* The relationship between the unborn child and the mother is an overwhelmingly natural, positive, healthful, and mutually beneficial one necessary for the procreation of the species.

The Patient-As-Vegetable Hoax

Several noteworthy challenges have been likewise presented to counter the widespread practice of reducing comatose and debilitated patients to "vegetables" or "persistent vegetative states." One of the most compelling voices is that of Sondra

Diamond, a counseling psychologist born with cerebral palsy. Diamond was appalled when she read in *Newsweek* (November 12, 1973) that doctors at the Yale University–New Haven Hospital intensive care nursery allowed forty-three babies born with disabilities to die by deliberately withholding life-sustaining medical treatment. She was equally appalled by Yale pediatrician Raymond Duff's characterization of these infants as "vegetated individuals who have no human potential."[4] Diamond wrote the following response, which was published in *Newsweek* on December 3, 1973:

Life-and-Death Decisions

I'll wager my entire root system and as much fertilizer as it would take to fill Yale University that you have never received a letter from a vegetable before this one, but, much as I resent the term, I must confess that I fit the description of a "vegetable" as defined in the article "Shall This Child Die?"

Due to severe brain damage incurred at birth, I am unable to dress myself, toilet myself, or write; my secretary is typing this letter. Many thousands of dollars had to be spent on my rehabilitation and education in order for me to reach my present professional status as a counseling psychologist. My parents were also told, 35 years ago, that there was "little or no hope of achieving meaningful 'humanhood'" for their daughter. Have I reached "humanhood?" Compared with Drs. Duff and Campbell, I believe I have surpassed it!

Instead of changing the law to make it legal to weed out us "vegetables," let us change the laws so that we may receive quality medical care, education and freedom to live as full and productive lives as our potentials allow.[5]

Hospice physician Dr. R. Lamerton strongly criticizes use of the word "vegetable" as a scientific classification for describing the bodily functions of decerebrate patients:

What is scientific about it? Wherein does an unconscious man resemble a vegetable? Photosynthesis? Roots? Edibility? Science implies precise observation, confirmed by demonstration, leading to logical conclusions. I challenge anyone to demonstrate to me the vegetable attributes of a man. (1974, 1184)

Lamerton suggests such replacements for the vegetable metaphor as "unconscious, decorticate, with only physical functions, decerebrate and so on." These expressions, he explains, "describe the lesion without questioning the patient's basic humanity" (ibid.).

Another penetrating critique of the "patient as vegetable" analogy comes from Dr. Thomas C. Oden, a pastoral counselor and professor of theology and ethics at Drew University:

Patient as Vegetable? One phrase that recurs incessantly in the medical descriptions of coma is "persistent vegetative state." Is this an accurate metaphor to describe comatose patients who have lost cognitive function but who continue to have many other forms of responsiveness? **Jewish and Christian moral thought should call upon neurologists to abandon the "patient as vegetable" analogy, and speak instead of a prolonged comatose condition or chronic state of low-level responsiveness.**

The analogy invites a particular set of moral responses, especially the treating of the living patient as if he or she were a vegetable. We do not even call deceased persons "vegetables" in our society, yet both popular language and neurological practice call living patients vegetables. This amounts to a linguistic predisposition and rationale to act as if the patient were a vegetable. It provides a convenient language for the thoughtless predisposition of crucial moral decisions. It is a pejorative, prejudicial, and dehumanizing use of metaphor. (1976, 60–61)

17

Statements of Semantic Impact: Assessing the Devastating Effects of Words on Deeds

Rachel Carson's *Silent Spring* (published in 1962) marked a watershed in awareness about how the widespread use and misuse of insecticides and poisonous chemicals were polluting the environment. Her damning and persuasive insights helped ignite a revolution of consciousness regarding the dangerous contamination of the air, water, land, and life wrought by a wide spectrum of environmental degradations: lethal fumes spewed from automobile exhausts; the dumping of industrial wastes into rivers, lakes, and streams; oil spills in the oceans; the hazards of nuclear waste storage and disposal. In response to these and other ecological concerns, the Environmental Protection Agency was established in 1970 to monitor environmental quality and control pollution caused by solid wastes, pesticides, toxic substances, noise, and radiation. An important tool for preserving a clean and safe environment was the development of *environmental impact statements,* reports designed to evaluate the probable effects of proposed projects—especially of an industrial or commercial nature—on local employment, services, and living standards as well as the more directly visible effects on the physical environment, such as noise, air pollution, visual intrusion, land degradation, and watercourse contamination.

Today there is another kind of toxicity loose upon the land—an avalanche of dehumanizing expressions. This semantic venom contaminates the perceptions of many people and readily leads to multiple types of violence, including destruction on an unprecedented scale. It also continues a longstanding legacy of name-calling that despoiled the social and psychological environment in times past. In *1984* George Orwell wrote about the indispensable role played by "newspeak"—an all-encompassing lexicon of semantic distortion—in perpetuating totalitarian regimes. Since then a heightened public awareness has developed with respect to the profound impact of disparaging words on the enhancement of malevolent deeds. Just as *environmental impact statements* reveal the disastrous effects of pollutants on the environment, there is a dire need to create *semantic impact statements* to demonstrate the devastating influence of linguistic toxin on human lives. This chapter represents an attempt to move in this direction: to delineate how some of the demeaning classifications in part 2 have affected the victims of these classifications.

Marginalized Human Lives

Consigning the unborn to the "rudimentary, insignificant, and inferior" stage of "potential life" has had a far-reaching effect on perpetuating the abortion liberty. The potential life doctrine proved to be such a potent force for the late Dr. Alan F. Guttmacher that it overrode his previous writings stressing the humanity of the unborn from the very onset of pregnancy. In *Having A Baby* (1947), he focused on "the new baby which is created at this exact moment [fertilization]" (p. 4). In another book, *Pregnancy and Birth: A Book for Expectant Parents* (1957), Guttmacher wrote: "A facet which makes the obstetrician's burden unique in the whole field of medicine is his double obligation: he simultaneously cares for two patients, the mother and infant. Each has an individual right to life." He concluded by wishing "babies yet unborn" a "triumphant entrance into the universe" (pp. xv, 321). In contrast, by 1973 Dr. Guttmacher defended abortion as the removal of "only potential life" (1973, 144). Thus, the "babies yet unborn" whom he had so enthusiastically welcomed into the universe in 1957, had by 1973 become *personae non gratae* unceremoniously exiled to the nether world of potentiality.

The rhetoric of "lives not worth living" has become increasingly responsible for the spread of contemporary euthanasia, particularly the imposed starvation deaths of patients in hospitals. A prime illustration is the 1982 case of "Baby Doe" in which the Supreme Court of Indiana ruled in favor of the parents' decision to deny life-sustaining surgery and nutrition to a child born with Down's syndrome and a deformed esophagus. An obstetrician, the child's parents, and the judge all relied upon the expression "a minimally accepted quality of life was never present" to justify what happened to this infant.[1]

The writings of German euthanasia proponents Ernst Haeckel, Karl Binding, Alfred Hoche, and others depicting the disabled as hopelessly defective lives not worth living had an enormous impact on the Nazi euthanasia program, which consumed some 275,000 patients in hospitals and psychiatric institutions. The demeaning concepts imposed on the handicapped in Binding and Hoche's 1920 book *Permitting the Destruction of Unworthy Life* were considered so significant that they formed part of the defense invoked by those who were tried for crimes against humanity at the Nuremberg War Crimes Trials.[2]

Perceptions of women, blacks, and Indians as members of an "inferior" race supplied a powerful rationalization for the many injustices and atrocities committed against these groups in times past. Scientists helped endow the inferiority stereotype with heightened authority by citing an array of skull measurements purporting to demonstrate "defects" in the capacities of these victims. Writing in the British monthly *The Nineteenth Century* (May 1887), physiologist George J. Romanes asserted that because "the average brain-weight of women is about five ounces less than that of men, on merely anatomical grounds we should be prepared to expect a marked inferiority of intellectual power in the former" (pp. 654–55). New Orleans physician Dr. Samuel A. Cartwright maintained that "his [the Negro's] brain is a ninth or tenth less than other races of man" and the "deficiency of red blood in the pulmonary and arterial systems . . .

conjoined with a deficiency of cerebral matter in the cranium" results in "that debasement of mind, which has rendered the people of Africa unable to take care of themselves" (1851, 65–66). In *Crania Americana* (1839), Philadelphia physician Dr. Samuel George Morton drew upon measurements selectively culled from the world's largest scientific collection of human skulls to conclude that the "intellectual faculties" of Indians "appear to be of a decidedly inferior cast when compared with those of the Caucasian or Mongolian races" (1839, 81).

Subhuman Creatures

Defining the unborn out of the human race is deemed a high priority justification for destructive actions performed inside the womb. During the late 1960s an obstetrician acknowledged that the perception of the unborn as "not a live human being" was essential for alleviating the stress of seeing "the dismembered limbs and so forth that you remove from the womb."[3] Physician abortionist Dr. Howard I. Diamond finds the phrase "a fetus is nothing" (Rosen 1977, 75) helpful to justify his assaults on the unborn. In 1985 a Minnesota district court judge used the statement "a fetus is not a human being" (Zack 1985, 21A) as grounds for dismissing a murder charge brought against a man who beat up his 8½-month-pregnant girlfriend and caused the death of her unborn baby. Portrayal of the four-week-old fetus as "patently inhuman" (1982, 5) furnishes the underpinnings for former Columbia University professor Robert Nisbet's defense of abortion.

Characterizations of unwanted, disabled patients as part of the nonhuman universe comprise an influential component in today's euthanasia advocacy and practice. Philosopher John Lachs's proposal for doing away with hydrocephalic children is based on a definition of them as "only human forms" and "not . . . human beings" (1976, 840). The expression "a sadly non- or un- or subhuman creature" serves as a foundation for biomedical ethicist Joseph Fletcher's opposition to medical treatment for those with Down's syndrome (1968, 62). Dehumanizing phrases—"she died as a human being a long time ago," "a monstrosity of human existence," "she is not a physical entity, a human being"—played a major role in the court-sanctioned starvation death of Nancy Ellen Jobes, a New Jersey woman dependent upon a feeding tube for survival.[4]

Invocation of the subhuman term "nothing" played a crucial role in the brutal rape and beating of a young woman in New York's Central Park by a gang of teenage boys on the evening of April 19, 1989. After their arrest the perpetrators joked about and described what they had done as "fun." One of them told the police that the woman was "nothing."[5] How often such dehumanizing designations get translated into violent actions is difficult to determine, but recent research indicates that they comprise a key justification in the vocabulary of motives constructed by rapists to rationalize their assaults (Scully and Marolla 1985, 260).

The extermination of European Jews and the Soviet people owed much of its success to the imposition of subhuman terminology on the victims. Judges at the Nuremberg War Crimes Trials considered the dehumanizing language and "obscene racial libels" churned out over a twenty-five-year period by Julius Streicher's anti-Semitic newspaper *Der Stuermer* important enough to have perverted the attitudes of countless Germans toward, and incited genocidal acts against, the Jewish people. For this and other activities, Streicher was hanged on October 15, 1946, under count four of the indictments: "Crimes against humanity" (Varga 1981, 92, 94). Soviet perpetrators acknowledged that "in order to massacre them, it was necessary to proclaim that kulaks are not human beings" (Grossman 1972, 144).

Views of African Americans and Native Americans as degraded races far beneath the threshold of humanity made up a prominent part of the justifications buttressing the inhumane treatment of these two groups. The American anti-slavery movement's extensively documented indictment of slavery, *American Slavery As It Is* (1839), highlights the indispensable relationship between dehumanizing terminology and the cruelties inherent in slavery: "He [the slaveowner] does not contemplate slaves as human beings, consequently does not treat them as such; and with entire indifference sees them suffer privations and writhe under blows, which, if inflicted upon whites, would fill him with horror and indignation" (p. 110). Newspaper accounts of Plains Indians as "heartless creatures . . . destitute of all the promptings of human nature" helped pave the way for the wholesale assaults on Native Americans by the American cavalry (Mardock 1971, 86).

Degrading Animal Metaphors

Animal metaphors are instrumental in affirming the legitimacy of abortion and the expansion of fetal research. Drawing analogies between fetal behavior and the responses of lower animals such as amoebas is considered to be an effective means of protecting the abortion liberty by minimizing the significance and humanity of human life before birth. It is often employed to offset abortion's most dreaded complication—an aborted baby with life signs—and the highly personalized images of the unborn projected by ultrasound.[6] Another use of animal references—the definition of aborted humans as guinea pigs—has had a profound effect on justifying experimentation on the unwanted unborn. As far back as the early 1960s the phrase "to see whether any animals had survived" was used to characterize a terminal experiment in which fifteen living aborted human fetuses were immersed in a solution to test their survival capabilities ("no fetus was living after a third period of immersion") (Goodlin 1963, 579). Since then, animal expressions imposed on the unborn have given a tremendous boost to the growing medical and ethical acceptance of research involving the harvesting of fetal tissues for transplantation.

Animal parallels have likewise become incorporated into the lexicon of contemporary euthanasia proponents and those in favor of experimenting on and harvesting spare parts from severely handicapped infants and brain-damaged patients. Philosopher John Lachs employs an invidious animal comparison in his proposal for "easing the death" of hydrocephalic children—"pigeons have more personality—the indigo bunting more intellect—than this unfortunate mooncalf in our midst" (1976, 840). Animal liberation philosopher Peter Singer's arguments in support of infant euthanasia are often accompanied by comments emphasizing the superiority of dogs and pigs to severely handicapped babies in terms of "rationality, self-consciousness, communication, and anything else that can plausibly be considered morally significant" (1983, 129). Yale University medical professor Robert Levine employed an animal analogy in reference to the case of Theresa Ann Campo, an anencephalic child whom her parents attempted to get declared brain dead so her organs could be donated for transplantation. Dr. Levine likened the brain of such an infant to that of "a fish" (Chartrand 1992, 12; Levine 1992, 24).

Down through the ages much physical and sexual aggression against women has been shaped by degrading animal metaphors. In 195 B.C. Marcus Porcius Cato's portrayal of the woman as "a violent and uncontrolled animal" was invoked to justify keeping her "on a tight rein" (O'Faolain and Martines 1973, 39). French poet Charles Baudelaire's reduction of women to "domestic animals" is followed by a prescription for domestic violence—regular beatings (Hays 1964, 201). Nineteenth-century adages comparing women to dogs functioned as an inducement for wife battering (Dobash and Dobash 1979, 55; Cobbe 1878, 79). A staple of contemporary pornography—images of females as unrestrained sexual animals and "bitches in heat" that crave unrelenting sexual debauchery and assaults—furnishes powerful stimulants for men to perpetrate all kinds of sexual violence (Miller 1965, 229, 181, 287, 126, 304; Mailer 1965, 34, 43).

Lowering Nazi and Soviet victims to the level of animals paved the way for the most barbaric actions. German lawmaker Hermann Ahlwardt's depiction of Jews as "beasts of prey" was a prelude to exterminating "those beasts of prey" (Massing 1949, 303–4). Nazi medic Dr. August Hirt's death-dealing concentration camp experiments proceeded from a perception of the subjects as "animals before all else" (Aziz 1976, 1:232). The mass killing of Soviet people was enhanced by Lenin and Stalin's frequent exhortations "to destroy" these "wild imperialist beasts" and ravenous "wolves" since they posed such a formidable threat to the "workers' revolution" (Lenin 1960–70, 10:219, 234; 28:159; Stalin 1953–55, 4:151).

Caricatures of African Americans as work animals and dangerous beasts gave a tremendous impetus to the establishment and expansion of two horrendous institutions: black slavery and the lynching of Negroes. The depiction of black people as a kind of domestic animal that operated on a strictly instinctual, reflexive level helped many slaveholders remain oblivious to the pain and suffering experienced by those held in bondage (Estes 1846, 79–80; Sawyer 1858, 222, 197). Historian George W. Fredrickson attributes the spate of lynchings during the late 1800s and early 1900s to widespread circulation of the stereotype that "many Negroes were literally wild beasts, with uncontrollable sexual passions and criminal natures stamped by heredity" (1971, 276).

Images of Native Americans as wild, primitive animals destined to disappear with the coming of civilization were used regularly by pioneers, settlers, the military, speculators, explorers, the federal government, and local governments to rationalize the relentless assaults on Indian lands and lives. Predictions such as "civilization is destined to exterminate them in common with the wild animals" (Caldwell 1830, 142) were repeatedly put forth to buttress the U.S. government's removal policy—a gigantic euphemism that involved robbing Indians of their lands on a massive scale. When the Indian people refused to fade away and began resisting the onslaught, they were labeled a "dangerous species of wild beast" that had to be hunted down and destroyed (Mardock 1971, 86).

Parasitic Growths

Contemporary depictions of the unborn as a repulsive, voracious, parasitic invader bent on destroying the autonomy, health, and life of the pregnant woman show signs of growing acceptance. For Dr. Warren Hern, the presentation of abortion as a "defense mechanism" against the "local invasion" of a "parasite" (1984a, 14–15) undoubtedly serves as a compelling justification for the thousands of abortions he has performed. The fetus as a "parasite in the woman's body" (Petchesky 1984, 346; Wahlberg 1987, 5) has become a standard tenet of feminist polemics, as well as an ideological construct that is becoming embedded in the academic world and other institutions of contemporary culture. Even broader credibility was conferred on the parasite analogy in *Parade Magazine* on April 22, 1990, when high-profile astronomer Carl Sagan and scientist-wife Ann Druyan etched a deeply degrading portrait of human life in the womb, including a reference to the unborn as "a kind of parasite" that "destroys tissue in its path" and "sucks blood from capillaries" (1990, 6). Sagan is possibly the best known scientist in America and *Parade Magazine* has the widest circulation of any weekly magazine.

Relegation of individuals after birth to the category of vegetative, parasitic creatures intent on draining the health care system of valuable resources is playing an increasingly significant role in justifying euthanasia for a broad spectrum of contemporary victims. The vegetable analogy undergirds much of the growing sentiment in favor of removing life-sustaining treatments from and administering lethal substances to expanding categories of patients. It has become so fully entrenched in the public consciousness that even individuals opposed to euthanasia are apt to say that the worst calamity to befall anyone is "to become a vegetable." The number of health care workers resorting to the parasite epithet is on the upswing. A veteran intensive care nurse identifies the phases associated with this form of semantic devaluation and its detrimental impact: "At first, calling patients 'parasites' provides an emotional release from stressful work situations. Soon the name-calling degenerates from a temporary response to a deeply-rooted pattern of perceiving certain groups of patients. It eventually results in the actual abuse of those tagged with the parasite label."[7]

For millennia the contention that women are naturally parasitic, subservient creatures ordained to serve men has been resorted to as an effective semantic standby for excusing all kinds of male-perpetrated abuse directed against females (Guyon 1958, 207, 263, 214, xi, 208, 212, 198). Married women who choose to be full-time homemakers find themselves being castigated as "parasites" by radical feminists (de Beauvoir 1974, 510, 123, 481, 777). This brand of name-calling represents a two-pronged attack—one against women who remain in the home and the other against the institution of marriage for keeping them in a state of parasitism.

Parasite analogies played an indispensable role in facilitating both the Nazi Holocaust and the Soviet Union's war against its own people. By 1942 Hitler's anti-Semitic propaganda chief Julius Streicher was publishing articles calling for "the elimination of these parasites" (Varga 1981, 291). The booklet *The Jew as Global Parasite* was considered so important that Nazi officials made sure copies got into the hands of those charged with implementing the Holocaust.[8] Holocaust scholar Raul Hilberg found a revealing connection between this repulsive terminology and the destructive technology actually employed: "Jews were parasites who had to be exterminated like vermin, and with the introduction of Zyklon into Auschwitz that thought had been translated into reality" (1967, 567). Lenin capped off his endless speeches reviling kulaks as parasitic "blood-suckers" by declaring: "Ruthless war on the kulaks! Death to them!" (1960–70, 28:56–58). The devastating consequences of such violent language became evident at the Communist Party Congress in 1934 with Stalin's announcement that the successful campaign against the kulaks had resulted in "elimination of the parasitic classes . . . the kulak exploiters, the blood-sucking usurer" (1953–55, 13:340, 342).

Parasitic imagery was imposed on black slaves in the antebellum American South and Indians on the American western frontier with telling effectiveness. Slaveowners found the phrase "a serving people, parasitic to the white man" (Drake 1940, 31) to be an indispensable characterization for keeping black people in a state of bondage. Cavalry officers created a special version of the parasite menace—"nits make lice"—to justify the deeply disturbing task of killing Indian women and children. The significance of this slogan is apparent in Colonel John M. Chivington's instructions to the militia just before slaughtering 163 peaceful Cheyenne at Sand Creek, Colorado, in 1864: "Kill and scalp all big and little; nits make lice" (Andrist 1964, 89).

Contagious Diseases

The definition of unwanted pregnancy as a disease of epidemic proportions has become an exceedingly potent form of devaluation. Not only has it helped elevate abortion to the legitimate realm of mainstream medical practice, but it has facilitated the transformation of abortion into a public health measure designed to combat the spread of an infectious disease. Little wonder that the American Public Health Association has been one of the staunchest supporters of abortion.[9] The numerous references in the medical literature to abortion as a medical or surgical procedure are premised on the presentation of pregnancy as a kind of disease, diseased condition, or contagious illness. The notion of unintended pregnancy as a disease is so influential that, according to abortionist Dr. Warren Hern, the percentage of American women who each year "define pregnancy as an illness for which they regard the appropriate treatment to be abortion" has increased to nearly one-third (1984a, 10).

Depicting today's seriously afflicted and elderly patients strictly in terms of their illnesses has had a detrimental effect on their treatment. In her study of the doctor-patient relationship in a major American medical center, sociologist Terry Mizrahi reveals that reducing patients to "disease entities" has led to such practices as avoiding patients in need of treatment, getting rid of patients by pawning them off on someone else, and other forms of abuse. "Most hospital staff," she found, "admitted treating less thoroughly those patients they labeled derogatorily and some admitted to making mistakes because of their attitude" (1986, 102). The common practice of labeling disoriented and delusional elderly patients with the incurable disease of "senility" has had a devastating impact. Since their condition is defined as intractable, older patients who present some of the symptoms associated with senility are likely to be denied necessary medical care and, instead, end up warehoused "in the socially unstimulating and medically nihilistic environment of the average nursing home where untreated pathology is more likely to reach the stage of irreversibility" (Wershow 1977, 297–98).

The portrayal of women—especially during their periods—
as diseased and highly contagious sources has led to numerous injustices. At the onset of their first menstruation, girls
from the Nootka of the Canadian northwestern coast were
supplied with private eating utensils and had to eat alone for
eight months. When Eskimo girls experienced the monthly
flow, they had to crouch in a corner, their faces to the wall,
and let their hair hang over their heads. Among the Australians
of Queensland, the menstruating girl was buried up to the
waist in a secluded spot. The soil was supposed to purify her
"contaminated" condition (Hays 1964, 40–41). As late as the
beginning of the twentieth century, a rule still existed forbid-
ding women afflicted with "the curse" from entering refineries
in northern France because it was feared they would cause the
sugar to blacken (de Beauvoir 1974, 168).

Disease metaphors played a significant role in furthering
Nazi genocide and Soviet tyranny. The drastic implications of
defining Jews as carriers of contagious diseases became evident at a health conference held on July 9, 1943, commemorating the deportation of over 400,000 Jews from the Warsaw
ghetto to the death camps. This meeting served to showcase
the announcement that "removal" of the Jewish "element"
made a significant contribution to the health of Europe
(Hilberg 1967, 657). The phrase "intensive struggle against the
propagation of infection" provided Auschwitz physician Dr.
Joseph Mengele with a public health rationale for dispatching
inmates with scarlet fever to the gas chambers (Aziz 1976,
2:114). Among the Bolsheviks, Lenin exhibited the most persistent predisposition toward describing the extermination of
ideas and people opposed to Soviet totalitarianism as equivalent to performing medical procedures on malignant afflictions. A typical example is an address given in 1920 before the
Second Congress of the Communist International in which he
reported that "enormous successes had been achieved in the
treatment [destruction] of this disease [members of the bour-
geoisie]" (1960–70, 31:230–31).

Equating black people with dangerous plagues contributed
greatly to the increase in various forms of violence aimed at

them. Perceptions of African Americans as being associated with virulent diseases that contaminated the white race led to segregation, a practice that had become a deeply entrenched public policy in the United States by the beginning of the twentieth century. Writing in the journal *Medicine* (1903), Baltimore physician Dr. William Lee Howard proposed "quarantine" to combat the spread of "sexual madness" (attacks on white women by black males)—a "disease" he described as intrinsic to "the African's birthright" (p. 424).

Descriptions of Native Americans as being consumed by "a warlike contagion" and as constituting "more deadly enemies than the pestilence" gave a sense of urgency to the necessity of waging all-out war against such a malevolent and disease-ridden foe (Parkman 1902a, 1:244; Parkman 1902b, 2:224).

Inanimate Objects

Characterizations of the unborn as nondescript "products" and "material" or a form of disposable "property" help endow abortion with widespread legitimacy. These images reverberate throughout the modern world. They comprise a foundation for the endless accounts of abortion in medical journals as merely the removal of inconsequential "pregnancy products" or "fetal material." They bolster the "right to choose" by consigning the unborn victims to the status of the woman's "property." They form the semantic backbone of the exploding fetal research industry by relegating aborted humans to experimental "material" and "tissue." They are even found in contemporary literary works such as John Irving's best-selling novel *The Cider House Rules* (1986), which glorifies abortionist-orphanage director Dr. Wilbur Larch as a secular saint who devotes a lifetime to carrying out "the Lord's will" by removing "the products of conception" and caring for orphans (pp. 65–66, 83).

The objectification of patients—particularly the elderly in nursing homes—has had a profound influence in furthering abusive behavior against these vulnerable seniors. A series of environmental stresses—the difficult nature of bed and body work, an overabundance of tasks to accomplish, and the

unstimulating and depressing atmosphere of institutional life—
press upon a low-paid and understaffed work force to view and
treat patients as "work objects." A frequent finding among studies of nursing home staff members is their acknowledgment of
the relationship between such degrading conditions and the
depiction of residents, not as people to be cared for, but as
"things" to be moved, lifted, and placed in some corner according to the dictates of a rigid work routine (Gubrium 1975,
151–52; Fontana 1977, 144, 155–56).

Perceptions of women as the man's rightful "possession" to
be used and abused as he sees fit have long served as a fundamental justification for the proliferation of wife battering, rape,
and other atrocities. No contemporary institution has had a
more disastrous influence on male perceptions of women, the
treatment of women, and women's perception of themselves
than the pornographic Goliath, an empire that thrives on
unremitting portrayals of women and young girls as dehumanized "objects," "property," "things," and impersonal "matter"
upon which males act out their aggression and lust. Robin
Morgan's observation that "pornography is the theory and rape
the practice" emphasizes the enormous impact of dehumanizing language and images on behavior.[10] It should hardly come
as a surprise that men who are raised on a steady diet of material overflowing with violence and sexual terrorism would be
readily disposed to act out these scenarios in real life. And millions of men have been exposed to this degrading fare. It is
more than coincidental that today—with wife battering, sexual
abuse, rape, and other sexual crimes running rampant—is also
an era when society is being polluted with a deluge of sexually arousing, degenerate, and violent imagery. Tragically,
many women have also become imprisoned by the demeaning
images of females as erotic slaves and sex objects constructed
by the purveyors of porn.

The lexicon of objectification—"material," "matter," "pieces,"
"the load," etc.—was instrumental in buttressing the massive
exploitation and destruction of human lives in the Nazi death
camps. Historian Nora Levin furnishes a penetrating insight into
the compelling relationship between the radical subversion of

language resulting in the reduction of Jews to nonhuman matter and the emotional detachment so indispensable for their mass extermination and exploitation: "For the Nazis, Jews became part of the non-human universe. . . . This new formulation enabled mass murderers to think of themselves as technicians following orders and to call mass murder 'special treatment.' The accompanying obliteration of all customary human feelings—remorse, guilt, or pity—created a new phenomenon in history which defied the judges at Nuremberg and made the trials an exasperating, if well-meant effort to lift international law to a new level, while the Nazi transvaluation of meaning in language left judges, prosecutors and spectators stupefied, as the victims themselves had been" (Levin 1973, xii).

The view of the human being as "a lump of material" in need of processing was a central tenet of the Soviet regime. Its most brutal application occurred in the arctic death camps of the Gulag where scores of innocent victims were worked to death under the guise of transforming the "nastiest human material" into productive builders of socialism. Sometimes this massive exploitation of "work material" even took hold beyond the grave. D. P. Vitkovsky, a work supervisor on the White Sea Canal, revealed that in the summer, bones from the corpses together with the gravel "got into the concrete mixer. And in this way they got into the concrete of the last lock . . . and will be preserved there forever" (Solzhenitsyn 1973–74, 2:99).

For centuries the definition of black people as "a species of property and merchandise" stood as a core element in the expansion of slavery and kindred injustices. It supplied the justification for converting human beings into possessions and objects to be bartered, sold, deeded, pledged, exchanged, auctioned, and awarded in lotteries. It provided the foundation for numerous state laws categorizing slaves as "personal property" along with furniture, farm utensils, books, and dishes. The United States Supreme Court in *Dred Scott* noted that such a classification had been so "fixed and universal in the civilized portions of the white race" that "it was regarded as an axiom in morals as well as politics, which no one thought of disputing or supposed to dispute."[11] A court so completely bogged down by the oppressive weight of prejudicial precedents and pejorative stereotypes proved to be totally devoid of the expansive vision essential for recognizing blacks as legitimate human beings entitled to the same rights and protection enjoyed by other members of the human community.

Objectification of Native Americans as "anthropological specimens," "relics," and "artifacts" has played a prominent part in giving credence to the oft-projected image of an outmoded people and way of life. The appearance of Indians and their wares at various events and exhibitions tended to solidify the impression of a national historical "property" on public display. The press helped reinforce these stereotypes at world's fairs of the past by satirizing Indians as harmless and amusing "anthropological specimens" and "exotic curiosities" (Hoxie 1979, 333–41).

Waste Products

Several factors combine to make waste analogies extraordinarily effective devices for bolstering abortion. First, they possess extensive legal affirmation, since numerous city health codes refer to the dismembered bodies of the unborn as simply "medical waste" or "pathological waste" (Thimmesch 1982, 5B; Effron and Floerchinger 1983, 2A). Second, the aborted remains resemble the kind of matter that needs to be disposed of along with the garbage and trash, thanks to the capacity of modern abortion technology to reduce the tiny preborn bodies to inconsequential fragments of tissue, blood, and fluid. Third, the definition of aborted babies as "waste products" destined for obliteration has given a boost to acceptance of fetal research and harvesting of fetal organs.[12]

Reduction of today's vulnerable hospitalized patients to a vulgar term for the body's waste products—"shit"—has become so commonplace that it is endowed with the acronym "SHPOSHs (*sub human pieces of sh*it)." Terry Mizrahi's research on physician-patient interaction reveals that the impact of this degrading slang expression on the treatment of patients is profound. A junior resident she interviewed put it this way:

"When you turn them into something other than human, you don't have to care about . . . this 'piece of shit' in the middle of the night." According to another resident doctor, "when you are a physician and someone tells you there is a SHPOSH—'a suhuman piece of s—'—needing treatment, automatically your relationship with that patient is damaged" (Mizrahi 1986, 34, 41; Ver Berkmoes 1988, sec. 5:12).

Although the comparison of a woman's body to a sewer for the disposal of waste is of longstanding duration, it is not utilized today as often as it was in the past. It still persists, nevertheless, in the writings of such modern authors as Henry Miller (1963, 144; 1978, 110). The sewer metaphor constitutes one among many terms of denigration employed by Miller to express contempt for female anatomy.

Portrayals of Jews and other Third Reich expendables as "trash," "garbage," and "rubbish" made a significant contribution to the success of the Holocaust. Reliance on these designations allowed Nazi perpetrators to carry out a variety of repulsive tasks with a minimum of psychological trauma: gunning down Jews in front of huge ditches, gassing victims in large chambers, burning bodies on an assembly-line basis in crematory ovens. Holocaust scholar Leon Poliakov found that the waste metaphor was so deeply imprinted on the German psyche that "even in their sub-conscious mind the Germans had been trained to consider the Jews as pariahs, as the refuse of humanity" (Poliakov 1979, 112).

The awesome effects of the foul waste epithets were played out on a vast scale in the arctic death camps of the Gulag. In a chapter from *The Gulag Archipelago* entitled "The History of Our Waste Disposal System," Aleksandr Solzhenitsyn compares the Gulag to a gigantic waste disposal project for consuming millions of victims and describes the waves of human lives "oozing in through gutters" and pulsing through prison sewers. In the wave of 1944 to 1946, he writes, the Soviet perpetrators "dumped whole *nations* down the sewer pipes" (1973–74, 1:24–25).

Consignment of African Americans to the status of "trash" proved to be an enduring and influential ingredient in the nomenclature of dehumanization constructed by whites. From the onset of the slave trade, black people considered of little market value due to various disabilities were dubbed "refuse."[13] Those killed by white mobs were denied burial and regularly viewed as only fit for disposal along with the trash (Brown 1968, 61). Long after emancipation even the heritage of black Americans was equated with "debris" (English 1903, 469).

Noxious waste metaphors capture, in a remarkably literal fashion, the harsh reality of the U.S. government's brutal "Indian removal" policy of the nineteenth century. Native Americans were forcibly dispatched to the barren, arid sites of the Far West in a manner resembling a vast garbage and waste disposal project. In retrospect, William Hubbard's portrayal of Indians as the "Dregs and Lees of Earth, and Dross of Mankind" (Drinnon 1980, 40) and Christopher Brooke's poem calling Indians "the very dregs, garbage, and spanne of Earth" (Berkhofer 1978, 20)—formulated during the colonial period— provided a prophetic image for the treatment of Native Americans two centuries later.

Legal Nonpersons

The term "nonperson" has emerged as the most far-reaching and disastrous epithet ever invoked to devalue human life in the womb. When the United States Supreme Court's *Roe v. Wade* decision (1973) declared that "the word 'person,' as used in the Fourteenth Amendment, does not include the unborn," it sounded the legalized death knell for huge numbers of unborn humans.[14] Since then the nonperson concept has served as a foundation for countless articles, conferences, and court rulings designed to uphold and expand the abortion lib- erty as well as bolster experimentation on the unwanted unborn and the harvesting of fetal organs for transplantation. *The Planned Parenthood of Southeastern Pennsylvania v. Casey* (1992) decision reaffirming *Roe v. Wade* and allowing only the most minor abortion restrictions reiterated the non- person doctrine promulgated in *Roe*. "Since the unborn have never been recognized as persons in the whole sense," reasoned Associate Justice John Paul Stevens, "an abortion is not 'the termination of life entitled to Fourteenth Amendment protection.'" In addition, he emphasized, "from this holding, there was no dissent, indeed, no member of the Court has ever questioned this fundamental proposition. Thus, as a matter of Federal constitutional law, a developing organism that is not yet a 'person' does not have what is sometimes described as a 'right to life.'"[15] This is the dogma responsible for enshrining into law the killing of megamillions inside the uterus.

The nonperson label shows increasing signs of threatening the survival of vulnerable individuals at all phases of the post-natal human life span as well. Leading philosophers, ethicists, and physicians are developing justifications for reducing handicapped children, comatose patients, and the debilitated elderly to the status of "nonpersons." Dr. Raanon Gillon invoked the nonperson doctrine in the case of Baby Pearson, an unwanted Down's syndrome infant who died in 1980 in a British hospital from overdosages of adult pain medication: "It is because the newly born infant is not a person that it is justifiable in cases of severe handicap to 'allow it to die' in . . . [this] way" (1986, 545). A group of physicians and ethicists has already recommended including in the medical school curriculum material on determining "When does a dying patient cease to be a person?" (Culver et al. 1985, 253–56). Neurologist Ronald Cranford is working toward the day when the PVS (persistent vegetative state) classification is equated with "nonpersonhood" (Lippman 1991, 66).

Throughout the annals of inhumanity "legal personhood" has had an enormous effect on furthering the legitimation of massive oppression against a wide spectrum of victims.

Women have long suffered from the effects of treatment as "nonpersons" before the law—rape, wife beating, enforced marriage, witch burning, denial of voting rights, and discrimination in education and employment. Among the many anti-female court rulings is a 1909 British case that denied voting rights to women because "the statutory word 'person' did not in these circumstances include women."[16]

Political scientist Hannah Arendt found that a characteristic common to totalitarian regimes such as Nazi Germany and the Soviet Union was the exclusion of individuals declared stateless from the ranks of "legal persons" (1973, 290). According to an analysis conducted by legal scholar Ernst Fraenkel, a 1936 German high court decision that "refused to recognize Jews living in Germany as 'persons' in the legal sense" established a wide-ranging legal precedent for the genocide that followed (Fraenkel 1941, 95). The Soviet relegation of victims to the nonexistent position of "unpersons" had particularly drastic consequences for millions of Ukrainian farmers who were starved to death in the terror-famine of 1932–33 because of their resistance to the Soviet collectivization of agriculture (Conquest 1986, 303).

"Legal nonpersonhood" was a major factor underlying the oppression directed against two of the most maligned groups in American history: African Americans and Native Americans. The definition of black people as "noncitizens" and "nonpeople" in the *Dred Scott* decision of 1857[17] and the Virginia Supreme Court declaration *(Bailey & als. v. Poindexter's Ex'or,* 1858) that "in the eyes of the law . . . the slave is not a person"[18] epitomized the influential role of the law in buttressing the institution of slavery. Writing in *The American Law Review* of 1881, George Canfield summed up the precarious legal standing of Indians that permitted the wholesale assaults on Indian lands and lives: "An Indian is not a person within the meaning of the Constitution" (1881, 28).

18

Toward a Vocabulary of Life-Affirming Images: Replacing Dehumanizing Language with a Language of Humanization and Divinization

Even when massive victimization and the most negative images of the victims dominate the public consciousness, a counterlanguage—one characterized by personalized, positive, and uplifting views of the victims—surfaces to challenge the dehumanizing expressions. While the oppressors are calling the oppressed "inferior," "nonhuman," "animals," "parasites," "objects," "garbage," and "nonpersons," countervailing voices refer to those victimized as "human beings," "brethren," "men," "women," "brothers," "sisters," "children of God," and other terms of endearment and respect.

Today many pro-life proponents, disability rights advocates, and like-minded defenders of society's most defenseless individuals are in the forefront of attempting to replace the degrading designations of the unwanted unborn and born with humanized and exalted portrayals. It is important to gain a historical perspective on what they are doing; they are continuing a time-honored legacy of activism pioneered by those human rights leaders who insisted that victims in times past—women, Jews and others in the Third Reich, Soviet people, blacks,

Indians, and children—were rightful members of the human community despite the prevailing norms of denigrating terminology. Moreover, a striking kinship also exists between the language employed in support of contemporary vulnerable human lives inside and outside the womb and the language invoked on behalf of history's most oppressed groups. This kinship requires an extended examination.

The Humanity of the Unborn

Some of the most memorable portraits of the preborn as genuine members of the human family have been etched by physicians and scientists. As far back as 1859 and 1871, the House of Delegates of the American Medical Association unanimously enacted strongly worded resolutions against abortion buttressed by numerous references to the unborn as "children," "human life," and "unborn infants." The AMA report of 1859 characterized abortion as "the slaughter of countless children" and "such unwarrantable destruction of human life" (Storer 1859, 75–78). The report of 1871 asserted that "physiology considers the foetus as much a living being immediately after conception as at any other time before delivery" and called abortion the "wholesale destruction of unborn infants" (O'Donnell and Attlee 1871, 250, 248).

Out of the ashes of the Nazi Holocaust in 1948 the World Medical Association felt compelled to reiterate the fact of human life beginning at conception and the physician as a healer by formulating the Declaration of Geneva in order to prevent "any repetition, anywhere in the world, of the German doctors' descent into savagery." The Declaration states in part: "I will maintain the utmost respect for *human life from the time of its conception* [italics mine]. Even under threat I will not use my medical skills contrary to the laws of humanity" (Deutsch 1949, xxxviii).

Dr. Hymie Gordon, a geneticist at the Mayo Clinic, states: "It is at the moment of conception that the individual's capacity to respond to these exogenous [environmental] influences is established. Even at this early stage, the complexity of the living cell is so great that it is beyond our comprehension. It is a privilege to be allowed to protect and nurture it" (1968, 729–30). Dr. A. W. Liley's characterization of the unborn as a splendidly functioning baby instead of a poorly functioning adult has provided much of the attitudinal and empirical legacy for today's dramatic increase in fetal therapy. Dr. Liley, the father of fetology and the first person to successfully perform the intrauterine blood transfusion procedure, steadfastly maintained that

> the foetus is not an inert, helpless, fragile thing, a poor fish with a mind like a clean washed slate, a rather unpromising piece of material who, with time and good luck, might eventually turn into something tolerable and respectable by adult standards. Instead we must regard him as a young human being, dynamic, plastic and resilient. . . . Our task as parents, doctors and educators is to make sure . . . that throughout his development we help and not hinder him to do as much as he can as well as he can. (1967, 1, 4)

Early American feminists repeatedly highlighted the humanity of the unborn child and the oppression of women as the main bases for their forceful, persistent, and unequivocal condemnations of abortion. Their writings are full of references to the human being before birth as "the unborn innocent," "children," "unborn child," "infant," and "child." Elizabeth Cady Stanton referred to both abortion and infanticide as "degrading" and called for an end to "this wholesale suffering and murder of helpless children." Susan B. Anthony portrayed abortion as "the horrible crime of child-murder" against "the unborn innocent." In her focus on male irresponsibility, Matilda Gage equated abortion with "child-murder" and "infanticide." Dr. Alice Bunker Stockham, a leading proponent of the feminist health agenda, set forth in 1887 the scientific foundation for the feminist opposition to abortion: "When the female germ and male sperm unite, then is the inception of a new life; all that goes to make up a human being—body, mind, and spirit, must be contained in embryo within this minute

organism. *Life must be present from the very moment of conception."* Dr. Stockham added that "the woman who produces abortion, or allows it to be produced . . . commits the highest crime in
the calendar, for she takes the life of her own child." Sarah F.
Norton characterized abortion as "ante-natal child murder" and a
"war . . . against the woman and the child." She castigated abortionists as "child murderers" and "slayers of infants" who "practice
their life-destroying trade" in "infant butcheries."

The above and other quotations documenting the strong
opposition of the feminist foremothers to abortion, including
the complete texts in which they originally appeared plus
insightful historical commentary, is the result of pioneering
research conducted by Mary Krane Derr in her booklet
*"Man's Inhumanity to Women, Makes Countless Infants Die":
The Early Feminist Case Against Abortion* (1991) (pp. 13–14,
24–25, 10, 31–34).

Derr's findings are especially pertinent since they stand in
direct contradiction to the obsessive anti-fetal, pro-abortion
rhetoric of many modern-day feminists. Ironically, as members
of the contemporary feminist establishment continue to make
common cause with the names and values of the feminist foremothers, they are simultaneously repudiating one of the core
tenets held steadfastly and passionately by their counterparts
in times past—an expansive and consistent ethic of life that
encompassed both the woman and her unborn child. On April
5, 1992, for example, the National Organization for Women
sponsored a pro-abortion march in Washington, D.C. that,
according to the march organizers, was intended "to tie our
current challenge to the historic fight for women's rights
waged by our foremothers" (Mathews-Green 1992, 1).

In response to this event, Frederica Mathews-Green, communications director for the National Women's Coalition for Life, a
pro-life organization that takes seriously the consistent pro-life
philosophy of the early feminists, wrote: "On April 5, women
will carry the banner of the suffragists to celebrate access to
abortion, but with little awareness of these women's words on
the subject. The suffragists would cut across the deadlocked

debate of woman vs. fetus, and call for a feminism of broader vision, one that links rejection of abortion with rejection of sexual exploitation, and support for women in preventing or continuing unplanned pregnancies." Furthermore, Mathews-Green concluded, "may the present-day champions of Susan B. Anthony, who march under her banner, pay her the ultimate compliment: listen to her" (ibid., 5).

God-centered perceptions of the unborn emanating from both clerical and lay auspices and cutting across many religious denominations comprise another significant repository of powerful imagery.

Leading Protestant theologians Dietrich Bonhoeffer and Karl Barth pointed to the human and divine origins of the person before birth as a basis for speaking out against abortion. Bonhoeffer—a Lutheran pastor, scholar, and activist whose opposition to Hitler cost him his life—said of the human being in utero: "The simple fact is that God intended to create a human being and that this human being has been deliberately deprived of his life. And this is nothing but murder" (1955, 130–31). Barth emphasized that "the unborn child is from the very first a child . . . not a thing, nor a mere part of the mother's body" (1961, 415–16).

Sacred images of the preborn continue to be disseminated in contemporary society. Dr. Margaret White, a leader of the pro-life forces in England, declares: "There's a war against the most weak and the most innocent of all God's children. . . . If we want to have peace in the world, we must have peace in the womb" (Mother Teresa, Francis A. Schaeffer, Malcolm Muggeridge, et al. 1984, 9–10). Pastor John O. Anderson cites Holy Scripture as an authoritative source for an exalted depiction of human life before birth. "The Bible is clear concerning the absolute protection that is to be accorded to innocent life," he asserted. "Our Heavenly Father, who cares even for sparrows and lilies and grass, cares deeply for all human life, and especially that which is helpless and innocent. The unborn child is the most helpless, the most innocent of the innocent" (1984, 74).

During her long and persevering dedication to serving the world's most destitute people, Mother Teresa of Calcutta has frequently highlighted the plight of the unborn, a segment of the human family she continually characterizes as children made in the image of God. This theme served as the cornerstone of her Nobel Peace Prize acceptance speech in 1979:

> We are talking of peace, but, I feel that the greatest destroyer of peace today is abortion. Because it is a direct war, a direct killing—direct murder by the mother herself. And we read in the Scripture, for God says very clearly: "Even if a mother could forget her child—I will not forget you—I have carved you in the palm of my hand" (she said, quoting Isaiah). We are all carved in the palm of His hand, so close to Him. That unborn child has been carved in the hand of God. (Egan 1986, 404–5)

The Intrinsic Worth of Vulnerable Postnatal Humans

In the midst of the many dehumanizing terms that facilitated the imposed starvation death of Nancy Ellen Jobes on August 7, 1987, neurologists and staff members at the Lincoln Park Nursing and Convalescent Home where Nancy had been cared for over a seven-year period testified that she was not a "vegetable" or a "nonhuman entity," but a human being who still possessed a range of human qualities and capacities (Hentoff 1987).

Lincoln Park administrator Jeryl Turco took out a newspaper advertisement appealing to the community and medical staff to reconnect Nancy's feeding tube. Turco used the expressions "human being," "patient," "citizen," "fellow human being," and "innocent, helpless vulnerable member" in her references to Jobes. She insisted that Nancy's demonstrable capacity to respond to both loving care and painful stimuli indicated "not the description of a vegetable but a human being who is deserving of food and water as you and I" (Turco 1987).

Portrayals of persons with disabilities as worthwhile human beings present a strong challenge to the longstanding depictions of them as functionless "objects." An article in *Newsweek* (March 28, 1988) entitled "Waking Sleeping Souls" features Down's syndrome children operating computers and participating in team sports. Such individuals, concluded the authors of this article, "are, literally, expanding our definition of who is human" (pp. 70–71).

What a striking contrast this is to the pervasive characterizations of individuals with Down's syndrome—like those with other types of mental and physical handicaps—as hopelessly retarded, subhuman entities destined for a lifetime of institutionalization!

A moving reaction against the depiction of patients on respirators as some kind of irreparable appliances that need to be unplugged was expressed by comedian Sal Richards on the *Sally Jessy Raphael* television talk show on March 10, 1989. Richards revealed that a doctor asked him if he wanted the plug pulled on his 20-year-old son, Sal Jr., who had lapsed into a coma. Despite the severity of his son's condition, Richards told the doctor that Sal Jr. was a human being to be cherished and cared for, and not a badly damaged object to be thrown away: "What plug? My son isn't a machine, he isn't electric, he's not an appliance, you don't pull the plug; you pull the plug on an appliance to shut it off."[1]

The Female Half of the Human Race

During the Renaissance (roughly the period from the 1400s to the 1600s), exalted portrayals of women were invoked as antidotes to the widespread images of females as "inferior beings," "plagues," and "wild animals." Holy Scripture served as a primary source for calling attention to the equality, nobility, humanity, spirituality, and worth of women.

According to an analysis of these highly positive perceptions by Katherine Usher Henderson and Barbara F. McManus in *Half Humankind* (1985), biblical evidence was often quoted to demonstrate a special, close relationship between women and God:

> God sent children to many women past the childbear-
> ing age who longed for them. The New Testament
> abounds with women who were greatly loved by God
> and who returned a deep devotion to Him: Elizabeth,
> Anna, Martha, and Mary Magdalene, among many oth-
> ers. Old Testament heroines Judith, Deborah, and
> Esther performed heroic feats by the grace of God. All
> of these instances of God's favor toward individual
> women serve to suggest the moral and spiritual worth
> of women in general. (p. 49)

In *Esther Hath Hanged Haman* (1617), Esther Sowernan defended "the worthiness and worth of women both in respect of their Creation as in the work of Redemption" and as "gracious instruments to derive God's blessings and benefits to mankind." "You are women," she declared, "in Creation, noble; in Redemption, gracious; in use, most blessed" (ibid., 219–20). In another pamphlet, also published in 1617, Constantia Munda wrote that God created women "to be the consumma-tion of his blessed week's work, the end, crown, and perfec-tion of the never sufficiently glorified creation" (ibid., 103–4).

Those who spearheaded the movement to obtain legal rights for women during the eighteenth and nineteenth cen-turies repeatedly emphasized the principle that females were authentic and equal members of the human community. Mary Wollstonecraft's *The Vindication of the Rights of Women* (1792) argued that women were made to feel inferior due to an oppressive social and legal structure that severely limited their rights. She called for opening up increased institutional oppor-tunities for women and insisted upon "JUSTICE for one half of the human race" (1967, 20). In *The Subjection of Women* (1869), philosopher John Stuart Mill refuted the theory of female inferiority and maintained that the granting of equal rights to women was a matter of basic justice since women, like men, are members of the same human race. His book is replete with depictions of women as "human beings," "half of the human race," and "human fellow-creatures" (pp. 78, 91, 95, 149, 182, 187–88).

Women have taken a leading role in actively opposing the flood of pornographic materials polluting contemporary society by demonstrating the profoundly damaging impact they have on the humanity of females. Anti-pornography activists rely on a potent weapon: the insistence that women are worthwhile human beings who will not tolerate the extreme misogynistic propaganda aimed at reducing them to degrading objects. Writer Beverly LaBelle refers to pornography as "the propaganda of misogyny." "As women," she stresses, "we must destroy the pornographic image in order to be seen and treated as full human beings."[2]

Defenders of female humanity and dignity also emphasize a spiritual component—the woman's soul—in their battle against pornography. Thus the staple of pornography—reduction of women to dehumanized objects of exploitation and violence— is viewed as not only profaning the body, but desecrating the soul as well. In the words of author Adrienne Rich, the essence of pornography involves "objectification, which increasingly includes cruelty, violence against women and children, the crushing out of the soul."[3]

The Human and Transcendental Nature of Nazi Victims

During the darkest years of the Nazi era when millions suffered grievously from the calamitous effects of dehumanizing rhetoric, some voices continued to uphold the innate value of the victims.

On August 3, 1941, in the Cathedral of Saint Lambert, Count Clemens August von Galen, the Catholic Bishop of Munster, spoke out against the Nazi extermination of mentally ill and handicapped patients. His powerful sermon countered the notion of these victims as expendable objects and animals not deserving of life with characterizations of them as human beings possessing inestimable value:

No, it is not for reasons of this kind [the commission of serious crimes] that these unhappy patients are to be killed: it is simply because in the opinion of some doctor, in the view of some committee, they are "unworthy to live" . . . and that they are like old machines which can no longer work, like an old horse which has become incurably lame or like a cow which can no longer give any milk. . . .

We are not here dealing with machines or horses or cows. . . . We are speaking here of human beings, of our neighbours, our brothers and sisters, poor people and invalids (1943, 43–45).

Nazi Germany provided an even less favorable climate for the expression of sentiments on behalf of Jews. And yet they could be heard throughout the Third Reich.

In the fall of 1942, the White Rose, a small group of German university students dedicated to overthrowing the Nazi regime, disseminated a series of anti-Nazi leaflets, one of which called the killing of Jews "the most frightful crime against human dignity, a crime that is unparalleled in the whole of history." The leaflet stressed that "Jews, too, are human beings . . . and a crime of this dimension has been perpetrated against human beings" (Scholl 1983, 78).

An uncompromising pastoral letter strongly protesting the persecution of Jews issued by Archbishop Jules-Gerard Saliege of Toulouse focused on a personalized depiction of the Jewish people:

Jews are men and women. . . . It is just as criminal to use violence against these men and women, these fathers and mothers with families, as it is against anyone else. They too are members of the human race. They are our brothers like so many others. A Christian cannot forget that. (Hallie 1979, 187)

Bolstered by the example of the biblical Good Samaritan who considered everyone his neighbor, Pastor Andre Trocme and the people of the village of Le Chambon saved the lives of many Jewish refugees during the Nazi occupation of France. In sermon after sermon, Pastor Trocme and his assistant, Pastor Edouard Theis, stressed the importance of cherishing "the preciousness of all human life," Jew and non-Jew alike. When Trocme was accused of disrupting national harmony by hiding Jews, he replied: "It cannot be a question of national harmony when our brothers are threatened with deportation." His rescue activities were guided by the principle that "it is evil to deliver a brother who has entrusted himself to us" (ibid., 85, 103–4, 183).

The Corrie Ten Boom family hid Jews in their home during the Nazi occupation of Holland. When a Jewish woman asked for help, Corrie's father responded: "In this household, God's people are always welcome." On another occasion, he greeted a Jewish man who had come for refuge with the salutation—"A Brother of the Chosen People!" (Ten Boom with Sherrill and Sherill 1971, 78, 101).

Most of the Ten Boom family lost their lives at the hands of the Nazis. Many other families who tried to aid the Jews also perished in the Nazi death camps. Some survived, like Corrie, to tell the story of the abiding love of non-Jews for "God's chosen people."

People of the Soviet Union

Aleksandr Solzhenitsyn and Andrei Sakharov, prominent critics of human rights violations perpetrated when the Soviet system of tyranny dominated Russia and other countries under the yoke of Communist oppression, repeatedly stressed the humanity and inherent dignity of the victims and openly protested their horrendous treatment at the hands of the Soviet government.

Solzhenitsyn's most graphic accounts of the infinite value of every human life are incorporated in *The Gulag Archipelago*. He describes the Arctic death camp victims as "at least human beings, yes, human beings" and "thin strands of human lives" whose suffering and humanity cry out to be commemorated.

The expressions "a silent people, without a literary voice," "the innocent," "courageous people," "my new friends," "proud sons of Russia," "my own brothers," and "our own people" are among the phrases Solzhenitsyn utilizes in his efforts to retrieve from oblivion those relegated to the status of "enemies" and "unpersons" by the Soviet regime (1973–74, 1:549, 517, 24, 76, 95, 239, 549, 614).

Integration of the human and sacred levels constitutes one of Solzhenitsyn's central themes. He referred to fellow prisoners as "wise spiritual beings—*human beings*" and, in contrast to Bolshevik propagandists who equated the extermination of fifteen million peasants with eradicating a "parasite," Solzhenitsyn identified them as "Fifteen million souls. Fifteen million lives." Reflecting on the horrors of life in the Gulag, he observed that even in a prison cell, "your soul would heal." In the second part of volume 2 of *The Gulag Archipelago,* entitled "The Soul and Barbed Wire," Solzhenitsyn concludes: "The meaning of earthly existence lies not, as we have grown used to thinking, in prospering, but . . . in the development of the soul" (ibid., 1:184; 3:350; 1:183; 2:613).

Andrei Sakharov, a physicist and leader in the development of the Soviet hydrogen bomb, forged a far-reaching nomenclature of human rights infused with the designations "humanity," "mankind," "human being," "human life," "peoples," "citizens," "brotherhood," "human personality," and "the innocent." He began his defense of human rights by opposing the Soviet testing of nuclear weapons. In 1968 he wrote that the cessation of testing would prevent the needless "sacrifice of human life" and "would directly preserve the life of hundreds of thousands of people" (Dornan 1975, 360–61).

Although Sakharov invoked, for the most part, humanistic terminology in spotlighting the predicament of oppressed people, he was not unmindful of the importance of the spiritual nature of existence. He often included the concepts "spiritual culture," "spiritual regeneration," and "the soul" in his writing and speeches. His "Postscript to Memorandum" (1972) pointed to a drastic need for "the country's spiritual regeneration." He characterized "the persecution and destruction of religion, which has been carried on with perseverance and cruelty for decades," as "one of the most serious infringements of the rights of man in our country" and described "freedom of religious belief" as "an integral part of intellectual freedom as a whole" (1974, 154, 156).

Some of those who continued Solzhenitsyn and Sakharov's legacy of humanizing the victims of Soviet tyranny had once been oppressors themselves. A Communist Party activist who had participated in the forced collectivization of agriculture reflects on how she came to the realization that those she persecuted were human beings: "What I said to myself at the time was 'They are not human beings, they are kulaks'. . . . But that is a lie. They are people! They are human beings!" (Grossman 1972, 144).

The Inestimable Value of Black Americans

The American anti-slavery movement built its case for freeing black people on a vocabulary of respect and esteem. Its beginnings can be traced back to 1688 when a group of Quakers in Germantown, Pennsylvania, declared that "the traffick of men-body" represented sinful assaults on human liberty and divine law.[4] A petition "for the state of liberty" submitted to the New Hampshire legislature on November 12, 1779, by nineteen slaves was based on the premise "that the *God* of nature gave them life and freedom, upon the terms of the most perfect equality with other men."[5]

The American abolitionist challenge to slavery during the nineteenth century was based on the definition of blacks as human beings and children of God who were entitled to the same freedom and protection enjoyed by others. William Lloyd Garrison called for "the immediate enfranchisement of our slave population" because of "the 'self-evident truth' maintained in the American Declaration of Independence, 'that all men are created equal, and endowed by their Creator with certain inalienable rights—among which are life, liberty and the pursuit of happiness'" (Garrison and Garrison 1885, 1:225). Angelina Grimke affirmed that "man cannot rightfully hold his fellow man as property" (1972, 59).

Frederick Douglass, a former slave who became one of the outstanding orators, writers, editors, and organizers in America during the nineteenth century, persistently high-lighted the human nature of fellow blacks in his untiring efforts to free them from bondage. "Under the skin," he declared, "we are all the same and every one of us must join in the fight to further human brotherhood." After purchasing his freedom in Europe in 1847, he stated: "I came as a slave; I go back as a free man. I came here a thing—I go back a human being." From that time on, Douglass decided, "wherever I go, I shall go as a man, and not as a slave . . . firmly and con-stantly endeavoring to assert my equal right as a man and a brother" (Foner 1968, 7, 20).

The Nobility of Native Americans

Within the maelstrom of degrading images that helped sustain the barbaric and treacherous actions taken against Indians throughout the nineteenth century—a period dubbed *A Century of Dishonor* (1881) by author Helen Hunt Jackson—influential voices could still be heard depicting Native Americans as legitimate members of the human com-munity whose rights and lives should be respected and safeguarded.

Henry Benjamin Whipple, the first Episcopalian Bishop (appointed in 1859) of the frontier diocese of Minnesota and widely known as the "apostle to the Indians," referred to Native Americans as "red Brethren," "human beings," and "intelligent creatures of God." "It was God our Father," he recalled, "who gave them those wonderful intuitions, those marvellous instincts, that true unwavering love" (1899, 90, 158, 317).

Lydia Maria Child's *An Appeal for the Indians* (1868) is founded on references to America's original inhabitants as "human beings," "members of the human family," and "red brethren" (pp. 8, 10, 14–15).

During the twentieth century, Indians have been increasingly characterized as honest, strong, reflective, and respectful people closely integrated with God, nature, and their surroundings.

John Collier, an influential United States Commissioner of Indian Affairs who served from 1933 to 1945, wrote extensively about the capabilities and humanity of Indians. In 1942 he emphasized that "the Indian has demonstrated, in the four centuries since Columbus, a capacity for every technological and social adaptation for which the rapidly changing European-influenced world has called" and concluded that "the Indian lives now in spirit as in flesh, one of the great races" (1942, 4, 10). Five years later Collier concentrated on the Native American's ancient "reverence and passion" for "human personality" and for "the earth and its web of life" (1947, 15, 17).

The 1960s, an era when the civil rights movement in the United States had become an effective instrument for advancing legislation in support of black people, also proved to be an auspicious decade for bringing to public awareness the long overdue need to rectify the deplorable plight of many Indians. A significant component of contemporary Indian activism underscores the need to communicate the humanity and profound spirituality of Native Americans. At a symposium on Indian education in June 1968, Joshua Wetsit, an Assiniboine Indian, talked about his people as being prayerful individuals who continually give thanks to "the Great Spirit for the Mother Earth." He recalled how his father "never neglected his thanks early in the morning" and at noon "gave thanks to the Great Spirit and asked to be blessed. Then again when the sun was going down" (Morey 1970, 48).

History's Most Priceless Possession: Children

In the midst of a pagan world where unwanted children were viewed as "inferior, subhuman entities" that could be disposed of at will, the early Christian Fathers argued that all human beings, particularly the youngest and most defenseless, were of inestimable value because they too were created in the image and likeness of God. George H. Payne's *The Child in History* (1916) highlights the indispensable role played by the Christian Church in forging revolutionary, human-divine images of the most vulnerable lives, especially those of children:

Its impassioned preachers and apostles vaunted the humanity of their new faith; for cast-out infants and the despised slaves the new priests fought such a battle of perseverance and martyrdom as the world had never seen before.

In the name of their new God, Jesus . . . they took all the truth there was in the aristocratic philosophy of the Romans and their emperors, and made it live indeed— they applied it to the lowest, and the most humble— even to children. "Nothing human is alien"—this was a verity in the lives of the men who fought the first battles of Christianity.

Every human being had a soul—that was a vital point in their fight. They asserted that children had souls, to which religious doctrine probably more is due in the way of checking the practice of infanticide than any other single idea. . . . The Fathers won the battle in that they convinced the Roman world that children had souls. (pp. 263–64)

John Boswell's history of child abandonment from the third to the eighteenth century, *The Kindness of Strangers* (1988), reveals that parents who abandoned their offspring did so largely in desperation: due to dire circumstances such as extreme poverty, famine, wars, social tumult, and other catastrophic events. Most of these parents exhibited a strong attachment to their children and viewed abandonment as "the first step in a large, informal adoption process. . . . They imagined that the children would be found by a loving couple and brought up." In many cases this is what happened. "The 'kindness of strangers' in every age," Boswell found, "seems to have been sufficient to rescue most abandoned children." These strangers were motivated by perceptions of infants as valuable human beings who deserved the best of care and protection. The esteem in which the *alumni* (rescued children) were held by those who found and reared them is embodied in the numerous terms of endearment still extant in inscriptions commemorating their deaths—"to the *alumnus* whom he always loved as his son"; "whom I love as my own daughter"; "For you, Claudius, Happily-Found, our *alumnus,* your family."[6]

In the heyday of the industrial revolutions in England and the United States—when widespread neglect, abandonment, cruelty, and exploitation were the lot of children looked upon as "beasts of burden" and "refuse"—various reformers, humanitarians, and child-saving organizations exposed the barbaric conditions under which these children lived and presented a contrasting image of them as worthwhile human beings who needed love and protection.

In 1861 Mary Carpenter, a leading advocate of education for England's poor and neglected children, countered the widespread view of these youngsters as "the dregs of the population" with a portrayal of them as "in reality immortal beings, children of one Father and heirs with Christ of eternal life!" (Housdan 1956, 75–76).

The Children's Aid Society of New York was founded in 1853 on a view of destitute and vagrant children as "the little ones of Christ" (Bremner 1970, 743). At the annual meeting of the National Conference of Charities and Corrections in 1882 Eldridge T. Gerry, president of the New York Society for the Prevention of Cruelty to Children, emphasized that laws for the protection of children were based on the principle "that man himself is but a reflection of the image of his maker, that the purity of the little child is the most beautiful type of the purity of God himself" (1974, 128).

Postscript
Thinking the Unthinkable: The Prospects for Expanding the Boundaries of Humanity

What is self-evident and beyond dispute today—the intrinsic humanity and worth of various groups—was not so apparent in times past. It was once considered unthinkable to grant legal rights to Native Americans, African Americans, Soviet people, European Jews, women, and children. These and other victims were defined as members of an "inferior race" or reduced to the subhuman level of "animals," "parasites," "diseases," "inanimate objects," "waste products," and "nonpersons." Imposition of the same degrading terminology makes it equally unthinkable in the view of many in contemporary society to safeguard other human lives such as the unwanted unborn, people with severe disabilities, and the seriously afflicted elderly.

Thinking the unthinkable—the conferral of basic protections onto individuals and groups previously deemed outside the pale of human empathy and the human community—requires an expansive moral vision, one involving a major transformation in language and awareness. This means a growing openness to the humanity and value of those obscured by and buried underneath the avalanche of disparaging designations.

Consciousness-Raising

Thinking the unthinkable will eventually necessitate at least four steps in increased awareness and action:

1. The veracity of the degrading expressions imposed on today's vulnerable individuals inside and outside the womb must be persistently challenged and refuted. Ample sources can be cited to expose the rank duplicity and outlandish absurdity of the derogatory terminology. A *California Medicine* editorial of 1970 acknowledges that a form of pathological lying called semantic gymnastics is an essential linguistic strategy for dehumanizing individuals before and after birth in order to promote abortion and euthanasia. Developments in the field of fetology comprise another invaluable basis for discrediting the demeaning images constructed of the unborn. Each time preborn humans become the recipients of medical treatment formerly confined to those after birth, a spotlight of increasing intensity is focused on the humanity of prenatal life. Such portrayals can serve as a powerful antidote to the depersonalized, anachronistic stereotypes of the unborn manufactured by members of the abortion culture.

2. Contemporary perpetrators and their proponents must be faced with the disturbing reality that the words they are using against the unwanted unborn and born are, in many instances, the *exact same words* employed to revile some of history's most victimized groups. These revelations furnish an indispensable historical perspective for understanding the horrendous nature of today's pejorative expressions—not only are they appalling in their own right, but they also share an uncomfortably close kinship with the most violence-inducing concepts from times past.

3. The public needs to become more conversant with how malevolent words lead to violent deeds. Never has the oft-repeated observation that words have consequences been more strikingly prevalent than in the full-scale war of words directed against today's most defenseless victims. Unborn children, women, infants with disabilities, the debilitated elderly, and those dependent for survival

on respirators and feeding tubes are among the most prominent targets of the semantic onslaught.

4. The lexicon of dehumanization needs to be replaced by a nomenclature featuring life-affirming and exalted portrayals of all human beings despite their status, condition, stage of development, gender, race, age, or place of residence. It is imperative to highlight how closely the positive images called upon to counter contemporary victimization resemble the worth-conferring language so successfully invoked to overturn the degrading rhetoric of the past. As such, these personalized portrayals draw their inspiration and strength from a powerful, longstanding legacy of semantic humanization and divinization.

A Titanic Struggle

Despite the capacity of reality and life-affirming language to counteract the juggernaut of dehumanization, disparaging terminology is still undermining the most significant advances made on behalf of society's most vulnerable citizens. Images of the preborn as authentic human beings and patients in need of humane treatment are continually thwarted by portrayals of human life before birth as "nonhuman," "a parasite," "property" of the woman's body, "waste products," and "nonpersons." Stereotypes of people with disabilities as worthwhile human beings deserving esteem and opportunities for optimal development are seriously eroded by definitions of the handicapped as "inferior," "vegetative," and "parasitic" lives not worth living. Depictions of women as equal members of the human race entitled to basic dignity and respect are repeatedly subverted by characterizations of females as an "inferior" species, "property" of the male, and prime "objects" for sexploitation and violence.

The major transformation of language necessary to bring about a magnanimous environment is a task of monumental proportions fraught with numerous obstacles. In all too many circumstances, the ultimate triumph of linguistic corruption—an inability to distinguish truth from error and the belief that the prevailing lies are undisputed facts—has been achieved. Even in situations where the reality (humanity of the victims) is so compelling that it contradicts the distorted semantic versions (subhumanity of the victims), it is the rhetorical fabrications that are often victorious. The endlessly repeated falsehoods thus have become so deeply ingrained in the public mindset that they remain impervious to any facts or evidence to the contrary, no matter how persuasive.

Unfortunately, too few people seem capable of or interested in reflecting upon the sinister nature of linguistic oppression, especially when it is disseminated by highly respected individuals and institutions. Name-calling is a two-edged sword afflicting victims and perpetrators alike. This is particularly the case regarding the widespread acceptance of abortion. Dehumanizing designations have resulted in millions of people becoming completely oblivious to the plight of the unborn in abortion. This posture of massive desensitization to large-scale violence in utero constitutes an alarming tragedy of far-reaching ramifications.

Disparaging rhetoric constitutes one of the most devastating forces of any era. In today's world where style so often passes for substance and pervasive slogans overwhelm reason and reality, it will take a persistent, herculean effort to overcome the awesome power of semantics to corrupt thought, undermine truth, and transform unwanted human beings into dangerous, despicable, insignificant, or totally worthless entities.

Toward an Expansive Definition of Humanity

The outlook for expanding the boundaries of the human community is simultaneously bleak and hopeful. The wholesale consignment of unwanted human beings before and after birth to a less-than-human status will make it exceedingly difficult to create a humane social order in which all people are respected and protected. On the other hand, every time the labels "human," "person," and "God's people" are conferred on a group previously denied such worth-endowing identities, the prospects are enhanced for recognizing the intrinsic value of other groups currently existing outside the recognized orbit of the human race.

The omnipresence of violence today—rape, wife beating, child abuse, genocide, enslavement, abortion, fetal experimentation, infanticide, and euthanasia—will never end or even diminish until its victims are at least recognized as members of the human family.

A growing awareness of how the verbal pollution of the past continues to contaminate the present will not alone halt the extensive oppression. Neither will an increase in positive, exalted, and life-affirming terminology. These, nonetheless, comprise essential steps toward the indispensable goal of protecting the lives of today's most defenseless victims.

A titanic struggle continues to be waged between two sharply contrasting versions of who is entitled to membership in the human community: one highly restrictive and the other greatly expansive. The condition of mankind in the future— whether it be primarily one of war or peace, enslavement or freedom, hatred or love, degradation or respect, discrimination or equality, annihilation or survival—will be largely contingent upon which of the opposing images prevails. The corrosive movement to define more and more individuals out of the human race in order to justify their oppression must be seen for what it really is—a severely constricted notion of the human community. An urgent need exists to foster an entirely different vision of the human family, one which is expansive rather than restrictive, democratic instead of elitist; a universe of humanity broad and generous enough to include the unborn as well as the born, the disabled as well as those without disabilities, the old as well as the young, women as well as men, people of color as well as Caucasians.

Human rights defenders of the past toiled for long periods of time—often against overwhelming odds—in their drive to widen the definition of humanity. It took centuries before much of their effort bore fruit. Such indomitable perseverance bequeathes a model of determination for those today who are likewise faced with enormous roadblocks in attempting to expand the boundaries of the human community. Contemporary proponents of an enlarged definition of the human race can derive strengthened resolve from the fact that their efforts continue a longstanding tradition of human rights advocacy on behalf of society's most vulnerable individuals.

Notes

Introduction

1. For an account of "the big lie" psychology, see the chapter on "War Propaganda" in Hitler 1971, 176–86.

2. "A New Ethic for Medicine and Society," *California Medicine* 113 (September 1970): 68.

3. Extensive accounts of the "Great Chain of Being" and its dehumanizing impact can be found in Jordan 1968, 219–39, 154, 304–5, 308, 482–511, and in Mosse 1978, 4–5, 7, 9, 14–15, 33.

4. Woodward 1992, 55; Leo 1990, 17; see also the series of articles on abortion in Shaw 1990.

Chapter 1

1. *The People of the State of California v. William Baxter Waddill, Jr.* Transcript of Preliminary Examination in the Municipal Court of the West Orange County Judicial District, State of California, Case N. 77W2085, 18 April 1977, 39–40.

2. A huge proportion of abortions today are performed, not because the woman's life or health is endangered by the pregnancy, but because of feminist ideology (i.e., reproductive freedom, the right to choose, etc.) or social and economic factors. This situation of abortion on demand for all nine months of pregnancy was made possible by the United States Supreme Court's *Roe v. Wade* and *Doe v. Bolton* decisions of 1973 which put forth an exceedingly broad definition of maternal health for justifying abortion even in the last trimester of pregnancy. See Associate Justice Harry Blackmun's pronouncements on this in *Doe v. Bolton,* 410 U.S. 192 (1973).

Chapter 2

1. "Parents Bar Surgery and Lose Son's Custody," *New York Times,* 9 August 1981, 21.

2. *Who Should Survive?* A film produced by the Guggenheim and Joseph P. Kennedy, Jr. Foundation, 1971. For an extensive analysis of the "Johns Hopkins Hospital Case" recreated in this film see Gustafson 1973, 529–57.

Chapter 3

1. "Wife-Beating Declines," *USA Today Newsview,* April 1986, 6.

2. For an analysis of how the "war against women" has become embedded on the cultural and institutional levels, see French 1992. An account of "femicide, the misogynous killing of women by men," and its association with patriarchal dominance, racism, the mass media, pornography, and the legal system, can be found in Radford and Russell 1992.

Chapter 4

1. Nuernberg Military Tribunals, *Trials of War Criminals,* 15 vols. (Washington, D.C.: U.S. Government Printing Office, 1945–47), 1:228–30, 236.

Chapter 5

1. "Soviet Newspaper Puts Death Toll from Stalin at 20 Million," *St. Louis Post-Dispatch,* 5 February 1989, 9A.

Chapter 6

1. *American Slavery As It Is: Testimony of a Thousand Witnesses* (1839; reprint, New York: Arno Press and The New York Times, 1968), 9.

2. *The Suppressed Book About Slavery* (1864; reprint, New York: Arno Press and The New York Times, 1968), 338–39.

3. A table summarizing the number of lynchings by year and race from 1882 to 1968 is included in Zangrando 1980, 6–7.

Chapter 7

1. Hoig 1961, 154, 162. For a fuller account of this positive press response, see *The Rocky Mountain News,* 17 December 1864.

Chapter 8

1. *Roe v. Wade,* 410 U.S. 159 (1973).

2. *Doe v. Bolton,* 410 U.S. 192 (1973).

3. "Declaratory Judgment in the Matter of the Treatment and Care of Infant Doe," Judge John G. Baker, Monroe County Circuit Court, 12 April 1982; also quoted in Manney and Blattner 1984, 4.

4. "Care for Retarded in Dispute on Coast," *New York Times,* 26 November 1978, 38.

5. "Eugenics in Germany," *Journal of the American Medical Association* 101 (July 22, 1933): 295.

6. Nuernberg Military Tribunals, *Trials of War Criminals,* 15 vols. (Washington, D.C.: U.S. Government Printing Office, 1945–47), 1:58.

7. *Dred Scott v. Sanford,* 19 Howard 404 (1857).

Chapter 9

1. "A Moral Paradox: Abortion and the Freeze," *Nightline,* Transcript # 712, 31 January 1984, 9–10.

2. Deposition of Carolyn V. Brown, M.D., in the Superior Court for the State of Alaska, Third Judicial District at Anchorage, 28 February 1983, 153–54.

3. In the Matter of Nancy Ellen Jobes, Stenographic Transcript of Proceedings, Superior Court of Morris County: Chancery Division, Morris County, Docket No. C–1971–85E, Morris County Courthouse, Morristown, New Jersey, 25 March 1986, 117, 113, 158; 24 March 1986, 124–25, 157.

4. Diana E. H. Russell with Laura Lederer, "Questions We Get Asked Most Often," in Lederer 1980, 24.

5. *Congressional Globe,* 27th Cong., 2nd sess., Appendix, vol. 11, 12 June 1842, 503.

Chapter 10

1. "Abortion Controversy—The Silent Scream,'" *Nightline* Transcript # 972, 12 February 1985, 3.

2. "The Facts Speak Louder: Planned Parenthood's Critique of 'The Silent Scream'" (Paper, 1985), 2–3.

3. Conversations with and material furnished by Dr. Judith A. Reisman. For an extensive account of cartoons depicting sex between wives and animals and other forms of sexual debasement, see the three-volume report in Reisman 1987. This research was sponsored by the Office of Juvenile Justice and Delinquency Prevention (OJJDP), United States Department of Justice, Project No. 84–JN–AX-K007, and conducted at The American University, Washington, D.C., from February 1984 to November 1985.

4. Jackson to Graham, 16 December 1817, U.S. Congress, *American State Papers, Indian Affairs,* 2 vols. (Washington, D.C., 1832–61), 2:162.

Chapter 11

1. Interview with Janine Thomas (pseudonym), intensive care nurse, 27 May 1989.

2. "Shall This Child Die?" *Newsweek,* 12 November 1973, 70.

3. "The Jew as Global Parasite," in *The Holocaust: Selected Documents in Eighteen Volumes, 4. Propaganda and Aryanization,* 1938–1944, ed. John Mendelsohn (New York and London: Garland Publishing, 1982), 86–89.

4. Interview with Janine Thomas.

Chapter 12

1. Terri L. Dasenbrock, "The World of the Handicapped Through the Eyes of a Symbolic Interactionist." (Paper submitted for graduate course credit, St. Louis University School of Social Service, St. Louis, Missouri, 12 December 1988), 5.

2. Hesiod, *Theogony,* trans. Norman O. Brown (Indianapolis: Bobbs-Merrill, 1953), 70.

3. See Lenin 1960–70, 17:346, 18:432, 24:54, 27:36–40. "Liquidationism" refers to a tendency among the Bolsheviks to disband their party; "otzovism" to a trend advocating withdrawing from all forms of legal work, and in particular from the Russian Duma (parliament); "ultimatumism" to the view that the Bolsheviks should continue working in the Duma only if its officials accepted certain demands that Lenin considered unattainable; and "defencism" to the position holding that workers should unite with the bourgeoisie and defend their countries in time of war, rather than uniting with workers in other countries and working for revolution.

Chapter 13

1. "Transplantation of Neural Tissue from Fetuses," *Science* 235 (13 March 1987): 1307–8; "Panel Backs Transplants of Aborted Fetuses' Tissue," *St. Louis Post-Dispatch,* 14 March 1987, 6A.

2. Nuernberg Military Tribunals, *Trials of War Criminals,* 15 vols. (Washington, D.C.: U.S. Government Printing Office, 1945–47), 1:142.

3. "Men Tell Why They Batter," *Donahue,* Transcript #2777, 19 September 1989, 4.

4. *Dred Scott v. Sanford,* 19 Howard 393 (1857).

5. Ibid., 411, 451.

Chapter 14

1. "Forum: Ethics in Embryo," *Harper's Magazine,* September 1987, 38.

2. Interview with Janine Thomas (pseudonym), intensive care nurse, 27 May 1989.

3. "William Fitzhugh Enlarges His Holdings," in Rose 1976, 40.

Chapter 15

1. *Roe v. Wade,* 410 U.S. 162 (1973).

2. See, for example, Walters 1992, vol. 6, no. 1:12–22; Goodman 1988; Scott 1988; "The Problem of Person-hood: Biomedical, Social, Legal, and Policy Views," Special Issue, *Millbank Memorial Fund Quarterly* 61 (1983): 1–147; Tauer 1985, 10:253–66; and Macklin 1983, 61:35–57.

3. Cited in *Commonwealth v. Welosky,* 177 *North Eastern Reporter* 660 (1931).

4. "1984 Revisited," a CBS television special, narrated by Walter Cronkite, 7 June 1983.

5. *Dred Scott v. Sanford,* 19 Howard 404 (1857).

6. *Bailey & als. v. Poindexter's Ex'or,* 14 Grattan 432 (1858).

7. *Tucker v. Alexandroff,* 183 U.S. 424 (1901).

8. *Santa Clara County v. Southern Pac. R. R.,* 118 U. S. 394 (1886).

9. *Sierra Club v. Morton,* 405 U.S. 742 (1972).

10. *Doe v. Bolton,* 410 U.S. 220 (1973).

Chapter 16

1. "A New Ethic for Medicine and Society," *California Medicine* 113 (September 1970): 68.

2. *Roe v. Wade,* 410 U.S. 159 (1973).

3. "Technological Advances to Make Pro-Abortion Tougher, Planned Parenthood Official Tells National Abortion Federation," *National Right to Life News,* 14 October 1982, 8.

4. "Shall This Child Die?" *Newsweek,* 12 November 1973, 70.

5. "Life and Death Decisions," *Newsweek,* 3 December 1973, 12.

Chapter 17

1. "Declaratory Judgment in the Matter of the Treatment and Care of Infant Doe," Judge John G. Baker, Monroe County Circuit Court, 12 April 1982; also quoted in Manney and Blattner 1984, 4; Lyon 1985, 31; Andrusko 1985, 36–7.

2. Nuremberg Military Tribunals, *Trials of War Criminals,* 15 vols. (Washington, D.C.: U.S. Government Printing Office, 1945–1947), 1:810, 827.

3. "Coping with Abortion: Six Panelists Compare Their Convictions, Experiences, and Predictions," *Mademoiselle,* October 1967, 173, 216.

4. In the Matter of Nancy Ellen Jobes, Stenographic Transcript of Proceedings, Superior Court of Morris County: Chancery Division, Morris County, Docket No. C-1971-85E, Morris County Courthouse, Morristown, New Jersey, 25 March 1986, 117; 24 March 1986, 124, 157.

5. Gibbs 1989, 20–21; "Rape of Jogger in Park Aggravates New York's Racial Tension," *St. Louis Post-Dispatch,* 30 April 1989, 6A.

6. Kibel 1972, 131; "Abortion Controversy—'The Silent Scream,'" *Nightline,* Transcript #972, 12 February 1985, 3.

7. Interview with Janine Thomas (pseudonym), intensive care nurse, 27 May 1989.

8. "The Jew As Global Parasite," in Mendelsohn 1982, 86–89.

9. "Recommended Standards for Abortion Services," *American Journal of Public Health* 61 (February 1971): 396–98.

10. Morgan 1980, 139. For more recent examples of the growing literature documenting the pernicious effects of degrading pornographic images of women, see Berger, Searles, and Cottle 1991; and Russell 1993.

11. *Dred Scott v. Sanford,* 19 Howard 407 (1857).

12. "Forum: Ethics in Embryo," *Harper's Magazine,* September 1987, 38.

13. "William Fitzhugh Enlarges His Holdings," in Rose 1976, 40.

14. *Roe v. Wade,* 410 U.S. 158 (1973).

15. "Excerpts From the Justices' Decision in the Pennsylvania Case," *New York Times,* 30 June 1992, A8.

16. *Nairn v. University of St. Andrews* (1909), cited in *Commonwealth v. Welosky, North Eastern Reporter* 177 (1931): 660.

17. *Dred Scott v. Sanford,* 19 Howard 404 (1857).

18. *Bailey & als. v. Poindexter's Ex'or,* 14 Grattan 432 (1858).

Chapter 18

1. "They Thought I Was Dead . . . Until I Woke Up," *Sally Jessy Raphael,* Transcript #135, 10 March 1989, 9.

2. Beverly LaBelle, "Snuff—The Ultimate in Woman-Hating," in Lederer 1980, 178.

3. Adrienne Rich, "Afterword," in Lederer 1980, 314.

4. "Germantown Friends' Protest Against Slavery, 1688," in Bruns 1977, 3.

5. "Petition of New Hampshire Slaves, November 12, 1779," in Bruns 1977, 452.

6. "The Unwanted Children of Times Past," *U.S. News & World Report,* 1 May 1989, 62; Boswell 1988, 429, 120–21.

References

Adamic, Louis. 1936. *Cradle of Life: The Story of One Man's Beginnings.* New York: Harper & Brothers.

Adams, Charles Francis, ed. 1874–77. *Memoirs of John Quincy Adams, Comprising Portions of His Diary from 1795 to 1848.* 12 vols. Philadelphia.

Allan, J. McGregor. 1869. "On the Real Differences in the Minds of Men and Women." *Journal of the Anthropological Society of London* 7:cxcv–ccxix.

Alexander, Leo. 1948. "War Crimes and Their Motivation: The Socio-Psychological Structure of the SS and the Criminalization of a Society." *Journal of Criminal Law and Criminology* 39 (September–October): 298–326.

———. 1949. "Medical Science Under Dictatorship." *The New England Journal of Medicine* 241 (14 July): 39–47.

Altman, Lawrence K. 1991. "Cell Channel Finding Earns Nobel Prize." *New York Times,* 8 October, C3.

American Fertility Society. 1984. "Ethical Statement on In Vitro Fertilization." *Fertility and Sterility* 41:12.

American Slavery As It Is: Testimony of a Thousand Witnesses. 1968. 1839. Reprint, New York: Arno Press and The New York Times.

Anderson, John O. 1984. *Cry of the Innocents: Abortion and the Race Towards Judgment.* South Plainfield, New Jersey: Bridge Publishing.

Andrews, Lori. 1986. "My Body, My Property." *Hastings Center Report* 16 (October): 28–38.

Andrist, Ralph K. 1964. *The Long Death: The Last Days of the Plains Indians.* New York: Macmillan.

Andrusko, Dave. 1985. "Abortion and Infanticide: America's Movement Away from Human Rights." *Lincoln Review* 5 (Winter): 31–39.

————. 1992. "Abortion-on-Demand Losing Proposition for Democrats." *National Right to Life News* (2 June): 13.

Arendt, Hannah. 1973. *The Origins of Totalitarianism*. New York: Harcourt Brace Jovanovich, A Harvest Book.

Ariel [Buckner H. Payne]. 1867. *The Negro: What Is His Ethnological Status?* Cincinnati, Ohio.

Aristotle. 1943. *Aristotle's Politics*. Translated by Benjamin Jowett. New York: Random House, Modern Library.

————. 1953. *Generation of Animals*. Translated by A. L. Peck. Rev. and reprinted ed. London: Heinemann; Cambridge, Mass.: Harvard University Press, Loeb Classical Library.

Aronsfeld, C. C. 1975. "The Nazi Design Was Extermination, Not Emigration." *Patterns of Prejudice* 9 (May–June): 20–24.

Aziz, Philippe. 1976. *Doctors of Death*. Translated by Edouard Bizub and Philip Haentzler. 4 vols. Geneva, Switzerland: Ferni.

Balikci, Asen. 1967. "Female Infanticide on the Arctic Coast." *Man* 2 (December): 615–25.

Ball, George H. 1981. "What Happens at Conception?" *Christianity and Crisis* 41, 19 October, 274, 286, 288.

Bannon, Anne. 1982. "The Case of the Bloomington Baby." *Human Life Review* 8 (Fall): 63–68.

Barnes, Robert. 1873. "Lumleian Lectures on the Convulsive Diseases of Women." *Lancet* (12 April): 513–16.

Barnett, Louise K. 1975. *The Ignoble Savage: American Literary Racism, 1790–1890*. Westport, Conn.: Greenwood Press.

Barr, Martin W. 1913. *Mental Defectives: Their History, Treatment and Training*. Philadelphia: P. Blakiston's Sons.

Barth, Karl. 1961. *Church Dogmatics: The Doctrine of Creation*. Translated by A. T. Mackay et al. Vol. 3. Edinburgh: T & T Clark.

Berg, Paul. 1973. "Battle Lines in a Moral and Legal Dispute." *Sunday Pictures—St. Louis Post-Dispatch,* 20 May, 1–15.

Berger, Ronald J., Patricia Searles, and Charles E. Cottle. 1991. *Feminism and Pornography.* New York: Praeger.

Berkhofer, Richard F. 1978. *The White Man's Indian: Images of the American Indian from Columbus to the Present.* New York: Alfred A. Knopf.

Binding, Karl, and Alfred Hoche. 1920. *Permitting the Destruction of Unworthy Life: Its Extent and Forms.* Translated by Walter E. Wright. Reprinted in *Issues in Law and Medicine* 18 (Fall 1992): 231–65.

Bird, Robert Montgomery. 1967. *Nick of the Woods or the Jibbenainosay.* Edited by Curtis Dahl. New Haven, Conn.: College & University Press.

Bonhoeffer, Dietrich. 1955. *Ethics.* New York: Macmillan.

Bopp, James. 1982. "The Death of Infant Doe." *National Right to Life News,* 20 May, 1, 8.

Borkin, Joseph. 1978. *The Crime and Punishment of I. G. Farben.* New York: Free Press.

Boswell, John. 1988. *The Kindness of Strangers: The Abandonment of Children in Western Europe from Late Antiquity to the Renaissance.* New York: Pantheon Books.

Bremner, Robert H., ed. 1970. *Children and Youth in America: A Documentary History, Volume I: 1600–1865.* Cambridge: Harvard University Press.

Breslow, Marvin A., ed. 1985. *The Political Writings of John Knox: The First Blast of the Trumpet Against the Monstrous Regiment of Women and Other Selected Works.* London and Toronto: Associated University Presses.

Brown, Dee. 1970. *Bury My Heart at Wounded Knee.* New York: Holt, Rinehart, and Winston.

Brown, Norman K., and Donavan J. Thompson. 1979. "Nontreatment of Fever in Extended-Care Facilities." *New England Journal of Medicine* 300 (31 May): 1246–50.

Brown, Sterling A. 1937. *The Negro in American Fiction.* Washington, D.C.: Associates in Negro Folk Education.

————. 1939. "American Race Problem as Reflected in American Literature." *Journal of Negro Education* 8 (July): 275–90.

Brown, William W. 1968. "Narrative of William W. Brown, A Fugitive Slave." In *Five Slave Narratives: A Compendium*. 1847. Reprint, New York: Arno Press and The New York Times.

Brownmiller, Susan. 1975. *Against Our Will: Men, Women and Rape*. New York: Simon and Schuster.

Bruns, Roger, ed. 1977. *Am I Not a Man and a Brother? The Antislavery Crusade of Revolutionary America, 1688–1788*. New York: Chelsea House.

Caldwell, Charles. 1830. *Thoughts on the Original Unity of the Human Race*. New York.

Callahan, Daniel. 1983. "On Feeding the Dying." *Hastings Center Report* 13 (October): 22.

Canfield, George F. 1881. "The Legal Position of the Indian." *American Law Review* 15 (January): 21–37.

"Care for Retarded in Dispute on Coast." 1978. *New York Times,* 26 November, 38.

Carroll, Charles. 1969. *"The Negro A Beast,"* or *"In the Image of God"*. 1900. Reprint, Miami: Mnemosyne Publishing Company.

Carroll, Lewis. 1872. *Through the Looking Glass and What Alice Found There*. London: Macmillan.

Carson, Rachel. 1962. *Silent Spring*. Boston: Houghton Mifflin.

Cartwright, Samuel A. 1851. "Diseases and Peculiarities of the Negro Race." *De Bow's Review* 11 (July): 65–66.

Cates, Willard, David A. Grimes, and Jack C. Smith. 1978. "Abortion as a Treatment for Unwanted Pregnancy: The Number Two Sexually-Transmitted Condition." *Advances in Planned Parenthood* 12, No. 3: 115–21.

Chartrand, Sabra. 1992. "Legal Definition of Death Is Questioned in Florida Infant Case." *New York Times,* 29 March, 12.

Child, Lydia Maria. 1868. *An Appeal for the Indians.* New York: William P. Tomlinson.

Cobbe, Frances Power. 1878. "Wife-Torture in England." *The Contemporary Review* (April): 55–87.

Collier, John. 1942. Introduction to *The Changing Indian.* Edited by Oliver Lafarge. Norman: University of Oklahoma Press.

———. 1947. *The Indians of the Americas.* New York: W. W. Norton.

Congressional Globe. 46 vols. Washington, D.C., 1834–73.

Conquest, Robert. 1978. *Kolyma: The Arctic Death Camps.* New York: Viking Press.

———. 1986. *The Harvest of Sorrow: Soviet Collectivization and the Terror-Famine.* New York: Oxford University Press.

———. 1990. *The Great Terror: A Reassessment.* New York: Oxford University Press.

Cook, Sherburne F. 1976. *The Conflict Between the California Indians and White Civilization.* Berkeley and Los Angeles: University of California Press.

Cooper, James Fenimore. 1951. *The Last of the Mohicans.* New York: Dodd, Meade & Company.

———. 1888. *The Redskins; or, Indian and Injin.* Chicago and New York: Belford, Clarke & Co.

"Coping with Abortion: Six Panelists Compare Their Convictions, Experiences, and Predictions." 1967. *Mademoiselle,* October, 172–73, 211–16.

Culver, Charles M., K. Danner Clouser, Bernard Gert, Howard Brody, John Fletcher, Albert Jonsen, Loretta Kopelman, Joanne Lynn, Mark Siegler, and Daniel Wikler. 1985. "Special Report: Basic Curricular Goals in Medical Ethics." *New England Journal of Medicine* 312 (24 January): 253–56.

Davis, David Brion. 1975. *The Problem of Slavery in the Age of Revolution, 1770–1823.* Ithaca and London: Cornell University Press.

de Beauvoir, Simone. 1974. *The Second Sex.* Translated by H. M. Parshley. New York: Vintage Books.

Deloria, Vine. 1974. *Behind the Trail of Broken Treaties: An Indian Declaration of Independence.* New York: Dell.

Derr, Mary Krane, ed. 1991. *"Man's Inhumanity to Woman, Makes Countless Infants Die": The Early Feminist Case Against Abortion.* Kansas City, Mo.: Feminists for Life Education Project.

De Sade, The Marquis. 1965. *The Complete Justine, Philosophy in the Bedroom, and Other Writings.* Compiled and translated by Richard Seaver and Austryn Wainhouse. New York: Grove Press.

Deutsch, Albert. 1949. "A Note on Medical Ethics (including the New Hippocratic Oath of the World Medical Association)." In Alexander Mitscherlich and Fred Norden, *Doctors of Infamy.* New York: Henry Schuman.

Dippie, Brian W. 1982. *The Vanishing American: White Attitudes and U.S. Indian Policy.* Middletown, Conn.: Wesleyan University Press.

"Disease of Unwanted Pregnancy." 1967. *Time,* 15 September, 84.

Dixon, Thomas. 1967. *The Leopard's Spots: A Romance of the White Man's Burden—1865–1900.* 1902. Reprint, Ridgewood, New Jersey: Gregg Press.

Dobash, R. Emerson, and Russell P. Dobash. 1977–78. "Wives: The 'Appropriate' Victims of Marital Violence." *Victimology: An International Journal* 2:426–42.

———. 1979. *Violence Against Wives: A Case Against the Patriarchy.* New York: Free Press.

Dornan, Peter. 1975. "Andrei Sakharov: The Conscience of a Liberal Scientist." In *Dissent in the USSR: Politics, Ideology, and People,* edited by Rudolf L. Tokes. Baltimore and London: Johns Hopkins University Press.

Drake, Daniel. 1940. *Letters on Slavery to Dr. John C. Warren, April 3, 5, and 6, 1851.* New York: Schuman's.

Drayton, William. 1969. *The South Vindicated from the Treason and Fanaticism of the Northern Abolitionists.* 1836. Reprint, New York: Negro Universities Press.

Drinnon, Richard. 1980. *Facing West: The Metaphysics of Indian-Hating and Empire Building.* New York: New American Library.

Duff, Raymond S., and A. G. M. Campbell. 1973. "Moral and Ethical Dilemmas in the Special-Care Nursery." *New England Journal of Medicine* 289 (25 October): 890–94.

Effron, Seth, and Jane Floerchinger. 1983. "Wichita Bans Burning Fetuses in Incinerator." *Wichita Eagle-Beacon,* 2 August, 2A.

Egan, Eileen. 1986. *Such A Vision of the Street: Mother Teresa—The Spirit and the Work.* Garden City, New York: Doubleday, Image.

Elby, Cecil. 1973. *"That Disgraceful Affair," The Black Hawk War.* New York: W. W. Norton.

Ellis, Havelock. 1914. *Man and Woman: A Study of Human Secondary Sexual Characters.* 5th ed., rev. & enl. New York: Charles Scribner's.

Emerson, Edward Waldo, and Waldo Emerson Forbes, eds. 1912. *Journals of Ralph Waldo Emerson, 1820–1872.* 10 vols. Boston and New York: Houghton Mifflin.

Engelhardt, H. Tristram. 1973. "Viability, Abortion, and the Differences Between a Fetus and Infant." *American Journal of Obstetrics and Gynecology* 116 (1 June): 429–34.

———. 1983. "Viability and the Use of the Fetus." In *Abortion and the Status of the Fetus,* edited by William B. Bondeson, H. Tristram Engelhardt, Stuart F. Spicker, and Daniel H. Winship. Dordrecht, Boston, and Lancaster: D. Reidel.

English, William T. 1903. "The Negro Problem from the Physician's Point of View." *Atlanta Journal-Record of Medicine* 5 (October): 459–72.

Estes, Matthew. 1846. *A Defence of Negro Slavery as it Exists in the United States*. Montgomery: Press of the "Alabama Journal."

Etzioni, Amitai. 1976. "A Review of the Ethics of Fetal Research." *Society* (March–April): 71–72.

"Eugenics in Germany." 1933. *Journal of the American Medical Association* 101 (22 July): 295.

"Excerpts from the Justices' Decision in the Pennsylvania Case." 1992. *New York Times,* 30 June, A8–9.

"The Facts Speak Louder: Planned Parenthood's Critique of 'The Silent Scream.'" 1985. Photocopy.

Fitzgerald, John F. 1901. "The Duty of the State Toward Its Idiots and Feeble-Minded." *Albany Medical Annals* 22 (March): 125–30.

Fletcher, John C., and Mark I. Evans. 1983. "Maternal Bonding in Early Fetal Ultrasound Examinations." *The New England Journal of Medicine* 308 (17 February): 392–93.

Fletcher, Joseph F. 1968. "The Right to Die: A Theologian Comments." *Atlantic Monthly,* April, 62.

———. 1973. "Ethics and Euthanasia." In *To Live and To Die: When, Why, and How.* Edited by Robert H. Williams. New York: Springer-Verlag.

———. 1979. *Humanhood: Essays in Biomedical Ethics.* Buffalo, New York: Prometheus Books.

Foner, Philip S., ed. 1968. *Frederick Douglass: Selections from His Writings.* New York: International Publishers.

Fontana, Andrea. 1977. *The Last Frontier: The Social Meaning of Growing Old.* Beverly Hills, Calif.: Sage Publications.

"Forum: Ethics in Embryo." 1987. *Harper's Magazine,* September, 37–47.

Fraenkel, Ernst. 1941. *The Dual State: A Contribution to the Theory of Dictatorship.* Translated by E. A. Shils, with Edith Lowenstein and Klaus Knorr. New York: Oxford University Press.

Fredrickson, George M. 1971. *The Black Image in the White Mind: The Debate on Afro-American Character and Destiny, 1817–1914.* New York: Harper & Row.

Fremont, Jack. 1984. "Rapists Speak for Themselves." In *The Politics of Rape: The Victim's Perspective,* edited by Diana E. H. Russell. New York: Stein and Day.

French, Marilyn. 1992. *The War Against Women.* New York: Summit Books.

Freud, Sigmund. 1959. "Some Psychological Consequences of the Anatomical Distinctions Between the Sexes." In *Collected Papers.* Vol. 5. Edited by James Strachey. New York: Basic Books.

Galen, Robert S., Prem Chauhan, Howard Wietzner, and Carlos Navarro. 1974. "Fetal Pathology and Mechanism of Fetal Death in Saline-Induced Abortion: A Study of 143 Gestations and Critical Review of the Literature." *American Journal of Obstetrics and Gynecology* 120 (1 October): 347–55.

Garrison, Wendell Phillips, and Francis Jackson Garrison. 1885. *William Lloyd Garrison, 1805–1879: The Story of His Life Told by His Children.* Vol. 1. New York: Century Company.

Garrison, William Lloyd. 1968. *Thoughts on African Colonization.* 1832. Reprint, New York: Arno Press and The New York Times.

Gaylin, Willard, and Marc Lappe. 1975. "Fetal Politics: The Debate on Experimenting with the Unborn." *Atlantic,* May, 66–71.

Gerry, Eldridge T. 1974. "The Relation of Societies for the Prevention of Cruelty to Children to Child-Saving Work." In *Care of Dependent Children in the Late Nineteenth and Early Twentieth Centuries,* edited by Robert H. Bremner. New York: Arno Press.

Gert, Bernard, and Charles M. Culver. 1984. "Moral Theory in Neurologic Practice." *Seminars in Neurology* 4 (March): 9–14.

Giannakoulopoulos, Xenophon, et al. 1994. "Fetal Plasma Cortisol and ß-endorphin Response to Intrauterine Needling." *The Lancet* 344 (9 July): 77–81.

Gibbs, Nancy. 1989. "Wilding in the Night." *Time,* 8 May, 20–21.

Gibson, William. 1962. *The Miracle Worker.* New York: Bantam.

Gillon, Raanan. 1986. "Conclusion: The Arthur Case Revisited." *British Medical Journal* 292 (22 February): 543–45.

Glassman, Marjorie. 1980. "Misdiagnosis of Senile Dementia: Denial of Care to the Elderly." *Social Work* 25 (July): 138–44.

Goldsmith, Sadja, Nancy B. Kaltreider, and Alan J. Margolis. 1977. "Second Trimester Abortion by Dilatation and Extraction (D&E): Surgical Techniques and Psychological Reactions." Paper presented at the annual meeting of the Association of Planned Parenthood Physicians, Atlanta, October.

Goodlin, Robert C. 1963. "Cutaneous Respiration in a Fetal Incubator." *American Journal of Obstetrics and Gynecology* 86 (1 July): 571–79.

Goodman, Michael F., ed. 1988. *What Is a Person?* Clifton, New Jersey: Humana Press.

Gordon, Hymie. 1968. "Genetical, Social and Medical Aspects of Abortion." *South African Medical Journal* (20 July): 721–30.

Gould, Stephen Jay. 1977. *Ever Since Darwin: Reflections in Natural History.* New York: W. W. Norton.

Griffin, Susan. 1981. *Pornography and Silence: Culture's Revenge Against Nature.* New York: Harper & Row.

Grimke, Angelina. 1972. "Letters to Catherine E. Beecher." In *The Abolitionists: Means, Ends, and Motivations,* edited by Hugh Hawkins. Lexington, Mass.: D. C. Heath.

Grossman, Vasily. 1972. *Forever Flowing.* Translated by Thomas P. Whitney. New York: Harper & Row.

Gubrium, Jaber F. 1975. *Living and Dying at Murray Manor.* New York: St. Martin's Press.

Gustafson, James M. 1973. "Mongolism, Parental Desires, and the Right to Life." *Perspectives in Biology and Medicine* 16 (Summer): 529–57.

Guttmacher, Alan F. 1947. *Having A Baby: A Guide for Expectant Parents*. New York: New American Library, A Signet Book.

———. 1957. *Pregnancy and Birth: A Book for Expectant Parents*. New York: Viking Press.

———. 1973. "Why I Favor Legalized Abortion." *Reader's Digest*, November, 143–47.

Guyon, Rene. 1958. *Sexual Freedom*. Translated by Eden and Cedar Paul. New York: Alfred A. Knopf.

Haeckel, Ernst. 1892. *The History of Creation or the Development of the Earth and Its Inhabitants by the Action of Natural Causes*. Translated by E. Ray Lankester. 4th ed., 2 vols. New York: D. Appleton.

———. 1904. *The Wonders of Life: A Popular Study of Biological Philosophy*. Translated by Joseph McCabe. London: Watts and Company.

Hakluyt, Richard. 1965. *The Principal Navigations, Voyages, Traffiques, & Discoveries of the English Nation: Made by Sea or Over Land to the Remote and Farthest Distant Quarters of the Earth at any time within the Compasse of these 1600 Yeeres*. 1598. 12 vols. Reprint, New York: AMS Press.

Hallie, Philip P. 1979. *Lest Innocent Blood Be Shed: The Story of the Village of Le Chambon and How Goodness Happened There*. New York: Harper & Row.

Hardin, Garrett. 1968. "Abortion—Or Compulsory Pregnancy?" *Journal of Marriage and the Family* 30 (May): 246–51.

Harris, Mrs. L. H. 1899. "A Southern Woman's View." *Independent* 51 (18 May): 1354–55.

Harris, Trudier. 1984. *Exorcising Blackness: Historical and Literary Lynching and Burning Rituals*. Bloomington: Indiana University Press.

Hart, Albert Bushnell, ed. 1925. *Source Book of American History*. New York: Macmillan.

Hays, H. R. 1964. *The Dangerous Sex: The Myth of Feminine Evil*. New York: G. P. Putnam's Sons.

Henderson, Katherine Usher, and Barbara F. McManus, eds. 1985. *Half Humankind: Contexts and Texts of the Controversy about Women in England, 1540–1640*. Urbana and Chicago: University of Illinois Press.

Henry, Clarissa, and Marc Hillel. 1976. *Of Pure Blood*. Translated by Eric Mossbacher. New York: McGraw-Hill.

Henshaw, Stanley K. 1986. "Induced Abortion: A Worldwide Perspective." *Family Planning Perspectives* 18 (November–December): 250–54.

Hentoff, Nat. 1987. "The American Death Squads." *Village Voice,* 25 August.

Hern, Warren M. 1971. "Is Pregnancy Really Normal?" *Family Planning Perspectives* 3 (January): 5–10.

———. 1984a. *Abortion Practice*. Philadelphia: J. B. Lippincott.

———. 1984b. "Correlation of Fetal Age and Measurements Between 10 and 26 Weeks of Gestation." *Obstetrics & Gynecology* 63 (January): 26–32.

Hern, Warren M., and Billie Corrigan. 1978. "What About Us? Staff Reactions to the D & E Procedure." Paper presented at the annual meeting of the Association of Planned Parenthood Physicians, San Diego, October.

Hesiod. *Theogony*. 1953. Translated by Norman O. Brown. Indianapolis: Bobbs-Merrill.

Hilberg, Raul. 1967. *The Destruction of the European Jews*. Chicago: Quadrangle Books.

Hitler, Adolf. 1971. *Mein Kampf*. Translated by Ralph Manheim. Boston: Houghton Mifflin.

Hochhuth, Rolf. 1980. *A German Love Story*. Translated by John Browjohn. Boston: Little, Brown.

Hoig, Stan. 1961. *The Sand Creek Massacre*. Norman: University of Oklahoma Press.

Housdan, Leslie George. 1956. *The Prevention of Cruelty to Children*. New York: Philosophical Library.

Howard, William Lee. 1903. "The Negro as a Distinct Ethnic Factor in Civilization." *Medicine* 60 (May): 423–26.

Howsden, Jackie L. 1981. *Work and the Helpless Self: The Social Organization of a Nursing Home*. Lanham, Md.: University Press of America.

Hoxie, Frederick E. 1979. "Red Man's Burden." *Antioch Review* 37 (Summer): 326–42.

Irving, John. 1986. *The Cider House Rules*. New York: Bantam Books.

Jackson, Helen Hunt. 1881. *A Century of Dishonor: A Sketch of the United States Government's Dealings with Some of the Indian Tribes*. New York: Harper and Brothers.

Jacobson, Eric S., and Martha Goetsch. 1985. "Cytologic Identification of Trophoblastic Epithelium in Products of First-Trimester Abortion." *Obstetrics & Gynecology* 66 (July): 124–26.

Jalland, Pat, and John Hooper. 1986. *Women from Birth to Death: The Female Life Cycle in Britain 1830–1914*. Atlantic Highlands, New Jersey: Humanities Press International.

Jefferson, Thomas. 1955. *Notes on the State of Virginia*. Edited by William Peden. Chapel Hill: University of North Carolina Press.

Jeffrey, Roger. 1979. "Normal Rubbish: Deviant Patients in Casualty Departments." *Sociology of Health and Illness* 1 (June): 90–106.

Jennings, Francis. 1975. *The Invasion of America: Indians, Colonialism, and the Cant of Conquest*. Chapel Hill: University of North Carolina Press.

"The Jew as Global Parasite." 1982. In *The Holocaust: Selected Documents in Eighteen Volumes, 4. Propaganda and*

Aryanization, 1938–1944, edited by John Mendelsohn. New York and London: Garland Publishing.

Joint Committee on the Conduct of the War. [1864] 1972. "Massacre at Sand Creek, 1864." In *This Country Was Ours: A Documentary History of the American Indian,* edited by Virgil Vogel. New York: Harper & Row.

Jordan, Winthrop D. 1968. *White Over Black: American Attitudes Toward the Negro, 1550–1812.* Chapel Hill: University of North Carolina Press.

Juvenal. 1982. *The Sixteen Satires.* Translated by Peter Green. New York: Penguin Classics.

Katz, Jacob. 1980. *From Prejudice to Destruction: Anti-Semitism, 1700–1933.* Cambridge: Harvard University Press.

Kaufmann, Donald A. 1975. "The Indian as Media Hand-Me-Down." *Colorado Quarterly* 23 (Spring): 489–504.

Keller, Helen. 1961. *The Story of My Life.* New York: Dell.

Kenrick, Donald, and Grattan Puxon. 1972. *The Destiny of Europe's Gypsies.* New York: Basic Books.

Kerslake, Dorothea, and Donn Casey. 1967. "Abortion Induced by Means of the Uterine Aspirator." *Obstetrics & Gynecology* 30 (July): 35–45.

Khrushchev, Nikita S. 1962. "The Crimes of the Stalinist Era: Special Report to the 20th Congress of the Communist Party of the Soviet Union." *The New Leader,* S1–S67.

Kibel, Howard D. 1972. "Staff Reactions to Abortion: A Psychiatric View." *Obstetrics & Gynecology* 39 (January): 128–33.

King, Henry V. 1992. "Snubbing of Casey Might Hurt Democratic Ticket." *The Wanderer,* 30 July, 7.

Kingston-Mann, Esther. 1981. "Marxism and Russian Rural Development: Problems of Evidence, Experience, and Culture." *American Historical Review* 4 (October): 731–52.

Knightley, Phillip. 1975. *The First Casualty: From the Crimea to Vietnam: The War Correspondent as Hero, Propagandist, and Myth Maker.* New York and London: Harcourt Brace Jovanovich, A Harvest Book.

Kogon, Eugen. 1950. *The Theory and Practice of Hell: The German Concentration Camps and the System Behind Them.* Translated by Heinz Norden. New York: Farrar, Straus.

Konner, Melvin. 1987. *Becoming a Doctor: A Journey of Initiation in Medical School.* New York: Viking Press, Elisabeth Sifton Books.

Kraus, Ota, and Erich Kulka. 1966. *The Death Factory: Document on Auschwitz.* Translated by Stephen Jolly. New York: Pergamon Press.

Kravchenko, Victor. 1946. *I Chose Freedom.* New York: C. Scribner's Sons.

Lachs, John. 1976. "Humane Treatment and the Treatment of Humans." *The New England Journal of Medicine* 294 (8 April): 838–40.

Lake, Alice. 1976. "For Teenagers Only: Confidential Birth Control Clinics." *Good Housekeeping,* June, 153.

Lamerton, R. 1974. "Vegetables?" *Nursing Times* 70 (1 August): 1184–85.

Langness, L. L. 1981. "Child Abuse and Cultural Values: The Case of New Guinea." In *Child Abuse and Neglect: Cross Cultural Perspectives,* edited by Jill E. Korbin. Berkeley and Los Angeles: University of California Press.

Lanzmann, Claude. 1975. *Shoah: An Oral History of the Holocaust, The Complete Text of the Film.* New York: Pantheon Books.

Laqueur, Walter. 1980. *The Terrible Secret: Suppression of the Truth about Hitler's "Final Solution."* Boston: Little, Brown.

Lederer, Laura, ed. 1980. *Take Back the Night: Women on Pornography.* New York: William Morrow.

Lejeune, Jerome. 1981. "In Re New Humans." *Human Life Review* 7 (Summer): 60–79.

Lengyel, Olga. 1947. *Five Chimneys: The Story of Auschwitz.* Chicago and New York: Ziff-Davis.

Lenin, V. I. 1960–70. *Collected Works.* 45 vols. Translated by Joe Fineberg and George Hanna. Moscow: Foreign Languages Publishing House.

Leo, John. 1990. "Is the Press Straight on Abortion?" *U.S. News & World Report,* 16 July, 17.

Levin, Nora. 1973. *The Holocaust: The Destruction of European Jewry.* New York: Schocken Books.

Levine, Robert. 1992. "A Question of Anatomy." *New York Times,* 14 April, 24.

"Life and Death Decisions." 1973. *Newsweek,* 3 December, 12.

Lifton, Robert Jay. 1986. *The Nazi Doctors: Medical Killing and the Psychology of Genocide.* New York: Basic Books.

Liley, A. W. 1967. "The Influence of Prenatal Development in Child Development." Paper presented at the Postgraduate School of Obstetrics and Gynecology, University of Auckland, New Zealand, 15 June.

Lippman, Helen. 1991. "After Cruzan: The Right to Die." *RN* (January): 65–73.

Lloyd-Jones, Hugh. 1975. *Females of the Species: Semonides on Women.* Park Ridge, New Jersey: Noyes Press.

Lovelace, Linda, with Mike McGrady. 1980. *Ordeal: An Autobiography.* Secaucus, New Jersey: Citadel Press.

Lurie, Edward. 1960. *Louis Agassiz, A Life in Science.* Chicago: University of Chicago Press.

Lyon, Jeff. 1985. *Playing God in the Nursery.* New York: W. W. Norton.

Macklin, Ruth. 1983. "Personhood in the Bioethics Literature." *Millbank Memorial Fund Quarterly* 61:35–57.

Mailer, Norman. 1960. *Advertisements for Myself.* New York: New American Library, Signet.

———. 1965. *An American Dream.* New York: Dial Press.

Manney, James, and John C. Blattner. 1984. *Death in the Nursery: The Secret Crime of Infanticide*. Ann Arbor, Mich.: Servant Books.

Marder, Daniel, ed. 1970. *A Hugh Henry Brackenridge Reader, 1770–1815*. Pittsburgh: University of Pittsburgh Press.

Mardock, Robert Winston. 1971. *The Reformers and the American Indians*. Columbia: University of Missouri Press.

Marx, Karl. 1965. *The Eighteenth Brumaire of Louis Bonaparte*. New York: International Publishers.

Massing, Paul W. 1949. *Rehearsal for Destruction: A Study of Political Anti-Semitism*. New York: Harper & Brothers.

Mather, Cotton. 1913. *Decennium Luctuosum: An History of Remarkable Occurrences in the Long War, which New England Hath Had with the Indian Salvages, From the Year 1688, to the Year 1698, Faithfully Composed and Improved*. In *Narratives of the Indian Wars*, edited by Charles H. Lincoln. New York: Charles Scribner's Sons.

———. 1967. *Magnalia Christi Americana; The Ecclesiastical History of New England; From its First Planting, In the Year 1620, Unto the Year of Our Lord 1698*. Vol. 1. New York: Russell & Russell.

Mathews-Green, Frederica. 1992. "Suffragists at the Abortion March." *Sisterlife: Feminists for Life of America* 12 (Spring): 1, 5.

McDermott, John Francis. 1971. "The Indian as Human Being." *Nebraska History* 52 (Spring): 45–49.

McKim, W. Duncan. 1901. *Heredity and Human Progress*. New York: G. P. Putnam's Sons.

Methvin, Eugene H. 1985. "Hitler and Stalin: 20th Century Superkillers." *National Review*, 31 May, 22–29.

Mill, John Stuart. 1869. *The Subjection of Women*. London: Longmans, Green, Reader, and Dyer.

Miller, Henry. 1963. *Black Spring*. New York: Grove Press, An Evergreen Black Cat Book.

————. 1961a. *Tropic of Cancer.* New York: Grove Press

————. 1961b. *Tropic of Capricorn.* New York: Grove Press.

————. 1965. *Sexus.* New York: Grove Press,

————. 1978. *Two Books, Quiet Days in Clichy and The World of Sex.* New York: Grove Press.

Millett, Kate. 1970. *Sexual Politics.* Garden City, New York: Doubleday.

Mitrany, David. 1961. *Marx Against the Peasant: A Study in Social Dogmatism.* New York: Collier Books.

Mitscherlich, Alexander, and Fred Mielke. 1949. *Doctors of Infamy: The Story of the Nazi Medical Crimes.* Translated by Heinz Norden. New York: Henry Schuman.

Mizrahi, Terry. 1986. *Getting Rid of Patients: Contradictions in the Socialization of Physicians.* New Brunswick, New Jersey: Rutgers University Press.

Moore, Keith L. 1989. *Before We Are Born.* 3rd ed. Philadelphia: W. B. Saunders.

Morey, Sylvester M., ed. 1970. *Can the Red Man Help the White Man? A Denver Conference with the Indian Elders.* New York: Gilbert Church.

Morgan, Robin. 1980. "Theory and Practice: Pornography and Rape." In Lederer 1980.

Morton, Samuel George. 1839. *Crania Americana; Or A Comparative View of the Skulls of Various Aboriginal Nations of North and South America: To Which is Prefixed an Essay on the Varieties of the Human Species.* Philadelphia.

Mosher, Stephen W. 1985. "How China Uses U.N. Aid for Forced Abortions." *Wall Street Journal,* 13 May, 1.

Mosse, George. 1978. *Toward the Final Solution: A History of European Racism.* New York: Howard Fertig.

Murrell, Thomas W. 1909. "Syphilis and the American Negro— A Medico-Sociological Study." *Transactions* (Medical Society of Virginia): 168–74.

Naftulin, Donald H., John E. Ware, and Frank A. Donnelly. 1973. "The Doctor Fox Lecture: A Paradigm of Educational Seduction." *Journal of Medical Education* 48 (July): 630–35.

"A New Attack on Abortion." 1987. *Newsweek,* 2 February, 32.

"A New Ethic for Medicine and Society." 1970. *California Medicine* 113 (September): 67–68.

Nisbet, Robert. 1982. *Prejudices: A Philosophical Dictionary.* Cambridge, Mass. and London: Harvard University Press.

Noonan, John T. 1979. *A Private Choice: Abortion in America in the Seventies.* New York: Free Press.

Nott, Josiah C. 1843. "The Mulatto a Hybrid—Probable Extermination of the Two Races if the Whites and Blacks are Allowed to Intermarry." *American Journal of the Medical Sciences* 11 (July): 252–56.

———. 1847. "Statistics of Southern Slave Population." *De Bow's Review* 4 (November): 280.

Nott, Josiah C., and George L. Gliddon. 1954. *Types of Mankind: Or, Ethnological Researches Based Upon the Ancient Monuments, Paintings, Sculptures, and Crania of Races.* 4th ed. Philadelphia: Lippincott, Grambo & Company.

Nove, Alec. 1993. "Victims of Stalinism: How Many?" In *Stalinist Terror: New Perspectives,* edited by J. Arch Getty and Roberta T. Manning. Cambridge, New York, and Victoria, Australia: Cambridge University Press.

Nuernberg Military Tribunals. 1945–47. *Trials of War Criminals.* 15 vols. Washington, D.C.: U.S. Government Printing Office.

Oden, Thomas C. 1976. *Should Treatment Be Terminated? Moral Guidelines for Christian Families and Pastors.* New York: Harper & Row.

O'Donnell, D. A., and W. L. Atlee. 1871. "Report on Criminal Abortion." *Transactions of the American Medical Association* 22:239–58.

O'Faolain, Julia, and Lauro Martines, eds. 1973. *Not in God's Image.* New York: Harper & Row.

Okie, Susan. 1989. "Medical Advances Complicate Abortion Debate." *Washington Post,* 24 April, 1, 4, 5.

Orwell, George. 1949. *1984.* New York: Harcourt, Brace and World.

————. 1956. "Politics and the English Language." In *The Orwell Reader: Fiction, Essays, and Reportage by George Orwell,* introduction by Richard H. Rovere. New York: Harcourt Brace Jovanovich, A Harvest Book.

"Panel Backs Transplants of Aborted Fetuses' Tissue." 1987. *St. Louis Post-Dispatch,* 14 March, 6A.

Parkman, Francis. 1897–98. *The Conspiracy of Pontiac and the Indian War After the Conquest of Canada.* 2 vols. Boston: Little, Brown.

————. 1902a. *A Half-Century of Conflict.* 2 vols. Frontenac ed. Boston: Little, Brown.

————. 1902b. *The Jesuits in North America in the Seventeenth Century.* 2 vols. Frontenac ed. Boston: Little, Brown.

————. 1925a. *Montcalm and Wolfe: France and England in North America.* 2 vols. Centenary ed. Boston: Little, Brown.

————. 1925b. *The Oregon Trail: Sketches of Prairie and Rocky-Mountain Life.* Centenary ed. Boston: Little, Brown.

Pasternak, Boris. 1958. *Doctor Zhivago.* Translated by Max Hayward et al. New York: Pantheon Books.

Payne, George Henry. 1916. *The Child in Human Progress.* New York and London: G. P. Putnam's Sons.

Pearce, Roy Harvey. 1965. *The Savages of America: A Study of the Indian and the Idea of Civilization.* Rev. ed. Baltimore: Johns Hopkins Press.

Petchesky, Rosalind Pollack. 1984. *Abortion and Women's Choice: The State, Sexuality, and Reproductive Freedom.* Boston: Northeastern University Press.

Planned Parenthood Federation of America. 1976. *11 Million Teenagers: What Can be Done About the Epidemic of Adolescent Pregnancies in the United States.* Booklet. New York.

Planned Parenthood of New York City. 1975. *Abortion: A Woman's Guide*. New York: Pocket Books.

Plato. 1974. *The Republic*. Translated by Desmond Lee. Book 5, 2nd rev. ed. New York: Penguin Books.

Poliakov, Leon. 1979. *Harvest of Hate: The Nazi Program for the Destruction of the Jews of Europe*. Rev. & exp. ed. New York: Schocken Books, Holocaust Library.

Pritchard, Jack A., Paul C. MacDonald, and Norman F. Grant. 1985. *Williams Obstetrics*. 17th ed. Norwalk, Conn.: Appleton-Crofts.

"The Problem of Personhood: Biomedical, Social, Legal, and Policy Views." 1983. Special Issue. *Millbank Memorial Fund Quarterly* 61:1–147.

Proctor, Robert. 1988. *Racial Hygiene: Medicine Under the Nazis*. Cambridge: Harvard University Press.

Radford, Jill, and Diana E. H. Russell, eds. 1992. *Femicide: The Politics of Woman Killing*. New York: Twayne Publishers.

"Rape of Jogger in Park Aggravates New York's Racial Tension." 1989. *St. Louis Post-Dispatch*, 30 April, 6A.

"Recommended Standards for Abortion Services." 1971. *American Journal of Public Health* 61 (February): 396–98.

Reich, Wilhelm. 1970. *The Mass Psychology of Fascism*. Translated by Vincent R. Carfagno. New York: Simon and Schuster, A Touchstone Book.

Reisman, Judith A. 1987. *Images of Children, Crime, and Violence in Playboy, Penthouse and Hustler Magazines*. 3 vols. Arlington, Va.: The Institute for Media Education.

Resch, Bela A., Julius G. Papp, Ferenc E. Szontagh, and Laszlo Szekeres. 1974. "Comparison of Spontaneous Contraction Rates of In Situ and Isolated Fetal Hearts in Early Pregnancy." *American Journal of Obstetrics and Gynecology* 118 (1 January): 73–76.

Rietlinger, Gerald. 1961. *The Final Solution: The Attempt to Exterminate the Jews of Europe 1939–1945*. New York: A. S. Barnes, A Perpetua Book.

Romanes, George J. 1887. "Mental Differences between Men and Women." *The Nineteenth Century* 21 (May): 654–72.

Rooke, Patricia T., and R. L. Schnell, 1981. "The 'King's Children' in English Canada: A Psychohistorical Study of Abandonment, Rejection, and Colonial Response (1869–1930)." *Journal of Psychohistory* 8 (Spring): 387–420.

Roosevelt, Theodore. 1889. *The Winning of the West.* 4 vols. New York: G. P. Putnam's Sons.

————. 1902. *The Strenuous Life: Essays and Addresses.* New York: Century Company.

Rose, Willie Lee, ed. 1976. *A Documentary History of Slavery in North America.* New York: Oxford University Press.

Rosen, Norma. 1977. "Between Guilt and Gratification: Abortion Doctors Reveal Their Feelings." *New York Times Magazine,* 17 April, 70, 71, 73–80.

Rush, Dr. Benjamin. 1799. "Observations Intended to Favour a Supposition that the Black Color (As It is Called) of the Negroes is Derived from the Leprosy." *Transactions* (American Philosophical Society) 4:289–97.

Russell, Diana E. H., ed. 1993. *Making Violence Sexy: Feminist Views on Pornography.* New York and London: Teachers College Press.

Sagan, Carl, and Ann Druyan. 1990. "Is it Possible to be Pro-Life and Pro-Choice?" *Parade Magazine,* 22 April, 4–8.

Sakharov, Andrei D. 1974. *Sakharov Speaks.* Edited by Harrison E. Salisbury. London: Collins & Harvill Press.

Sanger, Margaret. 1922. *The Pivot of Civilization.* New York: Bretano's.

Sawyer, George S. 1858. *Southern Institutes; Or, An Inquiry into the Origin and Early Prevalence of Slavery and the Slave-Trade.* Philadelphia: J. B. Lippincott.

Schaeffer, Francis A., and C. Everett Koop. 1979. *Whatever Happened to the Human Race?* Old Tappan, N.J.: Fleming H. Revell.

Scholl, Inge. 1983. *The White Rose: Munich, 1942–1943.* Translated by Arthur R. Schultz. 2nd ed. Middletown, Conn.: Wesleyan University Press.

Schopenhauer, Arthur. 1951. *Essays: From the Parerga and Paralipomena: Studies in Pessimism.* Translated by T. Bailey Saunders. London: George Allen and Unwin.

Schreiber, Bernhard. N.d. *The Men Behind Hitler: A German Warning to the World.* Translated by H. R. Martindale. Les Mureau, France.

Scott, G. E. 1988. *Moral Personhood: An Essay in the Pshilosophy of Moral Psychology.* New York: State University of New York Press.

Scrimshaw, Susan C. M. 1984. "Infanticide in Human Populations: Societal and Individual Concerns." In *Infanticide: Comparative and Evolutionary Perspectives,* edited by Glenn Hausfater and Sarah Blaffer Hrdy. New York: Aldine.

Scully, Diana. 1988. "Convicted Rapists' Perceptions of Self and Victim: Role Taking and Emotions." *Gender & Society* 2 (June): 200–13.

Scully, Diana, and Joseph Marolla. 1984. "Convicted Rapists' Vocabulary of Motives: Excuses and Justifications." *Social Problems* 31 (June): 530–44.

Scully, Diana, and Joseph Marolla. 1985. "'Riding the Bull at Gilley's: Convicted Rapists Describe the Rewards of Rape." *Social Problems* 32 (February): 251–63.

Sereny, Gitta. 1974. *Into that Darkness: From Mercy Killing to Mass Murder.* London: Andre Deutsch.

Shainess, Natalie. 1970. "Abortion Is No Man's Business." *Psychology Today,* May.

"Shall This Child Die?" 1973. *Newsweek,* 12 November, 70.

Shatz, Marshall S. 1980. *Soviet Dissent in Historical Perspective.* Cambridge, England: Cambridge University Press.

Shaw, David. 1990. "Abortion Bias Seeps Into News." *Los Angeles Times,* 1 July, A1, A50, A51.

Shaw, Margery W., and A. Edward Doudera, eds. 1983. *Defining Human Life: Medical, Legal, and Ethical Implications.* Ann Arbor, Mich.: Health Administration Press.

Shelp, Earl E. 1986. *Born to Die? Deciding the Fate of Critically Ill Newborns.* New York: Free Press.

Simkins, Francis Butler. 1937. "Ben Tillman's View of the Negro." *Journal of Southern History* 3 (February–November): 161–74.

Singer, Peter. 1983. "Sanctity of Life or Quality of Life?" *Pediatrics* 72 (July): 128–29.

Slotkin, Richard. 1973. *Regeneration Through Violence: The Mythology of the American Frontier, 1600–1860.* Middletown, Conn.: Wesleyan University Press.

Smith, Donald S., comp., and Don Tanner, ed. 1985. *The Silent Scream: The Complete Text of the Documentary Film with an Authoritative Response to the Critics.* Anaheim, Calif.: American Portrait Films Books.

Solzhenitsyn, Aleksandr I. 1973–74. *The Gulag Archipelago, 1918–1956: An Experiment in Literary Investigation.* 3 vols. Translated by Thomas P. Whitney. New York: Harper & Row.

Sontag, Susan. 1978. "Disease as Political Metaphor." *New York Review of Books* (23 February): 29–33.

Southard, E. E. 1915. "The Feeble-Minded as Subjects of Research in Efficiency." *Proceedings of the National Conference of Charities and Corrections,* 12–19 May, Baltimore, Md.

"Soviet Newspaper Puts Death Toll from Stalin at 20 Million." 1989. *St. Louis Post-Dispatch,* 5 February, 9A.

Stalin, Josef V. 1953–55. *Works.* 13 vols. Moscow: Foreign Languages Publishing House.

Stampp, Kenneth M. 1968. *That Peculiar Institution: Slavery in the Ante-Bellum South.* New York: Alfred A. Knopf.

Stone, Christopher D. 1972. "Should Trees Have Standing?— Toward Legal Rights for Natural Objects." *Southern California Law Review* 45 (Spring): 450–501.

Storer, Horatio R., et al. 1859. "Report on Criminal Abortion." *Transactions of the American Medical Association* 12:75–78.

Sumner, L. W. 1981. *Abortion and Moral Theory*. Princeton, New Jersey: Princeton University Press.

The Suppressed Book About Slavery. 1968. 1864. Reprint, New York: Arno Press and The New York Times.

Tannenbaum, Frank. 1947. *Slave and Citizen: The Negro in the Americas*. New York: Alfred A. Knopf.

Tauer, Carol A. 1985. "Personhood and Human Embryos and Fetuses." *Journal of Medicine and Philosophy* 10:253–66.

"Technological Advances to Make Pro-Abortion Tougher, Planned Parenthood Official Tells National Abortion Federation." 1982. *National Right to Life News,* 14 October, 8.

Ten Boom, Corrie, with John Sherrill and Elizabeth Sherrill. 1971. *The Hiding Place*. Old Tappan, New Jersey: Fleming H. Revell, Spire Books.

Teresa, Mother, Francis A. Schaeffer, Malcolm Muggeridge, et al. 1984. *Who Is For Life?* Westchester, Ill.: Crossway Books.

Thimmesch, Nick. 1982. "Bizarre Cases of Abortions Gone Awry." *St. Louis Globe-Democrat,* 19–20 June, 5B.

Thomas, P. 1964. *Indian Women Through the Ages*. Bombay: Asia Publishing House.

Thomson, Keith Stewart. 1988. "Ontogeny and Phylogeny Recapitulated." *American Scientist* 76 (May–June): 273–75.

Tooley, Michael. 1972. "Abortion and Infanticide." *Philosophy and Public Affairs* 2 (Fall): 37–65.

———. 1983. *Abortion and Infanticide*. Oxford: Oxford University Press.

"Transplantation of Neural Tissue from Fetuses." 1987. *Science* 235 (13 March): 1307–8.

Trevelyan, George Macaulay. 1952. *History of England*. 3rd ed. London: Longsman, Green.

Tucker, Robert C., and Stephen F. Cohen, eds. 1965. *The Great Purge Trial*. New York: Grosset & Dunlap.

Turco, Jeryl. 1987. "A Message to the Community and Staff of Morristown Memorial Hospital." Advertisement in *Daily Record* (Northwest New Jersey), 2 August.

"The Unwanted Children of Times Past." 1989. *U.S. News & World Report,* 1 May, 62.

U.S. Congress. 1990. Senate Committee on Labor and Human Resources. *Freedom of Choice Act of 1989.* 100th Cong., 2d sess., S. Rept. 1912.

U.S. Department of Justice. 1988. Federal Bureau of Investigation. *Crime in the United States: Uniform Crime Reports for the United States.* Washington, D.C.: U.S. Government Printing Office.

Varga, William P. 1981. *The Number One Nazi Jew-Baiter (A Political Biography of Julius Streicher, Hitler's Chief Anti-Semitic Propagandist).* New York: Carlton Press, A Hearthstone Book.

Ver Berkmoes, Ryan. 1988. "Verbal 'Malpractice': Joking About Death Eases the Hospital Life." *Chicago Tribune,* 11 December, Section 5:12.

Vietnam Veterans Against the War. 1972. *The Winter Soldier Investigation: An Inquiry into American War Crimes.* Boston: Beacon Press.

Vogelman, Lloyd. 1990. *The Sexual Face of Violence: Rapists on Rape.* Johannesburg: Ravan Press.

Von Galen, Clemens August. 1943. *The Bishop of Munster and the Nazis: The Documents in the Case.* Translated and edited by Patrick Smith. London: Burns Oates.

Wade, Naomi. 1980. "Aborted Babies Kept Alive for Bizarre Experiments." *National Examiner,* 19 August, 20–21.

Wahlberg, Rachel Conrad. 1987. "The Woman and the Fetus: One Flesh?" *New Women/New Church* (September–October): 4–5.

"Waking Sleeping Souls." 1988. *Newsweek,* 28 March, 70–71.

Walker, Benjamin. 1968. *The Hindu World: An Encyclopedic Survey of Hinduism.* 2 vols. New York: Frederick A. Praeger.

Walters, James W. 1992. "Proximate Personhood as a Standard for Making Difficult Treatment Decisions: Imperiled Newborns as a Case Study." *Bioethics* vol. 6, no. 1: 12–22.

Warren, Mary Anne. 1973. "On the Moral and Legal Status of Abortion." *The Monist* 57 (January): 43–61.

———. 1978. Commentary on "Can the Fetus be an Organ Farm?" *Hasting Center Report* (October): 23–24.

Weeks, Philip, and James B. Gidney. 1981. *Subjugation and Dishonor: A Brief History of the Travail of the Native Americans.* Huntington, New York: Robert E. Krieger.

Weininger, Otto. 1975. *Sex and Character.* 1906. Reprint, New York: AMS Press.

Wershow, Harold. 1977. "Comment: Reality Orientation for Gerontologists." *The Gerontologist* 17 (August): 297–98.

Whipple, Henry Benjamin. 1899. *Lights and Shadows of a Long Episcopate.* New York: Macmillan.

Who Should Survive? 1971. A film produced by the Guggenheim and Joseph P. Kennedy, Jr. Foundation.

"Wife-Beating Declines." 1986. *USA Today Newsview,* April, 6.

Williamson, Laila. 1978. "Infanticide: An Anthropological Analysis." In *Infanticide and the Value of Life,* edited by Marvin Kohl. Buffalo, New York: Prometheus Books.

Wilson, John. 1855. *History of the Suppression of Infanticide in Western India.* Bombay: Smith, Taylor, and Company.

Wollstonecraft, Mary. 1967. *A Vindication of the Rights of Women: With Strictures on Political and Moral Subjects.* New York: W. W. Norton.

Woodward, Kenneth L. 1992. "The Elite and How to Avoid It." *Newsweek,* 20 July, 55.

Woodward, Kenneth L., with Mark D. Uehling. 1985. "The Hardest Question." *Newsweek,* 14 January, 29.

Wyman, David S. 1984. *The Abandonment of the Jews: America and the Holocaust, 1941–1945.* New York: Pantheon Books.

Zack, Margaret. 1985. "Court Rules Fetus Not 'Human.'" *Minneapolis Star and Tribune,* 6 December, 21A.

Zangrando, Robert L. 1980. *The NAACP Crusade Against Lynching, 1909–1950.* Philadelphia: Temple University Press.

Index

Abernethy, Virginia, nonpersonhood defined by, 155
Abolitionist movement, 217–18
Aborted babies as garbage, *ix*
Abortion, 27–31. *See also* Unborn,
unwanted
animal metaphors for unwanted
unborn to defend, 98, 180–81
cultural elite's domination of
issue of, 15–16
excuses invoked for, 22
feminists against, 207–8
language of subhumanity to promote, 86–87, 226
media coverage of, 17–18
medical advances undermining,
178–80
nonpersonhood as defined by
advocates of, 156
in People's Republic of China, 31
portrayed as removal of insignificant "material," 127–28
resolutions by AMA against, 206
scope of, 31
semantic gymnastics used to justify, 11, 13, 175–76, 224
separated from idea of killing,
8–9, 11
"waste products" from, 139–40
as woman's right to control her
body, 134–35
Abortion: A Woman's Guide, 128
Abortion and Infanticide, 152–53,
168–69
Abortion Practice, 114
African Americans
as category of linguistically victimized groups, 4, 6
dehumanizing terms for, 3

dogma of inferiority imposed
on, 73–74
life-affirming images of, 217–18
as nonpersons, 160–61, 204
portrayed as diseases, 116–17,
121–22, 196–97
portrayed as inanimate objects,
136–37
portrayed as parasites, 108–9, 194
portrayed as subhuman, 84–85,
189–90
portrayed as waste products,
144–45, 201–2
raising public awareness before
the Civil War about, 19–21
rationalization for enslaving, 22,
95
slavery of, 51–55
"work animal" metaphors for,
95–97, 192
Africans shipped to the Americas,
horrors during transport of,
51–52
Agassiz, Louis, racist statements
by, 10, 84–85
Ahlwardt, Hermann, dehumanization of Jews by, 82, 93, 105,
191
Alan Guttmacher Institute (Planned
Parenthood), epidemic of
adolescent pregnancies
described by, 118
Alexander, Leo, summary of
notion of worthless life by, 71
Allan, J. McGregor, menstruation
as debilitating crisis according
to, 116
Alzheimer's patients, fetal brain
implants for, 140

Amalrik, Andrei, labor camp sentence for, 108
American Colonization Society, 121
American Fertility Society, 135
American Indian Movement (AIM), 57
American Medical Association (AMA), 206
American Public Health Association, 195
American Slavery As It Is: Testimony of a Thousand Witnesses, 52–53, 189–90
American Society of Law and Medicine, abortion liberty meeting held by, 149
Ancestral recapitulation theory, 180–81
Anderson, John O., scriptural source for human life before birth quoted by, 209
Andrews, Lori B., categorization of embryos by, 135
Animals, 190–92
  African Americans portrayed as, 95–97, 192
  as category of name-calling, 3
  disabled and dependent persons portrayed as, 90–91, 190–91
  humans equated with, 89–98
  Jews portrayed as, 93–94, 191
  Native Americans portrayed as, 97, 133, 192
  Soviet enemies portrayed as, 94–95, 191
  unwanted unborn portrayed as, 89–90, 180–81, 190
  women portrayed as, 91–93, 191
Anthony, Susan B., as antiabortion, 207, 209
Anti-Semitism, nomenclature of defamation used in, 14, 82–83
Antonov-Ovseyenko, Anton, deaths under Stalinist regime tallied by, 49

Appeal for the Indians, An, 218
Arendt, Hannah, hallmark of totalitarian society noted by, 158, 204
Aristotle
  defamation of disabled by, 68
  females as deformed according to, 116
Auschwitz
  burning of children at, 44
  laborers from, 131–32, 138
Averbakh, I. L., goal of Soviet "corrective labor" described by, 133

Baby Pearson, death by overdose of, 203
Bailey & als. v. Poindexter's Ex'or, 161, 204
Baker, John G., parents' right to choose starvation ruled by, 67
Ball, George H., lack of humanity for the nonself-conscious stated by, 80, 90
Barnes, Robert, linkage of epilepsy and hysteria with menstruation by, 120
Barr, Martin W., disparagement of mentally ill people by, 119
Barth, Karl, human and divine origins of the person before birth for, 209
Battered wives, 39–41
Baudelaire, Charles, animality of women for, 91, 191
Becker, Phillip, court battles about surgery for, 34–35, 67–68
Before We Are Born, 177–78
Beria, Lavrenti, process of becoming an "unperson" for, 158–59
Best, George, blackness of Africans as disease for, 116–17
Big lie, psychology of, 8–9, 229n1
Binding, Karl
  destruction of the disabled advocated by, 70

impact on Nazi euthanasia program of, 187

Bird, Robert Montgomery, image of Native Americans of, 111

Black Kettle, chief of Cheyenne at Sand Creek, 60

Blackmun, Harry, as main author of *Roe v. Wade* decision, 66, 161, 229n2

Blacks. *See* African Americans

Bonhoeffer, Dietrich, human and divine origins of the person before birth for, 209

Borkin, Joseph, concentration camp laborers studied by, 132

Boswell, John, history of child abandonment by, 220

Bouquet, Henry, Native Americans considered vermin by, 109

Brackenridge, Hugh Henry, subhumanity of Native Americans for, 86

Bradford, William, animal metaphors for Native Americans by, 97

Brady, E. T., African Americans as parasites to, 109

Brodsky, Joseph, forced labor for, 107

Brooke, Christopher, Native Americans described as garbage by, 146, 202

Brown, Carolyn, language of abortion stated by, 79

Brown, Dee, Wounded Knee massacre described by, 58

Brown, William Wells, treatment of African American as trash described by, 144–45

Brownmiller, Susan, objectification of women analyzed by, 130

Bukharin, Nicholas, protest against collectivization of agriculture by, 144

Caldwell, Charles, animal metaphors for Native Americans by, 97

Callahan, Daniel, imposed starvation of dependent or disabled people for life-support patients advocated by, 101

Camil, Scott, dehumanization of women described by, 82

Campbell, A. G. M., withholding of medical treatment described by, 34, 67

Campo, Theresa Ann, comparison with fish of, 91, 191

Cancer metaphor, purpose of, 113

Canfield, George F., link between "nonperson" concept and treatment of Native Americans noted by, 162, 171, 204

Carlin, David, starvation death of Nancy Ellen Jobes advocated by, 81

Carpenter, Mary, neglected children championed by, 221

Carroll, Charles, racist writings of, 85, 96

Cartwright, Samuel A., African Americans' brains and blood analyzed by, 187–88

Casey, Robert, pro-life actions of, 16–17

Cates, Willard
  unwanted pregnancies as an epidemic to, 118
  unwanted pregnancies as venereal diseases to, 123

Cato, Marcus Porcius, woman described as animal by, 191

Century of Dishonor, A, 218

Chain of being, labeling of human groups in developing, 12–13

Cherokee Indians
  disease metaphor used for, 122
  Trail of Tears of, 59–60

Child in History, The, 219–20

Child, Lydia Maria, humanity of
    Native Americans stressed by,
    218

Children
    life-affirming images of, 219–21
    oppression against, 33–36. *See
    also* Infanticide

Children's Aid Society of New
    York, 221

Chivington, John, massacre of
    Cheyenne at Sand Creek,
    Colorado, led by, 60, 109, 194

Clark, Tom, view of life of fetus as
    potential by, 167

Clay, Henry, description of inferior-
    ity of Native Americans by, 74

Cobbe, Frances Power
    assaults on women in England
    described by, 40
    consignment of women to status
    of property described by,
    135–36

Collier, John, capabilities and
    humanity of Native Americans
    described by, 219

Committees of Poor Peasants, 72

Commonwealth v. Walosky, 157

Computer-person of Michael
    Tooley, personhood of,
    169–79

Conlee, Mary Ellen, aborted
    fetuses as "pathological
    waste" to, 140

Conquest, Robert
    atrocities in labor camp at
    Kolyma described by, 49
    naming of kulaks as class enemy
    described by, 84
    numbers of those killed under
    the Stalinist regime tallied by,
    49
    Russian deaths during Terror-
    Famine tallied by, 47–48

Consciousness-raising to expand
    the boundaries of humanity,
    223–25

Conspiracy of Pontiac, The, 145

Cooper, David, animalization of
    African Americans by, 95

Cooper, James Fenimore, inferior-
    ity of Native Americans
    described by, 75, 111

Corporations, personification of,
    163–64, 165

Cranford, Ronald, persistent vegeta-
    tive state as synonymous with
    nonpersonhood for, 155, 203

Crick, Francis H., view of new-
    borns of, 79–80

Cultural elite
    as dominating leading societal
    institutions, 15–16
    media elite as branch of, 17

Dachau concentration camp,
    experimental research on
    humans at, 45–46

De Beauvoir, Simone, views of
    marriage and housewives of,
    104, 112, 193

De Sade, Marquis
    degrading images of women in
    writings of, 81
    female victims of, 69

Declaration of Geneva, 206

Defencism defined, 233n3

Deficient human as category of
    name-calling, 3

Dehumanizing rhetoric
    challenges to, 18–20, 173–228
    deliberateness of, 12
    dynamics of, 1–23
    replaced with a language of
    humanization and diviniza-
    tion, 205–21, 225
    socio-cultural context of, 14–17

as a strategy for justifying massive oppression, *ix*
verbal gymnastics of, *ix*
Democratic Party, cultural elitist
position of, 16
Dependent humans, 65–75
as category of linguistically victimized groups, 4, 7
as inanimate objects, 128–29,
197–98
intrinsic worth of, 210–11
Lexicon of Esteem for, 21
parasite metaphor for, 110
in quality-of-life ideology, 14
Derr, Mary Krane, case against
abortion made by, 208
Diamond, Howard I., view of the
unwanted unborn of, 78–79,
188
Diamond, Sondra, view of
imposed starvation of disabled
infants of, 181–82
Disabled humans, 65
as animals, 90–91, 190–91
assaults on, 33–36
as category of linguistically victimized groups, 4–5, 7
defined as worthless, 68
as diseases, 114–15, 118–19, 195
intrinsic worth of, 210–11, 225
Lexicon of Esteem for, 21
marginalization of, 67–68
Nazi killings of, 43, 69–71
nonhumanity of, 79–81, 188–89
as nonpersons, 152–56, 203
parasite metaphor to dehumanize, 101–3, 193
in quality-of-life ideology, 14
as vegetables, 102–3, 181–83
as waste products, 140–42,
200–201
Disease metaphors, 113–25,
195–97
for African Americans, 116–17,
121–22, 196–97

for disabled people and elderly,
114–15, 118–19, 195
for Jews, 120, 123–24, 158, 196
for Native Americans, 122,
124–25, 197
for Soviet enemies, 121, 196
for unwanted unborn, 113–14,
117–18, 123, 195
for women, 115–16, 119–20, 196
Divine law tradition of creation, 19
Dixon, Thomas, view of African
Americans as disease of, 122
Doctor Zhivago, 133
Doe v. Bolton decision, 66, 67,
166–67, 187, 229n2
Douglas, William O.
majority view in *Roe v. Wade*
and *Doe v. Bolton* of, 166–68
view of legal personhood of
environment of, 165–66, 169
Douglass, Frederick, human nature
of African Americans stressed
by, 218
Down's syndrome
denial of life-preserving treatment for infants with, 34, 67,
187, 188
discovered by Jerome Lejeune,
178
intrinsic worth of people having,
211
starvation of newborn having,
35–36
victims of, as nonpersons, 154,
203
view of treatment as waste of
resources for, 80
Drake, Daniel, African Americans
as parasites to, 108
Drayton, William, view of African
Americans of, 74, 121
Dred Scott v. Sanford decision, 74,
137, 160–61, 199, 204

Druyan, Ann
  animality of unwanted unborn
    for, 90, 181
  parasitism of unwanted unborn
    for, 110, 194
Duff, Raymond S.
  disabled infants as vegetated
    individuals for, 102, 182
  withholding of medical treat-
    ment described by, 34, 67
Dying patient, cessation of personhood for, 156

Eberstadt, Nick, Stalinist war on
  Soviet citizens described by, 50
Eclipse of Reason, The, 128
Eglfing-Haar mental hospital, 45
Einsatzgruppen, 43
Elderly people
  decision not to treat illnesses in,
    35
  as dependent humans, 4
  as diseases, 114–15, 118–19, 195
  as inanimate objects, 128–29,
    197–98
  parasite metaphor to dehuman-
    ize, 101–2
  in quality-of-life ideology, 14
Ellis, George E., waste by Native
  Americans described by, 145
Emerson, Ralph Waldo, view of
  Native Americans of, 137
Engelhardt, H. Tristram
  fetuses as nonpersons and sub-
    ject to *in vitro* experimenta-
    tion for, 151–52
  "potential life" doctrine adopted
    by, 66
English, William T.
  regard for African Americans as
    trash by, 145
  subhumanity of African
    Americans for, 85

Environment
  awareness about pollution of,
    185
  non-ecological approach to
    intrauterine, 166–68
  personhood bestowed on nat-
    ural, 164
Environmental impact statements,
  185–86
Environmental Protection Agency,
  establishment in 1970 of, 185
Estes, Matthew, animal metaphors
  for slaves by, 96
Etzioni, Amitai, view of fetuses of,
  78
European Jews, destruction of,
  43–46
Euthanasia
  animal metaphors to defend, 98,
    190–91
  basic attitude regarding, 71
  designation of the disabled or
    dependent as parasites or veg-
    etables by advocates of,
    101–3, 193
  excuses invoked for, 22
  language of subhumanity to pro-
    mote, 86–87
  Nazi program of, 187
  nonpersonhood as defined by
    advocates of, 156
  separated from idea of killing, 8
  spread of contemporary, 187
Evans, Mark I., power of ultrasound described by, 178–79
Ever Since Darwin, 180
Exploitation of people classified as
  inanimate objects, 127–38

Females. *See* Women
Femicide, 41, 230n2
Feminist rhetoric, 104–5
Feminists for Life of America, 208
Fennelly, Joseph, dehumanization
  of Nancy Ellen Jobes by, 81

Fertilization, human development beginning at, 176–78

Fetal surgery, 180

Feticide. *See* Unwanted, unborn

Fetology, advancements in field of, 224

Fetus versus *baby*, 79

Fiala, Fritz, picture story on Auschwitz by, 18

Fitzgerald, John F., contagiousness of mental handicap described by, 119

Fitzhugh, William, slaves referred to as refuse by, 144

Fletcher, John, power of ultrasound described by, 178–79

Fletcher, Joseph
    view of disabled people of, 80, 102, 188
    view of the unwanted pregnancy of, 123
    view of the unwanted unborn of, 78

Fontana, Andrea, objectification of patients studied by, 129

Fourteenth Amendment to the U.S. Constitution, meaning of "persons" in, 163–64

Fredrickson, George M., defamation of African Americans described by, 96–97

Fraenkel, Ernst, study of Jews' status in German high courts by, 171, 204

Fredrickson, George W., stereotypes of African Americans examined by, 192

Frenkel, Naftaly, "corrective labor" doctrine of Gulag described by, 133

Freudian view of women as defective, 116

Gage, Matilda, stance against abortion of, 207

Garrison, William Lloyd, enfranchisement of slaves advocated by, 217

Gaylin, Willard, abortion procedures characterized by, 29

Genocide
    by Nazis, 44–45
    of the Soviet people, 47–50

Germans, dehumanizing terms for, 3

Gerry, Eldridge T., basis of laws protecting children noted by, 221

Gerstley, Louis
    comparison of unwanted unborn's response to amoeba by, 90, 101
    unwanted unborn as "obligate parasite" for, 100–101

Gibbon, John, animal metaphors for Native Americans by, 97

Gillon, Raanon, nonperson doctrine invoked by, 203

Gingras, Thomas S., questions about language of abortion by, 79

Goebbels, Joseph, Jews as waste products for, 143

Goldsmith, Sadja, details regarding abortion procedure given by, 29–30

Gordon, Hymie, humanity beginning at conception for, 206–7

Gorky, Maxim
    fate of Russian villages described by, 72
    support for using Gulag slave laborers by, 133

Gould, Stephen Jay, collapse of ancestral recapitulation according to, 180

Graebe, Hermann, mass shootings
of Nazi victims witnessed by,
43–44

Grant, Lee, tradition of wife beating described by, 136

Grayson, William J., view of
African Americans as disease
of, 121–22

Great Chain of Being, dehumanizing impact of, 229n3

Great Purge Trial (Soviet Union),
144

Griffin, Susan
animality of women researched
by, 92–93
objectification of women in
pornography described by, 130

Grimke, Angelina, abolitionist
stance of, 217

Grossman, Vasily, description of
annihilation of kulaks by, 84

Gubrium, Jaber, objectification of
nursing home patients studied
by, 129

Guett, Arthur, description of inferior creatures by, 70

Gulag Archipelago, enemies of the
Soviet people sent to, 48–49,
199, 201

Gulag Archipelago, The, 201,
215–16

Guttmacher, Alan F., "potential
life" doctrine adopted by,
66–67, 186–87

Guyon, Rene, sexual license proclaimed by, 104

Gypsies
marginalization of, 70
Nazi description of solution for
question of, 106
Ritter's genealogical tables for
"hunting out," 93

Haeckel, Ernst
concepts of purifying Aryan race
of, 69–70, 103
impact on Nazi euthanasia program of, 187

Half Humankind, 211–12

Hallervorden, Julius, use of body
parts of Jews advocated by,
132

Handicapped people. *See* Disabled
humans

Hardin, Garrett, delineation
between fetus and humans
for, 77–78

Harris, L. H., animal metaphors for
African Americans by, 96

Having a Baby, 186

Henderson, Katherine Usher, study
of women's images by,
211–12

Hern, Warren M.
description of aborted remains
by, 31
destructiveness of abortion
described by, 30
fetus as invasive parasite for,
101, 192
pregnancy as illness for, 195
pregnancy called pathological
condition by, 114, 118

Hesiod, women as a plague for, 119

Hilberg, Raul
anti-Semitic stereotypes used by
Hitler studied by, 22, 194
significance of description of
Jews as non-Aryans described
by, 157

Himmler, Heinrich, Jewish possessions as germ-infected according to, 120

Hirt, August
collection of "material" (from
Jews in experiments)
described by, 132

concentration camp prisoners
considered animals by, 94, 191
skull measurements of Jews by,
46
*History of the Discovery of
America, The*, 111
Hitler, Adolf
animalization of Jews by, 93
Jews referred to as virus by, 120
Mein Kampf contents by, 93,
120, 123–24
nomenclature of anti-Semitic
stereotypes used by, 22, 82
repetition of lies by, 8
threat of "Jewish parasites" proclaimed by, 105, 110–11, 112
Hoche, Alfred
destruction of the disabled
advocated by, 70, 93
impact on Nazi euthanasia program of, 187
Hopkins, Samuel, view of African
Americans summarized by, 95
Hospitalized patients. *See*
Dependent people
Host
dependence of parasite on, 99
threat by parasite to survival of,
99
Howard, William Lee, quarantine
for sexual madness of African
American males advocated by,
197
Howsden, Jackie, terminology for
nursing home residents
described by, 141
Hoxie, Frederick E., Native
Americans as anthropological
specimens described by,
137–38
Hubbard, William, Native Americans
as trash for, 146, 202
Humanity
beginning at conception, 206–7

expanding boundaries of,
223–28
of Native Americans, 218–19
of the unborn denied, 78
of victims of the Nazi Holocaust,
213–15
Human embryos, ownership of, 135
Humans, handicapped. *See*
Disabled humans
Hydrocephalic children, designation of nonpersonhood for,
80, 91, 154

I. G. Farben Chemical Corporation,
concentration camp inmates
used as "work material" by,
132, 138
Inanimate objects, 197–200
African Americans portrayed as,
136–37, 199–200
as category of name-calling, 3
disabled and elderly portrayed
as, 128–29, 194–95
Jews portrayed as, 131–32,
198–99
Native Americans portrayed as,
133–34, 137–38, 200
people classified as, 127–38
Soviet people portrayed as,
132–33, 199
unwanted unborn portrayed as,
127–28, 134–35, 197
women portrayed as, 130–31,
135–36, 198
Indian Declaration of
Independence, 57
Indian nations. *See* Native
Americans
Infanticide
in ancient Carthage, 33
Eskimos as practicing, 22, 34
of females, 37
feminists against, 207
by Nazis, 45

nonpersonhood as foundation
for, 154
Plato's advocacy of, 10, 68
at Yale University-New Haven
Hospital, 34, 67, 182
Infants, assaults on, 33–36
Infectious disease as category of
name–calling, 3
Institute for the Interprofessional
Study of Health Law, abortion
liberty meeting held by, 149
Iroquois Indians, disease metaphor
used for, 122
Irving, John, description of abor-
tionist-orphanage director as
saint by, 197
Irwin, James, pregnancy called dis-
ease by, 114
Italians, dehumanizing terms for, 3

Jackson, Andrew, animal
metaphors for Native
Americans by, 97, 98
Jackson, Helen Hunt, nineteenth
century dubbed a century of
dishonor toward Native
Americans by, 218
Jefferson, Thomas, inferiority of
African Americans described
by, 73
Jeffrey, Roger, staff's regard for
patients as "rubbish" noted
by, 141
Jews
atrocities by Nazis of, 46
as category of linguistically victimized groups, 4, 7
dehumanizing terms for, 3
destruction of European, 43–46
human and transcendental
nature of Nazi-persecuted,
213–15
Lexicon of Esteem for, 21
as nonhumans under the Third
Reich, 157–58

as nonpersons, 157–58, 204
portrayed as animals, 93–94
portrayed as diseases, 120,
123–24, 158, 196
portrayed as inanimate objects,
131–32
portrayed as parasites, 105–6,
110–11, 194
portrayed as subhumans, 22,
82–83, 189
portrayed as waste products, 143
Jobes, Nancy Ellen, starvation
death of, 80–81, 189, 210
Jordan, Winthrop D., Jefferson's
derogation of African
Americans described by, 73
Juvenal, animality of women for, 91

Kaufmann, Donald A., typecasting
of Native Americans described
by, 138
Kekomaki, Martti
support for decapitating live
aborted babies by, 140
use of parts of aborted humans
by, 30
Keller, Helen, acquisition of lan-
guage by, 1–2
Kelman, Wolfe, humanity of the
unborn denied by, 78
Kindness of Strangers, The, 220–21
"Knight of the La Tour Landry,
The," 39–40
Knightly, Phillip, casualty of truth
in war described by, 8
Knox, John, misogyny of, 68–69,
119
Koestler, Arthur, silence about
Soviet famine noted by, 159
Kolyma, labor camp at, 49
Krushchev, Nikita S., Stalin
denounced by, 47
Kulaks. *See* Peasants, Soviet
(kulaks)

LaBelle, Beverly, pornography as propaganda of misogyny for, 213

Lachs, John
  disabled people viewed as unconscious vegetables by, 102
  view of hydrocephalic children of, 80, 91, 154, 188

Lamerton, R., purpose of "vegetable" labeling described by, 102–3, 182–83

Lapham, Lewis H., rationale for using fetal brain implants by, 140

Lappe, Marc, abortion procedures characterized by, 29

Last of the Mohicans, The, 111

Lejeune, Jerome, human beings as beginning at conception for, 178

Lenin, Vladimir Ilych
  enemies called parasites by, 106, 111, 112
  enemies called wild animals by, 94–95, 98, 191
  ideas of God as a contagion for, 121
  lexicon of derogation fashioned by, 87
  petty-bourgeois socialism disparaged by, 144
  victims exterminated by, 159, 196
  view of rural life of, 72

Less than human as category of name-calling, 3

Levin, Nora, relationship between language and reduction of Jews to nonhumans described by, 198–99

Levine, Robert, animal analogy in describing Theresa Ann Campo used by, 191

Levy, David, subhumanity of Native Americans for, 86

Lexicon of dehumanization, 225

Lexicon of Esteem, 20–21

Lichter, Robert, studies of media by, 17

Life-affirming images
  as countering dehumanizing expressions, x, 225
  vocabulary for, 205–21

Liley, A. W., characterization of the unborn as splendidly functioning baby, 207

Linguistic devaluation. *See* Dehumanizing rhetoric

Linguistic warfare
  classification of, 2–4
  dynamics of, 1–23
  psychology of, 8–9

Liquidationism defined, 233n3

Liss, Henry, dehumanization of Nancy Ellen Jobes by, 81

Louisiana Purchase Exposition (1904), 137

Lovelace, Linda, objectification described by, 131

McDuffie, George, view of African Americans of, 73–74

McGee, W. J., view of Native Americans of, 137

McKim, W. Duncan, contamination by diseased people described by, 119

McManus, Barbara F., study of women's images by, 211–12

Mahowald, Mary, position on using "fetal material" of, 128

Mailer, Norman, debasement of women by, 92, 191

Male supremacy, dogma of, 13

Marginalization, 65–75, 186–88
  of African Americans, 73–74
  of disabled humans, 67–68, 69–71
  of Native American, 74–75

of Soviet peasants, 71–72
of unwanted unborn, 65–67
of women, 68–69
Marx, Karl
  capitalist state clogged by
    medieval rubbish for, 143
  view of peasants of, 72
Mather, Cotton
  animal metaphors for Native
    Americans by, 97
  objectification of Native
    Americans by, 133
Mathews-Green, Frederica, feminist pro-life stance of, 208–9
Means, Russell, Indian Declaration
  of Independence declared by,
  57
Media elite, 17–18
Medical treatment, denial of, 34–35
Medvedev, Roy, victims under
  Stalinist regime tallied by,
  49–50
Mein Kampf, 120, 123
Menendez, Erik, *ix*
Menendez, Lyle, *ix*
Mengele, Joseph, rationale for send-
  ing inmates with scarlet fever
  to the gas chambers of, 196
Menstruation
  blamed for host of problems,
    119–20
  women's uncleanness during, 196
Metellus, Egnatius, 39
Mill, John Stuart, female inferiority
  refuted by, 212–13
Miller, Henry, debasement of
  women by, 92, 116, 130, 142,
  191
Mitrany, David, prejudices of
  Marxism described by, 72
Mizrahi, Terry, dehumanizing lan-
  guage toward patients analyzed by, 115, 140–41, 195,
  200–201

Moore, Keith L., human development process according to,
  177–78
Moran, Alfred F., changes in perceptions of fetal viability
  noted by, 179
Morgan, Robin, view of rape of, 198
Morton, Samuel George, skull
  measurements by, 188
Mosse, George L.
  analysis of robbing races of
    humanity by, 94
  significance of Jews losing legal
    personalities described by, 158
Mother Teresa of Calcutta, plight
  of the unborn championed
  by, 210
Muller, Filip, labor at Auschwitz of,
  131
Munda, Constantia, positive images
  of women given by, 212

Nairn v. University of St. Andrews,
  156
Name-calling
  categories of, 3–4
  by children, 2–3
  ideological foundations of, 11–14
  of Jews, 105–6
  refusal to accept prevailing
    norms of, 18–19
  victims and perpetrators alike
    afflicted by, 226
  of women, 193–94
Nathanson, Bernard N.
  film by, 128
  position on abortion of, 27–29
National Abortion Federation, 179
National Commission for the
  Protection of Human Subjects
  of Biomedical and Behavioral
  Research, 150
National Organization for Women,
  208

Native Americans
animal metaphors to describe, 97, 133, 192
annihilation of, 57–61
as category of linguistically victimized groups, 4, 6
described as inferior, 74–75
expropriation of lands of, beginnings of, 161–62
infected with venereal diseases, 124–25
Lexicon of Esteem for, 21
massacre at Sand Creek, Colorado, of, 60–61
nobility of, 218–19
as nonpersons, 161–62, 204
portrayed as diseases, 122, 124–25
portrayed as inanimate objects, 133–34, 137–38
portrayed as parasites, nits, and lice, 109, 111, 194
portrayed as subhuman, 85–86, 189–90
portrayed as waste products, 145–46
Trail of Tears of, 59–60
warlike contagion of, accusations of, 197
at Wounded Knee, South Dakota, 57–59
Natural law perspective of creation, 19
Nazi Holocaust, 43–46. *See also* Jews *and* Third Reich
AMA declaration of humanity and responsibilities of physicians issued following, 206
dehumanization and name-calling of Jews before and during, 105–6
experimental brutalities during, 45–46, 132
humanity of victims of, 213–15
imposed starvation of children in hospitals during, 45
linguistic victimization of those exterminated in, 4–5, 7, 103
plans to exterminate Slavic people during, 44–45
role of parasite analogies in, 194
treatment of Jews as diseased during, 120
victims viewed as trash during, 143, 201
Netsilek Eskimos, infanticide among, 22
"Newspeak," 186
Nick of the Woods, 111
Nisbet, Robert, description of fetus by, 13, 188
Nobel committee, beginning of life for, 178
Nonhuman entities. *See also* Inanimate objects
classifying humans as, 77–87, 197–200
expanding universe of, 168–71
Nonpersons, 202–4
African Americans as, 160–61, 204
as category of name-calling, 3
disabled people as, 152–56, 203
Jews as, 157–58, 204
legal, 147–71
Native Americans as, 161–62, 204
Soviet enemies as, 158–59, 204
unwanted unborn as, 148–52, 166–68, 202–3
women as, 156–57, 203
Noonan, John T., beginning of life for, 178
Notes, 229–37
Nott, Josiah C.
animal metaphors for Native Americans by, 97
"hybrid mulatto" as doomed to destruction for, 122

Nove, Alex, victims of Leninist and
Stalinist regimes tallied by, 50
Nuremberg War Crimes Trial,
International, 44–45, 187

Oakie, Susan, positive view of
fetus emerging from medical
advancements according to,
179–80
Objectification of undesired
human beings. *See* Inanimate
objects
Oden, Thomas C., critique of the
"patient as vegetable" analogy
by, 183
Oppression
against children, 33–36
against Russians under Lenin
and Stalin, scope of, 49–50
against the dependent and disabled, 33. *See also* Dependent
humans and Disabled humans
against women, 156, 207
facilitated by parasite metaphor
for human victims, 99
name-calling as component of
large-scale, 3
profiles of victims of, 25–61
Orwell, George
"newspeak" described in *1984*
by, 186
unpersons described in *1984* by,
158
Ottawa Indians, disease metaphor
used for, 122
Otzovism defined, 233n3
Owens, Walter, quality of life argument by, 67

Parasitic creatures, 99–112, 192–94
African Americans as, 108–9, 194
as category of name-calling, 3
defined, 99
disabled and dependent as,
101–3, 110, 193

Gypsies as, 106
Jews as, 105–6, 110–11, 194
kulaks and Soviet enemies as,
106–8, 111, 194
Native Americans as, 109, 111,
194
unwanted unborn as, 100–101,
110, 181, 192–93
women as, 103–5, 193–94
Parkman, Francis
view of African Americans of, 10
view of Native Americans of, 86,
97, 122, 133–34, 145
Pasternak, Boris, portrayal of
results of Bolshevik
Revolution by, 132–33
Patterson, Henry, Native Americans
considered vermin by, 109
Payne, Buckner, assaults on
humanity of African
Americans by, 85, 96
Payne, George H., role of Christian
Church in forging positive
images of children described
by, 219–20
Peasants, Soviet (kulaks)
portrayed as nonhuman, 83–84,
189, 217
portrayed as parasites, 106–8,
111, 194
Soviet characterization and marginalization of, 71–72
mass killing under Stalin of,
47–48, 159
starvation during terror-famine
of, 47–48, 107, 159
unpersonhood of, 159
Pendleton, John, African
Americans as parasites to, 108
People of the State of California v.
William Baxter Waddill, Jr.,
229n1
Pequot Indians described as trash,
146

Permitting the Destruction of Unworthy Life, 187

Persistent vegetative state (PVS), 102, 155, 181–83, 203

Personification
  of corporations, 163–64, 165
  of environment, 164
  of ships, 163–64, 165

Petchesky, Rosalind Pollack, fetus as parasite according to, 100

Peterson, Hart, portrayal of aborted baby as animal by, 89–90

Pfaff, Christoph Heinrich, name-calling of Jews by, 105

Pfannmuller, Hermann, imposed starvation of "deficient" children demonstrated by, 45

Pilpel, Harriet F., rights of abortion discussed by, 149

Pivot of Civilization, The, 142

Planned Parenthood Federation of America, 90, 114

Planned Parenthood of Southeastern Pennsylvania v. Casey, The, 202–3

Plato, defamation of disabled by, 10, 68

Plekhanov, George V., view of Russian peasantry of, 72

Pliny, menstruating women blamed for harm to crops by, 119–20

Poland as the "trashcan of Europe," 143

Poliakov, Leon, Germans' waste metaphor for Jews studied by, 201

Pornography
  animality of women in cartoons of, 93
  damaging impact of, 213, 236n10

  as medium for depicting women as less-than-human, 81
  objectification of women in, 130–31, 198

"Potential life" doctrine, 65–67
  fallacy of, 176–78
  force for Alan F. Guttmacher of, 186

Pregnancy
  fetus as actual human being living during, 176–78
  as an illness, 113–14, 117–18
  as a venereal disease, 123

Pregnancy and Birth: A Book for Expectant Parents, 186

Property, treatment of humans as. *See* Inanimate objects

Quakers, antislavery stance of, 217

Quality-of-life ideology
  directed against disabled infants, 67
  directed against the vulnerable, 13–14

"Quasi-persons," classes of humans as, 152–53

Ramm, Rudolph, anti-Semitism of, 70–71

Rape of Nanking, 38–39

Rapes
  dehumanizing images of women as underlying, 82
  by Japanese of women in Nanking, China, 38
  of the New York jogger, 189
  as the practice of pornography, 198
  as robbery of property, 135
  of slaves, 55
  in United States, statistics of, 39

Rascher, Sigmund, view of Jews as "experimental material" of, 132

Reality test for refuting the validity
of disparaging designations,
175–83
Redskins, The, 75
References, 239–66
Reich, Wilhelm, sources of Nazis'
political views discussed by,
124
Reisman, Judith A., female bestiality research by, 93, 232n3
Reproductive technology industry,
134–35
Revolutionary phrase-making as a
disease for Lenin, 121
Rich, Adrienne, pornography as
objectification for, 213
Richards, Sal, humanity of the
dependent person for, 211
Ritter, Robert, Gypsies "hunted out"
by genealogical tables of, 93
Roe v. Wade decision by U.S.
Supreme Court, 27
definition of maternal health
under, 229n2
potential life doctrine
expounded in, 66–67, 176, 178
unborn not considered "person"
under, 202
as ushering in era of legal nonpersonhood, 148, 160, 166–67
Romanes, George J., women's
brain-weights analyzed by, 187
Romans, Bernard, description of
Native Americans as inherently defective by, 74
Roosevelt, Theodore, liberating
territories from Native
Americans described by,
145–46
Rugg, C. J., decision not to allow
women on juries by, 157
Rush, Benjamin, explanation of
blackness by, 117

Ryan, George M., medical implications of personhood discussed
by, 149–50
Ryan, Kenneth J., unwanted pregnancy called disease by, 114
Rye, Maria, role in child emigration
movement of, 141

Sac Indians, massacre in Wisconsin
woods of, 86
Sagan, Carl
animality of unwanted unborn
for, 90, 181
parasitism of unwanted unborn
for, 110, 193
Sakharov, Andrei, as critic of
human rights violations, 215,
216–17
Saliege, Jules-Gerard, positive
depiction of Jews by, 214
Sanctity-of-environment-life orientation of William O. Douglas,
166
Sanctity of life
ethic of, 13, 164–66
natural and supernatural orders
of creation as furnishing basis
of, 19–20
Sand Creek, Colorado, massacre of
Cheyenne at, 60–61
Sanger, Margaret, disabled people
as "dead weight of human
waste" for, 142
Sawyer, George S., animal
metaphors for slaves by, 96
Schmidt, Paul Karl, interpretation of
"The Jewish question" by, 83
Schopenhauer, Arthur, misogyny
of, 69
Scott, Winfield, Cherokee removed
from their lands by, 59
Scrimshaw, Susan C. M., study of
infanticide by, 22

Self-consciousness as requirement for attaining humanhood, 80

Semantic gymnastics, 8–9, 11, 13, 175–76, 224

Semantic impact of words, 1–4, 185–204

Semantic impact statements, call for, 186

Seminole Indians, animal metaphors to justify assault on, 97

Semonides, women as a plague for, 119

Senile dementia, 115

Sexploitation, 37–41

Sexual assaults on women, 38–39

Shainess, Natalie, disease metaphors for pregnancy used by, 117–18

Shelp, Earl E., nonpersonhood as foundation for infanticide for, 154–55

Ships, personification of, 163–64, 165

SHPOSHs, 200–201

Sickles, Emma, campaign against representing Native Americans as "specimens" by, 137

Sierra Club v. Morton, 164–65, 167

Silent Scream, The, 27, 89–90

Silent Spring, 185

Singer, Peter, disabled infants compared with animals by, 91, 190–91

Sioux Indians, massacre at Wounded Knee of, 58

Slavery of blacks, 51–55
  horrors of, in United States, 52–53

Slaves, African American
  hunting down of escaped, 53–54
  lynching and mob violence toward, 54–55
  merchandising of, 136
  punishments of, 52–53

right of property in, 137
  transport to the Americas of, 51–52

Slaves, Soviet, 132–33

Solzhenitsyn, Aleksandr
  as critic of human rights violations, 215–16
  Gulag compared to waste disposal system by, 201
  insights about ideology by, 12
  lives lost under Stalinist oppressors tallied by, 49

Sontag, Susan, purpose of disease metaphors analyzed by, 113

Southard, E. E., "feeble-minded" as "waste materials" to, 141–42

Southern Pacific Railroad, Supreme Court ruling in favor of, 163–64

Soviet people
  as category of linguistically victimized groups, 4, 6
  genocide of, 47–50
  as inanimate objects, 132–33
  Lexicon of Esteem for, 21
  Marxist-Leninist doctrine invoked against, 14

Soviet Union
  erasing purged "unpersons" from records in, 158–59
  metaphor of parasites for enemies of, 106–8, 111, 194
  metaphor as waste products for enemies of, 143–44
  name-calling in, 15
  treatment of peasants in, 47–48, 71–72
  wild-animal analogies for imperialists and enemies of, 94–95

Sowernan, Ester, worthiness of women defended by, 212

Spina bifida
  denial of life-preserving treatment for infants with, 34
  victims of, as nonpersons, 154

Stalin, Joseph
  enemies called parasites by, 107,
    111, 112, 194
  enemies called wild animals by,
    94–95, 98, 191
  Krushchev's denunciation of, 47
  lexicon of derogation fashioned
    by, 87
  mass killing of peasants and
    Ukrainians by, 47–48
  Trotsky's teachings as infecting
    youth for, 121
  victims exterminated by, 159
Stanton, Elizabeth Cady, abortion
    and infanticide for, 207
Starvation, imposed
  of farmers who opposed collec-
    tive farming, 48
  of unwanted children by Nazis,
    45
  of unwanted children in
    England and Europe, 33–34
  of unwanted handicapped chil-
    dren, 35–36
Stereotypes, dehumanizing, 63–172
  transformed into "truth," 8
Stevens, John Paul, unborn not
    considered whole people by,
    202–3
Stockham, Alice Bunker, stance
    against abortion of, 207–8
Stone, Christopher D., advocacy of
    bestowing legal personhood to
    environment by, 164, 165, 169
Straus, Murray, statistics of assaults
    on wives given by, 41
Streicher, Julius
  claim of the Jew's subhumanity
    by, 82–83, 189
  description of Jews as disease
    by, 120
  description of Jews as parasites
    by, 105–6, 194

Subhuman, The (Der
    Untermensch), 83
Subhumans, 77–87, 188–90
  portrayal of African Americans
    as, 84–85, 189–90
  portrayal of disabled humans as,
    79–81, 188–89
  portrayal of Jews as, 22, 82–83,
    189
  portrayal of Native Americans
    as, 85–86, 189–90
  portrayal of Soviet peasants as,
    83–84, 189
  portrayal of unwanted unborn
    as, 77–79, 188
  portrayal of women as, 81–82
Subjection of Women, The, 212
Sumner, L. W., host-parasite anal-
    ogy applied to pregnancy by,
    100
Suttee (widow burning), 37–38
Switzer, Chuck, wife considered
    property to, 136
Syphilis
  "Jewification" of, 123–24
  Native Americans portrayed as
    tainted with, 124–25

Taney, Roger Brooke
  African Americans not citizens
    according to, 160
  involuntary migration of Africans
    to United States described by,
    137
Ten Boom, Corrie, Jews hidden
    by, 215
Terror-famine for uncooperative
    Soviet farmers, 47–48, 107, 159
Theis, Edouard, movement to save
    Jewish refugees by, 214–15
Third Reich. *See also* Nazi
    Holocaust
  death factories (gas chambers)
    of, 44–45

disabled people and Jews portrayed as animals during, 93–94

disabled people and Jews portrayed as parasites during, 103

disabled people and Jews portrayed as subhumans during, 82–83

experimental brutalities during, 45–46

imposed starvation of children during, 45

Jews as nonpersons under, 157–58

mobile killing units of, 43–44

name-calling during, 15

sentiments on behalf of Jews spoken during, 214

victims as "not worth living" under, 69–71

Thompson, Keith, collapse of ancestral recapitulation theory noted by, 180

Tillman, Benjamin R., animal metaphors for African Americans by, 96

Tilt, E. J., women's life cycle as infirmities for, 116

Tom Quick, the Indian Slayer, 109

Tooley, Michael, designation of "human" for, 80, 148, 152–53, 168–70

Totalitarian social structures, degrading semantics by, 15

Trail of Tears of Cherokee Indians, 59–60

Trans-Disciplinary Symposium on Philosophy and Medicine, 150

"Transport material," Jews as, 131–32

Treblinka, Poland, body disposal at killing center of, 143

Trocme, Andre, movement to save Jewish refugees by, 214–15

Trotsky, Leon, Stalin's campaign against teachings of, 121

Tucker v. Alexandroff, 163

Turco, Jeryl, plea on behalf of Nancy Ellen Jobes by, 210

Twentieth Soviet Party Congress, 47

Ultimatumism defined, 233n3

Unborn, humanity of, 206–10, 225

Unborn, unwanted, 89–91. *See also* Abortion

as animals, 98, 180–81, 191

as a category of linguistically victimized groups, 4–5, 7

deaths of, 27–31

depersonalization of, 160–61

as diseases, 113–14, 117–18, 123, 195

effects of "potential life" doctrine on, 186–87

expanding the boundaries of humanity to include, 223–28

humanness and marginalization of, 65–67

as inanimate objects, 127–28, 134–35, 197

Lexicon of Esteem for, 21

as nonpersons, 148–52, 166–68, 202–3

as parasites in women's bodies, 100–101, 110, 181, 192–93

in quality-of-life ideology, 14

semantic gymnastics about, 8

as subhumans, 77–79, 188

as waste products, 139–40, 200

"Unperson." *See also* Nonpersons

process of becoming, 158–59

as rationalization for annihilation of Soviet people, 158–59, 171

Validity of disparaging designations, refuting, 175–83

Vegetables

disabled people labeled as, 102–3, 181–83, 193

replacements for the metaphor
of, 183
Vegetative state, nonpersonhood
of patients in, 155
Victims
of linguistic oppression, 4–7
linguistic reduction of, 3
plight of, 25–61
renaming former, 19
Vietnamese, dehumanizing terms
for, 3
*Vindication of the Rights of
Women, The*, 212
Violence
against females, 13, 37–41,
81–82, 189, 198
against slaves, mob, 54–55
name-calling resulting in, 3
omnipresence of, 227
Viscountess Rhondda's Claim,
156–57
Vision of the human family,
expansive, 227
Vitpvsky, D. P., disposal of
corpses at Gulag described
by, 199
Vocabulary of life, developing, *x*,
205–21
Von Galen, Clemens August, con-
demnation of Nazi extermina-
tions by, 213–14
Von Verschuer, Otmar, view of
Gypsies of, 70
Vyshinsky, Andrei, garbage
metaphor used for defendants
at Great Purge Trial by, 144

Waddill, William, destructive
impact of saline on unborn
child described by, 29
Wahlberg, Rachel Conrad
semantic assault on unwanted
unborn by, 100

woman's ownership of fetus
supported by, 134
Warren, Mary Ann
moral rights of nonpersons
advocated by, 170
nonpersonhood of fetus for,
149, 150
Washington, George, view of
slaves of, 136
Waste products, 200–202
African Americans as, 144–45,
201–2
as category of name-calling, 3
disabled people as, 140–42,
200–201
enemies of Soviet state as,
143–44, 201
Jews as, 143, 201
Native Americans as, 145–46
people as, 139–46
unwanted unborn as, 139–40, 200
women as, 142, 201
Weasel Bear, Louise, massacre at
Wounded Knee described by,
58
Weininger, Otto, misogyny of, 69,
81
Wet nurses, infanticide by, 33–34
Wetsit, Joshua, praise of Mother
Earth by Native Americans
described by, 219
Whipple, Henry Benjamin, humanity of Native Americans
stressed by, 218
White, Margaret, war against chil-
dren described by, 209
White Rose, 214
Who Should Survive?, 35–36
Widow burning, 37–38
Wife beating, 39–41, 135–36
Williams Obstetrics, 179
Williamson, Laila, view of infanti-
cide of, 34, 68

Wilson, Richard, description of disposal of dead fetuses by, 139–40

Wirth, Christian, bodies from Treblinka regarded as garbage by, 143

Wollstonecraft, Mary, social and legal structure oppressive to women according to, 212

Women
as category of linguistically victimized groups, 4–5, 7
as inferior sex, 68–69, 81–82
Lexicon of Esteem for, 21
life-affirming images of, 211–13, 225
as nonpersons, 156–57, 203
portrayed as diseases, 115–16, 119–20, 196
portrayed as inanimate objects, 130–31, 135–36, 198
portrayed as sexual parasites, 103–5, 193–94
portrayed as species of lower animal, 91–93
portrayed as waste products, 142, 201

violence against, 13, 37–41, 81–82, 189

Women Against Violence in Pornography and Media, subhuman portrayal of women described by, 81

Words
to describe unborn and born victims, linkage to other victimized groups of, 23

Words, devastating effects of, 185–204
consciousness-raising about, 224–25
dynamics of, 1–23
on victims and perpetrators, *ix–x*

"Work animal" metaphors for African Americans, 95–97, 192

World Columbian Exposition (1893), 137

Wounded Knee, South Dakota, takeover of, 57–59

Yale University-New Haven Hospital intensive care nursery, 34, 67, 182